BATTLE ROYAL

The Parliament of Edward I. An engraving after an ancient picture in the possession of the Society of Antiquaries

(Reproduced by kind permission of the Radio Times Hulton Picture Library)

BATTLE ROYAL

A NEW ACCOUNT OF
SIMON DE MONTFORT'S STRUGGLE
AGAINST KING HENRY III

TUFTON BEAMISH

with a foreword by
SIR CHARLES PETRIE

FREDERICK MULLER LIMITED
LONDON

First published in Great Britain 1965 by
Frederick Muller Limited
Printed in Great Britain by Ebenezer Baylis and Son, Ltd.
The Trinity Press, Worcester, and London

TO THE PEOPLE OF LEWES

That is not true liberty which is totally unlimited. On the contrary, true liberty is not lost by wholesome restraint, true power does not disappear under regulated compulsion . . . Mutual dependence is right. Let a prince so reign that he may never find it necessary to avoid depending on his subjects . . . Law is like fire, for it lights as truth, warms as charity, burns as zeal; with these virtues as his guides the king will rule well.

from *The Song of Lewes*

CONTENTS

ILLUSTRATIONS

All illustrations, except those acknowledged individually in the captions, are reproduced by kind permission of the Trustees of the British Museum.

MAPS

INTRODUCTION AND ACKNOWLEDGMENTS

WHEN I decided that the seven hundredth anniversary of the Battle of Lewes should be marked by the publication of a fresh account of it, I began a study of everything written on the subject. My first intention was limited to the story of the battle itself, but the more I read, the more fascinated I became: as a soldier, with the battle itself, and as a politician with the constitutional struggle of which it was the climax. Almost before I knew where I was I found I had embarked on a full scale history book, the writing of which involved a very careful and detailed study of the thirteenth century. Without the help of a really able researcher I could not possibly have covered the necessary ground in the time. Here I was very lucky indeed. Alison Christopher has been indefatigable in her research efforts under my guidance. No would-be historian can ever have had a more intelligent, enthusiastic and painstaking helper. The team stays together, as I have already started work on another fascinating subject.

I owe much to the historians and other writers whose names appear in the Bibliography, but above all to the chroniclers. These monks, the political journalists and gossip writers of their day, collected the comments jotted in the diary kept in each monastery library, added the news and rumours brought by visitors and wayfarers and, no doubt, some guesswork and imagination, in order to compile their stories. Outstanding among them during the troubled first half of the thirteenth century was Matthew Paris, a Benedictine of Saint Albans. His monastery was a popular meeting place, visited by the King and many leaders of opinion, and so he gathered much of his material at first hand. But he did far more than keep a well-informed and penetrating record of events, for he brought to his work an amused detachment and a lively style that make him one of the most readable of historians. I have quoted shamelessly from his chronicles, for it is Paris, who "loved to adorn a tale", who has illuminated for me the thirteenth century stage. I acknowledge my debt to him with gratitude.

Returning to the present, I thank most warmly Sir Charles Petrie, who has given me the friendliest encouragement and honoured my book by adding his Foreword to it. I also thank Jane Hodlin who translated so sympathetically *The Song of Lewes* and other medieval works which I have incorporated. Only an expert could have tackled such a difficult task and succeeded so brilliantly. M. Awais Khan has taken infinite pains in reproducing my plans of the battle and the maps of Lewes as it was in the thirteenth century and as it is today.

It is by kind permission of Methuen and Company that I have borrowed my chapter headings from one of the most inspired of all history books: *1066 And All That* by W. C. Sellar and R. J. Yeatman. Messrs. Longmans, Green and Company Limited have kindly allowed me to include passages of translation by Margaret A. Hennings from her book, *England Under Henry III*. I also thank Mrs. M. A. Berry who has agreed to my quoting from two books, *The Misrule of Henry III* and *Simon de Montfort and his Cause* published by her late husband's firm of David Nutt.

Among many others who have given me generous and valuable help I would like to mention L. S. Davey, whose knowledge of the history of Lewes is so extensive and who has allowed me to draw on it constantly; Richard F. Dell, the County Archivist for East Sussex; the Curator and staff of Barbican House, Lewes; the staff of the Department of Manuscripts in the British Museum and the staff of the Public Records Office; the Librarian and staff of the House of Commons Library and of Fulham Public Library; and all others who have contributed in numerous ways.

If this book gives its readers even half the pleasure gained from writing it, I shall feel amply rewarded.

Chelworth House
Chelwood Gate
Sussex
14 May 1964

TUFTON BEAMISH

BATTLE ROYAL

FOREWORD

by

Sir CHARLES PETRIE Bt

CBE MA (OXON) FR HIST SOC

It was a happy thought on the part of Sir Tufton Beamish to commemorate the septicentennial of the battle of Lewes by writing this account of the events which led up to, and those which immediately followed that event. For forty years Sir Tufton, and his father the late Rear-Admiral Beamish before him, have represented Lewes in the House of Commons, so it is particularly fitting that he should have set his hand to this task. In these days it is all too rare for the politician and the historian to be combined in the same individual, but in these pages Sir Tufton has shown us that it can still be done; and just as Gibbon found that his service as a captain of Hampshire grenadiers had "not been useless to the historian of the Roman Empire", so Sir Tufton has discovered that his years as a soldier and as a politician have been an asset when it came to analysing the struggle between Henry III and Simon de Montfort. He has written primarily for the layman, but his book is one of which any professional historian might well be proud.

Sir Tufton has rightly followed the late H. A. L. Fisher in stressing the cosmopolitanism of the age, and in particular the close connection which existed between England and France. The Norman Conquest had made England a province of French civilization: the language of the aristocracy, of the government and of the law-courts was French; it was from the Ile de France that England derived its Gothic architecture; while a great part of France—first Normandy, and then the Angevin Empire of Henry II—was ruled by English kings until the early years of the thirteenth century. Nor was this all, for feudalism, chivalry and the Crusades were French, and the university movement, at any rate so far as England was concerned, had its origin in Paris. It was the same with theories as with facts, for the general ideas about law and government, about society and religion, which were prevalent on one side of the Channel were equally familiar on the other. Indeed, so close was the connection between the two countries that more than one English town received a charter based on a French model.

Indeed, a traveller passing from one country to the other in the reign of Henry III would have found no very marked contrast between the French and English scene. In both kingdoms he would see majestic cathedrals being built, and upon closer examination he would discover that they were being erected by corporations of master masons under the direction of a bishop or abbot. He would find monasteries in either country obedient to the French rule, farming wide acres, and dispensing lavish hospitality; he would meet monks travelling to fair, market or tournament; and he would come across a group of gaping rustics listening to the eloquence of a travelling friar. To the Frenchman of this period England was hardly a foreign country, for although the mass of the people spoke a tongue which was unintelligible to him the gentry were of a world that was familiar, and they could make themselves understood in their provincial French. In these circumstances it is not so strange as it might otherwise appear that the barons of Magna Carta should have invited the future Louis VIII to accept the English crown, or that, as described in these pages, his son Saint Louis should have been called upon to arbitrate in an English political crisis. The close connection between England and France also explains why Simon de Montfort, an able adventurer of Norman French stock, was able to play so prominent a part in English history.

France, however, was not the only Continental country by which England was influenced in the thirteenth century, for down to the end of the Middle Ages the bulk of the population was to be found in London, Essex and East Anglia, and the trade of this part of the country was not mainly with France but with the Low Countries and the Rhineland, with Scandinavia and the Baltic: indeed, the greatest of all English medieval trades was with Flanders, for it was in Bruges and Ghent that the English wool was worked into cloth, and sent far and wide through Europe. It is to be noted that it was from London, Essex and East Anglia that Simon de Montfort drew his main support, just as Oliver Cromwell was to do four centuries later. For the rest, the general picture of the period with which Sir Tufton is concerned shows the English aristocratic and cultural connections to have been with France, while the commercial ones were with people of Teutonic stock.

The same cosmopolitan trend is to be observed in matters institutional as in those cultural, social and economic. The author rightly refuses to rate too highly the importance of de Montfort's Parliament which sat in London from January to March in 1265, for from the circumstances of the case it could only be a meeting of the supporters of the existing government. Indeed, so scanty was its following among the magnates that writs of summons were only issued to five earls and eighteen barons, though the strong muster of bishops, abbots and priors was proof that the Papal thunders had done little to shake the fidelity of the clergy to de Montfort's cause. The special feature of the gathering, however, was the summoning of two knights from every shire, side by side with the Barons of the Cinque Ports and two representatives from every city and borough, convened by writs sent, not to the sheriff as was later to be the case, but to the cities and boroughs directly. It was the presence of this strong popular element which in Victorian times caused this parliament to be regarded as the first really representative assembly in English history, and gained for de Montfort himself the credit of being the creator of the House of Commons. Modern research has shown that neither of these claims can be substantiated, but in the links which connect the early baronial councils with the assemblies of the three Estates of the fourteenth century not one is more important than de Montfort's Parliament.

The medieval idea of representation was basically functional, that is to say that it regarded man as an economic rather than as a purely political animal in the narrower sense of the term, and this is exemplified in the institutions of England, Spain, Sweden and France, to quote but four examples.

In the Model Parliament of 1295 there were gathered together the great lay and spiritual peers in person, the representatives of the lower clergy, two knights from each shire and a varying number of members, generally two, from each town and borough: in this way every interest in the kingdom was represented in Parliament. The lower clergy, it is true, soon preferred to sit in Convocation by themselves, and this proved to be the first step in the direction of representation by geography rather than by corporations, but that the latter was the original basis of the system is abundantly clear. In the reigns of Henry III and Edward I there were three occupations, and three only: namely that of the agriculturalist, of the trader, and of the priest, and they were all represented in de Montfort's and the Model Parliament. The landed interest spoke through the mouths of the lay peers and the knights of the shire; trade and industry were represented by the borough members; while the bishops, mitred abbots, and the nominees of the lower clergy stood for the Church and its interests. If it be objected that the constituencies were divided into rural and urban areas, the answer is that the division in those days was economic as well as geographical, for the primitive means of transport and the insecurity of travel, that were so prominent a feature of the Middle Ages, did not permit of the London business-man living in some rural district of Sussex or Hertfordshire fifty miles from his office.

To turn to Spain is to find the same principles at work. Representation there was slightly earlier than in England, for in Navarre it can be dated as far back as the fourth decade of the twelfth century. The late Antonio Goicoechea had no doubt whatever concerning the basis upon which the medieval *Cortes* of his country rested, for in *El Problema de Las Limitaciones de la Soberánia en el Derecho Público Contemporáneo* he wrote, "Medieval Spain regarded the social elements represented in its *Cortes* as parts of a living entity, with a separate and autonomous individuality, but subordinate to the existence of the whole". A brief survey of the conditions obtaining in the various Spanish kingdoms can but serve to emphasize the similarity between them and those existing in contemporary England. In León the borough representatives had sat with those of the nobles and clergy ever since 1188, and in Castile from a slightly later date. In Aragón the *Cortes* was composed of four *brazos* or estates—the high nobility, the knights or landed gentry, the clergy, and the towns and universities, though it is to be noted that all the nobles had not the right to attend unless specially summoned by the king. In Catalonia the organization was on somewhat similar lines, with the exception that there were three *brazos* instead of four, and in Valencia it was the same as in Catalonia. It will thus be seen that although the composition of the *Cortes* varied slightly in the different kingdoms it always, like the English Parliament, represented all the interests in the country, and it represented them by corporations. The queen of Edward I would find the institutions of England strangely reminiscent of her native Castile.

In Sweden the *Riksdag* was until very recent times divided into four estates—nobles, priests, burgesses and peasants—which sat and deliberated apart: each estate was ruled by its *talmon* or speaker, who was elected at the beginning of each Diet, with the exception that the Archbishop of Upsala was *ex officio* the *talmon* of the clergy. When the estates met in congress, as they did from time to time, the speaker of the nobility took the chair, and he also presided over the select committee which really carried on the administration of the country; this body consisted of fifty representatives of the nobility and twenty-five from each of the other three estates.

The States-General of medieval France never enjoyed the power either of the English Parliament or of the Spanish *Cortes*, but this cannot blind us to the fact that the principle by which it was recruited was the same. There was in France an absence of a rural middle class accustomed to shouldering public responsibilities. In England the main tasks of local government were carried out by knights of the shire or country gentlemen of moderate fortune, who attended the county courts, presented criminals to the judges, acted as jurors in civil suits and ultimately came to represent their respective counties in the national Parliament. In France there was no such amateur class of local jurors, justices and administrators comparable with the knights of the shire, and no such popular local institutions as the shire courts: the administration of the French monarchy was, in effect, carried on by professionals. The strength of the English Parliament, and the feature which gave it a permanent and continuous role in the government of the country, was that from the beginning it was in the main an assemblage of persons of intermediate social rank, who were accustomed to the discharge of public business in their respective localities. The French States-General was not rooted in local government in this way, nor was it closely fused by the presence of a class of representatives who, while they shared the rural tastes and pursuits of the noble, were in point of wealth and station more closely allied with the burgess. Consisting, as it did, of three distinct orders—the nobles, the clergy and the burgesses—the States-General progressively failed to play a decisive and formative part in the moulding of French policy.

It is against this background that Sir Tufton's story is set. In the thirteenth century the unity of Christendom was very real, and it explains, not least in England, many things which would otherwise be inexplicable. This unity of Christendom, however, was essentially a unity in diversity, and it nowhere approached uniformity save, perhaps, in the doctrines expounded in the pulpit. The difficulty experienced by the national leaders, cosmopolitan in outlook as they were themselves, as well as by such international authorities as the Pope and the Emperor, was to detect the subtle differences between the nations which lay beneath the surface, and in the pages of this book will be found more than one instance of their miscalculation in this respect.

It was only in a society of this nature that Simon de Montfort could have become an English national leader. He was, in origin, an able adventurer of Norman-French stock, and it is impossible to read Sir Tufton's narrative without coming to the conclusion that Simon owed a good deal to his opportune marriage with the King's sister, though whether he had previously seduced the lady is still wrapped in mystery. He was no inconsiderable soldier, and he was also a man of some learning himself, as well as being the friend of Robert Grosseteste, Bishop of Lincoln, who was the champion of the national party in the English Church against Papal exactions by foreign-born bishops. Simon had tried his fortune around Europe, and even in Palestine, before he played a leading part in English politics. In 1248 he was made Governor of Gascony, and constant complaints reached Henry III of his severity in that office, whether rightly or wrongly it is hard to say, for the Gascons were a turbulent race, and a strong hand was no doubt necessary in dealing with them. It would appear to be extremely doubtful if Simon spoke a word of English, but he has nevertheless obtained a niche in English history, and popular legend has termed him "Sir Simon the Righteous", chiefly because he led the opposition to the Pope and to an extravagant king. He seems to have been a difficult man to get on with, and even in the hour of victory he quarrelled with nearly every one of his leading supporters. Simon also had some unpleasant sons, whose behaviour did him a lot of harm.

Belloc well described him when he wrote that he was "a man made after a mould not unfamiliar to those who have studied the various types of the Gallic temperament when it is affected by military ambition".

> Brutal in discipline, of an indomitable physical tenacity which could force him to endure more than all he imposed upon his followers, perpetually considering death, and above all persuaded of something sacred in his career and capable of informing with a sense of mission any object of arms he had before him, Simon de Montfort repeats what half a dozen of the northern French leaders in the First Crusade exhibited, and what you may find later in the recovery of France from the Plantagenets, in the Wars of Religion, and conspicuously in the enthusiasms of the Revolution, with its mystical creed and its enormous and permanent achievement.
>
> It was his personality around which the next eighteen months of fighting were to turn: his ceaseless confidence in a divine selec-

tion, and his fierce insistence upon religion in his forces, between them determine the character of the struggle: his corresponding lack of equity, which was all merged in fanaticism, drove him and his: his eye for arrangement and for chance made him in particular a leader of cavalry.

Consonant with the character of such a man came, after the Mise of Amiens, an immediate repudiation by him of his own pledges.

A very different character was his brother-in-law, Henry III, and a good deal of importance should be attached to the fact that the two men were closely related. Even in the most exalted circles relations by no means always agree, as we have seen in the present century in the case of King Edward VII and the Kaiser Wilhelm II: indeed it is hard to say to what extent personal grudges against the King played their part in inducing Simon to take the leadership of the opposition to him. Henry was not at all a bad fellow, but he was not a success as a king: he was impatient, restless and hot-tempered, as became an Angevin, but he was fussy rather than businesslike, learned rather than clever; he was pious after his own lights, which unfortunately led him to look to Rome for guidance in temporal matters. Two really bad qualities he had inherited from his father, namely untruthfulness and extravagance; he did not mean consciously to lie, as John did, but he forgot his promises as soon as made, or explained them away, or got the Pope to absolve him from them, while as for his extravagance, it was boundless. On the whole he was a spirited, active, untrustworthy man, but posterity owes him a debt of gratitude for having rebuilt Westminster Abbey.

It is difficult for a modern Englishman, even if he be a member of the Church of Rome, to visualize a state of affairs when that Church in England should be in a continual conflict with the Papacy, yet such was the situation in the reign of Henry III, and it vitiated his relations with his subjects. His grandfather, Henry II, had enjoyed a very bad reputation at Rome for a variety of reasons, not least on account of the murder of Becket, to which it was widely believed on the Continent that he had been a party. John had gone too far in the opposite direction: he had promised to hold England and Ireland as fiefs of the Pope, and to pay tribute for them. This was too much for English churchmen, especially when it became clear that John's foolish concession was being interpreted at Rome as a licence to treat England as a farm out of which the Pope could squeeze rents at his pleasure. Whether it was that the leaders of the English Church—and the barons too, for that matter—resented the influx of foreigners for selfish reasons, or whether they were actuated by more patriotic motives, is a moot point, but the King's subservience to the Papacy unquestionably lost him a great deal of support, and such actions as the appointment of one of the queen's relations, Boniface of Savoy, to the See of Canterbury provoked universal discontent, especially when Boniface proved to be quite unsuited to the post.

Successive popes certainly drove Henry hard, but he had to give way to them because they were his only support against his own subjects. There were endless payments demanded by Rome from the English clergy such as annates, first-fruits, and tenths, while there were demands that one canonry in every cathedral should be reserved for the Pope who would thereupon present to it some Italian who never came to England but merely took the money. Similarly one or two good livings in each diocese had to be "reserved". All this was bad enough, but whenever the Pope got himself involved in a war, which was a by no means infrequent occurrence, he termed it a crusade, and called on England to give him a subsidy. In his age-old struggle with the Empire he persuaded Henry to allow his younger son, Edmund, to be put forward as a puppet King of Sicily, but little came of this project for the barons refused to provide any money. Then there was Henry's brother, Richard, who got himself elected to the vacant imperial throne, and who is known in English history as King of the Romans, though he never got hold of a rood of German soil. The age might be cosmopolitan, but there were limits, and it became impressed upon the barons that the royal family were squandering English resources upon matters which were no concern of England. If ever a monarch was his own worst enemy that monarch was Henry III.

It is a relief to turn from him to his eldest son, Edward, who was to become what Sir Arthur Bryant has termed "the beau-ideal of a medieval king". The distinguished historian goes on to say of him:

> From his father he had inherited a drooping left eyelid and a faint stammer. When aroused, the impediment vanished, and he spoke with an intensity that could move men to tears. A warrior from boyhood he had read few books, but he wrote French, and rather less certainly, Latin, and corresponded with his Castilian brother-in-law in Spanish. His mastery of legal argument was as formidable as his prowess in arms . . . Hard-working and orderly, this French-speaking king with an English name brought to his task habits of the strictest business. He disliked every form of waste and extravagance.

In the period covered by this present work Edward was only on the threshold of his career: as his ill-advised pursuit of de Montfort's London levies at Lewes clearly demonstrates, he had not yet learnt how to control his violent and overbearing temper, the legacy of the Angevin race, derived, men said, from their ancestor, the devil himself. Nevertheless even in these early days he was learning, and he was coming to know as his father had never known how to work with men of different opinions and make them his friends. Sir Tufton recalls that when Simon saw Edward, who was his own nephew, advancing against him at Evesham he exclaimed, "By the arm of Saint James they come on well. They learned that order from us." He was right, but Edward gained by experience in peace as well as in war, and de Montfort's Parliament of 1265 proved to be only a rehearsal for the Model Parliament of Edward I thirty years later.

The last, but by no means the least great figure to appear in this book is the King of France, Louis IX—Saint Louis. Throughout his reign he was connected with England to an extent that seems exceedingly strange to the modern mind, for not only did he defeat at Taillebourg the last despairing attempt of Henry III to recover his French possessions, but he came to be regarded in England itself as a permanent referee in the disputes between the king and the barons. A monarch him-self, it is often assumed that his sympathies must naturally have led him to support the royal authority across the Channel, as in the main he did, and that there is no more to it than that: such a judgment, however, does less than justice to the French king's character, and it is surely more likely that in the attitude he adopted where English politics were concerned he was led astray by false analogies.

As we have seen, England in the thirteenth century so closely resembled France that the differences between the two countries could easily be overlooked: furthermore, her recent history bore a remarkable similarity to that of her neighbour. On the unexpected death of Louis VIII after a reign of a mere three years the throne was occupied by a boy of twelve, namely Louis IX, under the regency of Blanche of Castile, one of the most remarkable women in history and a fit compatriot of Isabella the Catholic. It required all her skill and courage to preserve for her son even the semblance of authority, and the dispositions of her husband's will did not render her task any easier, for he broke with the tradition of the early Capetians by assigning a large territorial appanage to each of his younger children. Nor was this all, for a great feudal coalition quickly formed against the Regent, and several years of civil war ensued before it was broken, thus proving for the world to see that the French monarchy was now strong enough to survive a minority and the rule of a foreign woman. It is also to be noted that Pope Honorius III gave his full support to the Regent.

These events had naturally made no inconsiderable impression on Louis IX, and they unquestionably affected his judgment at the Mise of Amiens. He saw, or thought he saw, England going the same way as France in the days of his youth, and he had acquired a wholesome distrust of centrifugal tendencies in a medieval kingdom. Separatism seemed to him to be the real danger. As we have seen, the basis of representation in the States-General was the same as in the English Parliament, but for local reasons its composition was different: Louis did not realize this, and he saw behind the English barons, not country gentlemen accustomed to the tasks of local government, but the great feudatories whose aim it was to pull his own country asunder, and therefore he gave his decision in favour of the Crown. At the same time no one could be blamed for referring a problem to his arbitration. No man in Europe commanded, or perhaps has ever since commanded, the universal respect which Saint Louis enjoyed in the middle of the thirteenth century. Certainly no man was more permeated with that conception of government which satisfied the happy and stable society of the Middle Ages, nor could the decision of any other man be compared with his for the integrity upon which it would unquestionably be founded.

Finally, there is the account of the fighting itself, and here Sir Tufton shows himself to be an extremely competent military historian, also as one who thoroughly realizes the inter-action of politics and strategy in a civil conflict such as that which he is describing. On both sides the political object was to obtain control of the executive machinery of the country, and of the power to issue writs and to garrison fortresses. To effect this the first act of the victor in any decisive action was to secure custody of the person of the king, and it is no exaggeration to say that the varying fortunes of the campaign turned upon the physical possession of Henry III, of such moment was still the executive power of the hereditary monarch.

The twenty-six months of the war from June 1263 to August 1265 may be said to fall into three quite distinct military phases. The first, preliminary, phase was of no great importance save that it brought de Montfort's army into the field, and inaugurated a state of war. It covered the last six months of 1263, to be succeeded by a truce and the consent of both parties to the arbitration of Saint Louis. The second phase followed when the barons rejected the Mise of Amiens, and it closed with de Montfort's great victory at Lewes on May 14th 1264. For just over a year from that date Simon was the real ruler of England, and although there was some sporadic fighting among individuals locally, mainly for loot, the whole of that year may be excluded from the military history of the country, for no definite campaign was in progress, and no warfare on a national scale was taking place. The third phase began on May 28th 1265 when Prince Edward escaped from de Montfort's custody, collected an army, and after a brief campaign of the highest strategical interest brought Simon to action at Evesham, where he destroyed the baronial forces, killed their leader and restored the independence of the Crown.

The part played by London in the struggle should not be overlooked, and it testified to the growing importance of that city in the national life: as soldiers, the Londoners certainly made a poor show at Lewes, but London itself was both a base of supply for de Montfort and a nodal point of communication. The attitude of its inhabitants would be easier to determine if the accounts of contemporary witnesses were less partisan, but it would probably be a shrewd guess that though some of the richest merchants probably favoured Henry for the sake of peace, the mass of the commercial interests worked actively for his rival: to these latter must be added the populace, which in the thirteenth century was a powerful economic body of small owners strongly organized into co-operative associations. It is also to be noted that the prolonged royalist occupation of the Tower was far from having the same effect as the possession of the local castle in the case of the smaller towns: it carried with it neither control over the immensely larger population of the capital, nor any power of commanding its supplies and wealth. In this war, as in so many other civil conflicts, London acted as a virtually autonomous military element, and the scale into which it threw its weight in the main preponderated.

It is not easy in this latter half of the twentieth century to recapture the spirit of the Middle Ages, yet so far as institutions are concerned we are its heirs. For all their glamour the Athenian Assembly and the Roman Senate are mere names today, and the governments of England, France and the United States have their roots, not in the systems that flourished on the Acropolis or by the Tiber, but in those that were slowly and painfully evolved by Angles, Saxons and Franks, in a stage of civilization which to the cultured Athenian or Roman would have appeared little, if at all, removed from barbarism. The British monarchy looks back, not to the glories of Imperial Rome, but to rude chieftains like Cerdic. On the other hand, the thought of the Middle Ages is now a subject for the scholar rather than for the statesman, and to read the works of Duns

Scotus or of Thomas Aquinas is to pass at once into another world.

This is what Froude had in mind when he wrote—in an exaggerated vein—of the medieval era:

> And now it is all gone—like an unsubstantial pageant faded; and between us and the old English there lies a gulf of mystery which the prose of the historian will never adequately bridge. They cannot come to us, and our imagination can but feebly penetrate to them. Only among the aisles of the cathedral, only as we gaze upon their silent figures sleeping on their tombs, some faint conceptions float before us of what these men were when they were alive: and perhaps in the sound of church bells, that peculiar creation of medieval age, which falls upon the ear like the echo of a vanished world.

It is the supreme merit of Sir Tufton's narrative that he gives the lie to Froude, for in these pages the "gulf of mystery" is bridged, and the men and women of the Middle Ages very definitely "come to us".

CHARLES PETRIE

I

> "The Chapters between William I (1066) and the Tudors (Henry VIII, etc.) are always called the *Middle Ages*, on account of their coming at the beginning . . ." (*1066 And All That.*)

EACH CENTURY, seen in perspective, has its own unique pattern. The thirteenth century was one of sharp contrasts: of consummate skill and rich elegance side by side with barbaric and primitive ignorance; of cruelty and corruption on the one hand and saintly courage on the other. During that hundred years the English rebelled against authority. England struggled to free herself in some measure from the domination of Rome, ignored the warnings and strictures of King Louis of France and used physical violence against her own monarch. She demanded a greater say in her own affairs and began to recognize and assert her own national character.

For any country this early stage of growing up must bring suffering and humiliation. Out of it may come certain rewards: a better understanding between governor and governed; a greater flexibility and tolerance on both sides and certain laws and customs that form a basis for more stable government. England was fortunate. The lessons she learned during the thirteenth century have never been entirely forgotten, for they are absorbed into our parliamentary and judicial system and our way of life. The dangers still to be faced, both from foreign attack and internal rebellion, remained just as great in the centuries that followed, but she was better equipped to face them.

It is tempting to describe it as a century that "came in like a lion and went out like a lamb", but its peaceful end was marred by ferocious fighting against Scotland. King John at the beginning was one of the most hated of our monarchs, but his reign produced *Magna Carta*. Edward I at the end was certainly one of the most beloved. He was the first truly English king, sharing the characteristics of his people, and it was he who laid down the firm foundations of our present Parliament. Between them came Henry III, weak, vain and capricious, whose vacillations brought misery and bloodshed. Yet during his reign England gained greatly from one of the most profitable invasions of her history.

From the beginning this country had been colonized first by one marauding people and then another. Traces of their varied cultures remained, but at the Norman Conquest England was just a barbaric offshore island. By the thirteenth century the first small waves of the Renaissance were lapping the shores of Europe's mainland. Crusaders and merchants brought back to the west some of the beauties, crafts and philosophies of the east, and many glorious legacies of the past were reaching those countries that were ready to accept them. Monks, scholars, soldiers and traders were like the birds that broadcast seed, often in unexpected places.

England was late in arriving at this point of development. She lived mainly by her agriculture, and the sea limited her contact with the outside world. The royal court lived much of the time in France, for a king was not inclined to endure an uncouth way of life in a poor climate when he could enjoy sunshine and luxury on his own soil. When Henry III, deprived of his empire, was compelled to stay at home, he devoted his considerable talents and more money than his country could afford to artistic causes. His alien favourites, hated for their greed and ostentation, were also scorned for their dandyish tastes. The whiff of the exotic that surrounded them, the taste and care lavished on their clothes and furnishings, houses and accoutrements, were quite foreign to the more stolid Anglo-Norman aristocracy who sprang from rugged Norse stock.

The gothic movement had reached its peak across the Channel, and its vigour and freedom reflected the buoyant spirit which pervaded Europe. Delicate, sublime cathedrals rose throughout northern France, giving opportunities for craftsmen to exercise their highest skills, and man achieved marvels for the greater glory of God. The windows of Chartres cathedral, for instance, are one of the world's miracles. They shimmer like jewellery, flashing every shade and depth of blue, and suggesting perpetual sunshine behind a kaleidoscope of colour. England has her own fine examples of this art, especially at Canterbury and York, and she was already famous for ecclesiastical embroidery. *Opus Anglicanum* was renowned throughout Europe. It was worked in gold and silver threads, and that interweave of gold and silk known as samite, in intricate filgree designs and finest stitchery.

Most of this craftsmanship, like the enamel work at Limoges, much of the jewellery, the carvings in wood and ivory, the tapestries and frescoes, were sponsored by the Church. A taste for elegance, however, was spreading to the houses of the rich, where everything that could be decorated, enlivened with colour, painted with pretty and romantic scenes or given some new touch of gaiety or charm came under the craftsman's hand.

England was already enjoying this sense of adventure in art, but the influx of foreigners during Henry III's reign, and the increase in trade, brought impetus to the movement. Her own great cathedrals were rising, and by 1300 she was almost as rich in them as she is today. During Henry's reign cathedrals were built, or were in the process of building at Durham, Ely, Gloucester, Lichfield, Salisbury, Wells, Winchester and Worcester, as well as Saint Paul's and some 157 other religious houses. To see them as they were then, soot or grime and the patina of the years must be washed away. The west front of Saint Paul's Cathedral has already been restored to the brilliant, sunlit masterpiece that Wren created. The change is magical. And now the porch of the west door of Westminster Abbey has been cleaned and the warm, golden stone is once again as Henry III saw it.

Imagination must do the same for many other Norman and Gothic buildings, as well as restoring a wealth of colour that is now lost. The life-size figures on the west front of Wells Cathedral, for instance, were once brilliantly painted. Many frescoes have not survived the centuries, and only descriptions are left of the elaborate and richly jewelled church furnishings that brought colour and magnificence to the interior of these graceful buildings. Perhaps only inside Westminster Abbey, the realization of Henry III's great dream, can we guess at a former glory. "As the Rose is to other flowers, so this House is among buildings," is inscribed on the floor of the Chapter House.

The Norman Conquest was followed by wave after wave of monastic invasions, each making its own mark on English life. Most of them were quickly integrated, and by the thirteenth century there were rich and powerful monasteries established throughout the country by Cistercians, Benedictines, Austin or "black" canons, and many others. Only the Cluniacs kept their foreign allegiance and were never wholly accepted here. This strict branch of the Benedictine Order had spread throughout western Christendom from their first foundation at Cluny in Burgundy. The Priory of Saint Pancras at Lewes, built on the same plans as buildings just completed at Cluny, was started in 1077 and was most prosperous during the first half of the thirteenth century.

All these monasteries were enclosed communities with the position of rich and powerful landlords and employers. In the 1220s a fresh invasion brought something in the nature of a religious revival. The Dominicans, or Friars Preachers (known as the Black Friars) and the Franciscans or Friars Minor (known as the Grey Friars) arrived to spread new learning and religious teaching. They lived in small groups among the urban populations, teaching and preaching, and from their work sprang the universities at Oxford and Cambridge as well as the unfamiliar and dangerous habit of political argument.

This was an age of intrepid men who combined scholarship with statesmanship. Rome, always wary of strange doctrines, banned the teaching of Aristotle and threatened excommunication to those who disobeyed. Many established scholars themselves resented the "moderns" with their new and disturbing theories. Men like Robert Grosseteste, who was the first head of the Greyfriars' school at Oxford, and Adam Marsh (also called Adam de Marisco) who followed him, proclaimed the teaching of the church under Rome and yet taught men to think boldly for themselves. They and many others who had studied in Paris or Chartres, or in the Pope's Household, passed on their knowledge for a small fee. England, like other developing countries, showed a passionate desire for learning. It fired boys of all classes, and Edmund Rich of Abingdon, later Archbishop of Canterbury, was one of the many who begged or worked their way and joined small groups living in a boarding-house under a tutor. Weekly tuition fees were only a few pence, with handwriting as an "extra", but wages were comparably low and many boarding-house keepers were ready to exploit the struggling scholar.

The Osney Chronicle recorded that as early as 1133 Master Robert Puleyn was delivering public lectures in divinity at Oxford, but it was not until the thirteenth century that the first colleges were founded and the university gained international respect as a centre of learning. Both Oxford and Cambridge enjoyed royal encouragement because they could provide the expert knowledge and skill needed by a king in framing laws to further his own ends. Yet not only did they retain their independence, but they did not hesitate to join the anti-monarchist cause in time of civil war.

Students have always been inattentive at times. "A certain excellent lecturer, who studied with me at Oxford, used often when in the schools, while a master was lecturing or holding a disputation, to attend to other things than the lecture, even compiling works of his own. And behold, when he himself had been made a lecturer, his hearers were so inattentive that, as he said, he would as soon shut his book and go away, as lecture. And filled with remorse he said, 'It is by God's just judgment that nobody will listen to me, for I never used to listen to any teacher.' "[1]

Along with other "modern ideas", inflammatory political theories were kindling fires throughout Europe. Some of the tracts that passed surreptitiously from hand to hand were as advanced as the revolutionary pamphlets, like *Vindicia Contra Tyrannos*, of the sixteenth century. As early as 1159 John of

Salisbury, in his *Policraticus*, set out a philosophy based on the responsibility of the king for the welfare of his people, and the subjection of his will to the good of his subjects. The writer of the Song of the Battle of Lewes defined quite clearly the difference between liberty and licence:

"But whoever is truly king is truly free, if he rule himself and his kingdom rightly; let him know that all things are lawful for him which are fitting for ruling the kingdom, but not for destroying it. It is one thing to rule, which is the duty of a king, another to destroy by resisting the law. Law is so called from binding (*lex a ligando*), which is so perfectly described as the law of liberty, as it is freely served."[2]

How far Simon de Montfort was influenced by these theories, and how far he was a man of action who ruled empirically during his brief term of office, it is difficult to say. He may not have played a leading part in the drawing up of the Provisions of Oxford though his name was conspicuous among the signatories. He chose Robert Grosseteste, Adam Marsh (who was tutor and chaplain to his household), Walter de Cantelupe the saintly Bishop of Worcester, and other learned and thoughtful men, as his closest friends. He must often have listened to their discussions and been much influenced by their principles. But when he found himself, after the Battle of Lewes, the virtual dictator of England, with at least an outline of his plan of government, the forces ranged against him were so powerful that he had no chance to translate his advanced political theories into reality.

There has been a good deal of speculation about the "Paper Constitution" which Paris inserted in his chronicle for 1244 but which Denholm-Young suggests should correctly be attributed to 1238. Some sort of tract, which may have dealt only with church affairs but more probably referred to a plan for government reform, was sent by Adam Marsh to Robert Grosseteste from de Montfort's home at Leicester Castle:

"I return to your lordship that abbreviation which you have written '*de principatu regni et tyrannidis*' (the principles of kingship and tyranny) as you sent it, affixed with the seal of the Earl of Leicester . . ."

Marsh continues in such obscure and cautious terms that it is reasonable to think that the missing document was radical and highly dangerous. This is no place to examine the arguments, but like R. F. Treharne, who writes of "the great design", I believe that de Montfort and his friends, in advance of their time, were groping for some sort of constitutional pattern that would adjust the balance of power. Perhaps this was the blueprint for the Oxford Statutes of 1258.

Feudalism to some extent matched responsibility against obligation, but with its decline the scales were weighted too heavily on the side of the central government. However, as Bagehot wrote in 1867, "Of all nations in the world the English are perhaps the least a nation of pure philosophers", and the political development of the thirteenth century no doubt sprang from circumstance, ambition, and all the freaks and hazards of nature and of human behaviour, as much as from rational planning.

In the thirteenth century England was only groping towards a comprehensive political system, but her legal system was already established and complex. Even before Henry II's reign Westminster was a high court of justice. Knights came as representatives from the shires, and burgesses from the towns, to present petitions and answer writs of summons. Men came from the county courts or courts of the eyre to lodge appeals. They came also to settle the claims of the Exchequer for feudal dues, or taxes. Parliament, which is still the highest court of appeal, was no new institution. It developed its unique character over the centuries out of the growing needs of both king and people, and provided a vital link for communication between them.

Sir Charles Petrie points out in his foreword that it was the rooting of the central government in the new middle classes and through them in local authority that gave the English medieval parliamentary system lasting strength.

GROSSETESTE was not only a master of theology, philosophy

and languages. He also led a revolutionary movement in the sphere of science, and Oxford became a famous centre for the teaching of mathematics and physics. He and his colleagues were concerned with explaining natural phenomena in scientific terms, and they examined the rainbow, the properties of metals, the laws of refraction and the behaviour of heavenly bodies. Grosseteste apparently saw Halley's Comet in 1228. Medical knowledge and skill were growing too, with improvements in diagnosis and the wider use of surgery.

The most versatile genius of them all was Roger Bacon, who suffered persecution and imprisonment because of his revolutionary ideas. Whether in fact he invented gunpowder is not certain, but he fully understood its possibilities.

"By the flash and burning of fire, and by the horror of noises, wonderful things can be done, at any distance which we wish, so that no mortal man can avoid or endure it. A childish example is that noise and fire which are made in various parts of the world by the powder of saltpetre and sulphur and hazelwood charcoal. If this powder is enclosed in a tube of parchment as thick as one's finger, it makes such a noise as greatly vexes the ear, especially of one who does not understand it, and the terrible flash is also very alarming. Now if a tube of great size were made, nobody would be able to bear either the shock or the noise, or the flash; and if the instrument were made of solid substance, then the violence would be far greater."[3]

He looked into the future and accurately foretold many marvels. He wrote about ships "borne on under the guidance of a single man, with greater speed than if they had been full of sailors. Carriages also may be made so as to be moved without any animal force, with an incalculable impetus". He described glasses for long distance viewing of an enemy, "so also we might make the sun, moon and stars come down lower here. Contrivances also may be made to walk at the bottom of the sea or rivers without danger to the body. Bridges also may be made across rivers, without piers or other support. Machines also for flying may be made, so that a man seated in the middle may turn round a certain mechanism by which artificial wings may beat the air, flying like a bird." More than two hundred years later another genius, Leonardo da Vinci, shared Bacon's vision.

It is still fashionable to glorify the romance and chivalry of the Middle Ages. The picture of "Merrie England" is attractive, but it is no more true than it would be today. The same ingredients were there that make up our present world: poverty, affluence, brutality, tenderness, self-interest and compassion, learning and ignorance. Because the image is blurred by time we fail to see in the medieval mirror of the past a reflection of ourselves. But the differences between their world and ours were perhaps greater than the similarities.

Wars tended to be more negotiating manœuvres than the savage orgies of destruction they are now. There was an element of ritual, as in a violent game of chess. Serfs, or pawns, were expendable. Kings, bishops, knights and castles were jealously guarded, and their captors used them as bargaining counters at the end. The commander probably held his position by reason of his rank rather than his fighting qualities, and usually depended on skill at arms and weight of numbers instead of a knowledge of strategy or tactics. Apart from an occasional ambush and the inevitable skirmishing, a battle usually took the form of one army frontally assaulting the other, without any attempt at surprise or subterfuge.

Soldiers were mainly untrained men fulfilling their feudal service, and the "battle season" was a short one because of the demands of harvesting. When Henry III entered into long campaigns against France, or civil war was prolonged, he hired mercenaries. In fact, during the thirteenth century the role of the soldier was changing. It became common for a money payment to be substituted for military service, and feudalism was in any case declining. Armour became more elaborate and costly, and its greater weight meant a heavier and more expensive horse. Fewer and fewer men could afford the honour of knighthood.

The well-accoutred knight wore a mail *hauberk* or tunic, with a mail *coif* or close cap, reaching to the shoulders, and mail gloves and hose. Helmets were changing from flat-topped to round-topped design and enclosed the head with only slits to allow air and vision. Plate was just coming into fashion as reinforcements at the shoulder and elbow. A few would wear over their armour the loose, sleeveless surcoat, emblazoned with their arms, but they were not in general use yet. When the knights were dressed and mounted the servants handed up their arms. Each carried a triangular or kite-shaped shield made of wood covered with leather and strengthened with horn or metal; a lance sixteen feet long; and a short sword. Some perhaps had battle-axes with several vicious blades or a heavy spiked mace for close fighting.

Horses were valuable, and they also wore some chain mail protection. The art of breeding them was well understood, and both Henry II and King John imported stallions, mainly from Normandy and the low countries, to improve the English breed. The comment by Matthew Paris, referring to another occasion, "He had with him a very numerous and powerful force, consisting of a thousand knights sufficiently well mounted, though not on Spanish, Italian, or other costly horses, and properly equipped in mail and linen accoutrements . . ." suggests that some foreign horses were more highly prized than the English cross-breed. They would need to be bred for strength, for the weight of armour worn by cavalry was steadily increasing.

The ordinary ranks of cavalry and the foot soldiers would consider themselves lucky to have a tunic of quilted leather or cloth. At one time personal military service was for a certain period, usually two months in time of war or forty days in time of peace, each year. The habit had grown of replacing personal service by a sum of money paid in compensation which the lord collected from his feudal tenants and in turn paid to the king, or used for the hiring of mercenaries. At a time of civil war most of the men of military age would be called on for a period of service, whether they were well armed or not. Some of them would have to wear their ordinary clothes, adding protective padding where they could. Some had bows and arrows, but the use of massed archers had not yet been developed and many only had sticks with a leather loop for slinging stones, or stout poles, as much for self defence as for damaging the enemy.

At this period, the foot soldier was of little importance. Battles were fought mainly by mailed horsemen, and although massed archers might be drawn up in formation behind a palisade to meet the first onslaught of the enemy, their own cavalry would not hesitate to ride over them. Armed with longbows or slings, and perhaps a knife or club for in-fighting, they rarely made an effective fighting force. Their main use was in duties around the camp and in siege warfare. It is easy to imagine that when it came to the allocation of rations, the infantry came off badly.

For the knight and his mounted followers war was a very different matter. Every boy in a family of substance was educated primarily as a soldier, and jousting, although from time to time forbidden by the church and the state, was the popular sport. War was therefore something of an adventure, offering a young man a chance to exercise his talents and prove his manhood. The Crusades may have sprung from religious fanaticism (though some Frenchmen have claimed that the main purpose was to discover new varieties of vine) but to the ambitious young man they offered danger, experience, prestige, and if he were lucky, material gain. And just as today political disagreement is not inconsistent with personal friendship, so in the thirteenth century wars could be conducted without rancour.

The cavalry was normally formed into three divisions known as "battles" and drawn up to face the "battles" of the enemy. Keeping a fourth in reserve was unusual and probably unpopular, as no knight would willingly risk losing his share of the glory and spoils. It was also anything but easy to establish a workable hierarchy of command among many jealous factions. In fact then, as now, wars must have been ninety-five per cent boredom enlivened by five per cent danger. Sometimes hostile armies failed to meet because of their lack of reconnaissance or geographical knowledge. An unexpected river was enough to send them off course, and as few if any plans were made for provisions they followed a scorched earth policy wherever they went. Siege, minor skirmishes, stalemate, disease and hunger made up much of the story. For the infantryman there was little else to hope for. Only occasionally a great battle gave a knight the chance to prove his valour.

These were the early days of heraldry. As knights became more and more enclosed in the anonymity of armour, distinguishing marks grew more necessary. First the shield bore an insignia, and presently the device was repeated on the surcoat and later on the tabard, and an heraldic figure was worn on the crest of the helmet. Anthony Wagner, as Richmond Herald, has written "Crusade and the tournament which now brought together knights who were strangers yet rivals; the growth of feudalism and the emphasis on the knight's hereditary attachment to his lord and land; the efflorescence of romantic chivalry and its poetical expression; and the simultaneous culmination of the decorative arts all seem to join together to bring heraldry to birth and thereafter in one century to perfection".[4]

Chivalry can flourish without patriotism. Pollard wrote in *The Evolution of Parliament.* "English nationalism cannot, indeed, be assumed before the reign of Edward I. The cry against aliens was loud in the land under Henry III but it was raised by men who were hardly more English than the aliens they denounced." But men are not slow to develop local loyalty. Two hundred years proved more than long enough for national pride to take root in America and in many Commonwealth countries. The Normans who came to England on William the Conqueror's bandwagon and were rewarded with estates made it their home, and it is clear from the song-writers of the time that the name "England" was beginning to evoke a sense of patriotism. When Simon de Montfort raised the flag the news spread throughout the country, and citizens of all classes, though for many and diverse motives, rallied to his support. To the writer of the Song of the Battle of Lewes, all that gallant army were true patriots:

"May the power of the Almighty complete what He has commenced, and may He restore the kingdom of the English nation! . . . Read this, ye English, concerning Lewes' fight, under the protection whereof ye live defended. Because if victory had yielded to those who are now vanquished, the remembrance of the English would have been vanquished and become worthless."[2]

The ordinary poor villager of thirteenth century England had a greatly circumscribed view of the world if he knew of it at all. He was bounded by disciplines and fears. God, in the person of the Pope and through the agency of the priest largely governed his behaviour in this world and his hope of redemption in the next, but the powers of nature, superstitions, witchcraft and folklore powerfully influenced his mind. He watched a constant tussle between Satan, in the form of lightning, tempest, flood, frost, disease and pest, and God, and too often Satan proved the stronger. His feudal lord, of course, laid down the pattern of his working life and demanded a share of his labour, his production and his income. The king was just a remote, shadowy figure, representing the highest feudal power, the fount of unattainable justice and the embodiment of semi-divinity.

If a man broke the law he came under a code of punishment which was harsh but intelligible. A butcher selling tainted meat might find himself in the pillory while the offending goods were burned under his nose. The counterfeiter of money would lose his hand, and a poacher would suffer some amputation or even lose his life. Fines were levied for such sins as lying, selling under weight, practising magic, slandering and petty theft, and each town drew up a list of by-laws to govern the behaviour of its citizens and tried to enforce some standards of hygiene. For serious crimes or for extorting information there were various forms of torture, crushing the body in a narrow chest or stretching it on the rack, exposing it to extreme cold, or the horrible death by hanging, drawing and quartering.

The Church imposed periods of penance and fasting on bread and water, for periods varying from a few days to many years, for offences such as gluttony, drunkenness, witchcraft, sorcery, fortune telling, dressing in animal skins to celebrate the New Year, idolatry, or making love potions.

Even in this cruel age, however, there were signs of a social conscience. The Church led the way by providing care for the sick and poor, and although a leper was treated as an outcast and an untouchable, yet it was the duty of a priest to lead the sick man to church to hear Mass, and to comfort him. On certain holy days the King would feed hundreds of the poor in the precincts of his palace at Westminster, and many barons followed the royal example. The sick and maimed were accepted as a burden on the community, and although many of the medical remedies were still founded in superstition and witchcraft there was a glimmering of understanding of some elementary facts about diet and infection.

One of the greatest influences on a man's life was the money-lender. Like peasant subsistence farmers in all countries and at all times, he found it difficult to evade the clutches of the usurers: one bad harvest put him into debt, and he was seldom able to recover. The Jews were certainly chief among them, but their race was made the scapegoat for them all. With their long experience of the world and its ways, and their propensity for making money, they found their own niche in the machinery of feudal England. Henry III, who was always in money difficculties, glad to find a regular source of income, cheerfully exploited them by claiming a share of the money-lenders' profits. For some years this was said to amount to a fifth of his total income. Smallholdings held as security were sold to the powerful landowners, the great barons, the monasteries and rich merchants.

It is not surprising that the radical party, in their petition to the King in 1258, should include this grievance, "Also they seek remedy for this, because the Jews sometimes transfer their debts and the lands pledged to them to the nobles and more powerful people of the realm, who enter, in consequence, upon the lands of the lesser people; and although those who owe the debt are prepared to discharge it with interest, the said nobles put off the business so that the said lands and holdings may in some way or other remain with them, saying that without the Jew, to whom the debt was owed, they neither know nor can do anything; and always put off the discharge of the said money, so that, in case of death or any other accident, evident peril and manifest disinheritance hangs over those whose the said holdings were."[5]

It was an age in which it was too easy for the strong to batten on the weak, but the moneylenders also played a useful role by providing capital for expanding trade. Jews were singled out for harsh and vindictive treatment. Large numbers were massacred, their coffers were frequently robbed and in 1290 every Jew left in England was expelled. The practice of usury went on through the Gascons and Italians who took their place.

For the villein, the countryman with little or no freedom, and the cottager who held a small plot of land, life was a constant struggle for survival. He spoke in his local Saxon dialect, barely understanding the French of his feudal lord or the Latin of the Church. One matter was clearly laid down: the extent of his feudal rights and duties. He rented his plot from the lord of the manor and paid for it by working a stated number of days or half-days each week on the manorial fields. He also paid an agreed sum of money and perhaps some payment in kind. At Easter, for instance, he might deliver the "Easter eggs" to which his master was entitled.

A village was a small world, almost entirely self-sufficient. There were roads or tracks of a sort between one community and another, but there was probably nothing so coherent as a medieval road system. In Roman times roads were a military necessity, and no doubt some of their great highways such as Watling Street, Icknield Way, Fosse Way and Ermine Street were still in use. Henry I laid down regulations for the King's highways, including a standard width: "wide enough for two wagons to pass upon them, two oxherds to make their goads touch across them, and sixteen armed knights to ride abreast on them." The cartographer who made the famous "Gough Map" (now in the Bodleian Library at Oxford) during the first half of the fourteenth century shows a number of main arteries and cross country roads. So does Matthew Paris, whose distorted map of England shows the mouth of the Thames on the south coast. But it is the rivers that are marked so conspicuously. In good weather they were useful waterways for merchandise or travellers, and a source of income to bridge builders and toll keepers. In bad weather they were often an obstruction and a danger.

Each village family owned a few animals and poultry which in winter would share the shelter of their timber and clay cottage. They spun and wove their own wool and wore simple smocks of rough, undyed material. It was far from idyllic. Hunger was never far round the corner and the poacher who tried to improve his diet by going after the game that abounded in the royal forests risked losing a limb if not his life. On working days a serf might get a midday meal at the manor, but the staple diet of the villager was coarse black bread with cheese made from the milk of his sheep or goat, and a pottage of beans or peas.

Meat was therefore a great luxury although prices sound cheap enough today. The records of the household expenses of Eleanor de Montfort in 1265 show such items as two calves for 1*s.* 6*d.*, a calf and a sheep for 3*s.* 3*d.*, ten geese for 2*s.* 3*d.* and six dozen fowls for 3*s.* Eggs are shown as 400 for 18*d.* Even so, these prices set them out of reach of the poor agricultural community, living mainly by barter and their own efforts. An occasional pigeon or rabbit, or eggs from their underfed poultry were a treat. Sheep were kept mainly for their wool, and cows were doubly useful as they provided milk and dragged the plough. Men brewed their ale, and no doubt distilled their spirits at home from any grain available, usually barley or oats, and as hops were unknown then (and until two hundred years or so later) they seasoned it with pepper, a habit not unknown today. The price of ale was ½*d.* to ¾*d.* a gallon.

It is quite impossible, however, to interpret thirteenth-century prices in modern terms. Money was little used in village communities, and as coins were liable to be debased or clipped their value fluctuated. In the tenth century under King Athelstan there was only one official coin, the silver penny, but it was minted by moneyers all over the country. Canterbury had seven mints: four owned by the King, two by the Bishop and one by the Abbot. London had eight, Winchester six, Lewes in Sussex had two and there were one or more in every borough in the country. The number declined during the twelfth century

Two illuminations from the *Luttrell Psalter*, 1340, (British Museum reference No. MS Add 42130) and an illustration of boat building from *Li Livre des Ansienes Estoires*, written, probably in Italy, in the late thirteenth century

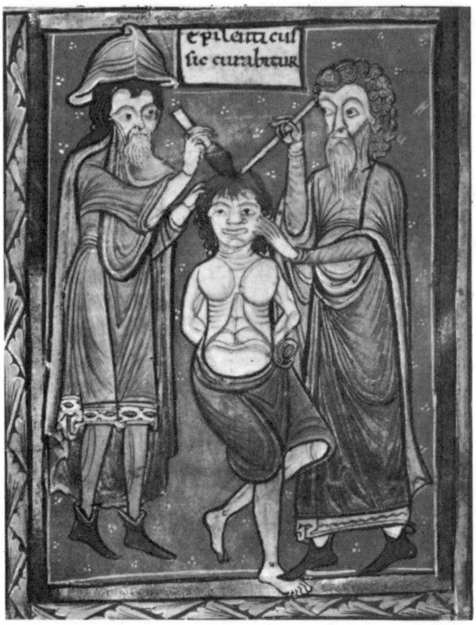

Left, a cure for epilepsy, from a twelfth-century collection of medical and herbal treatises (MS Sloane 1975). *Centre*, a boar hunt, from a fourteenth-century French manuscript, *Livre du roy Modas*. *Bottom*, an illustration of bear baiting, from the *Luttrell Psalter*

(Both reproduced by kind permission of the Radio Times Hulton Picture Library)

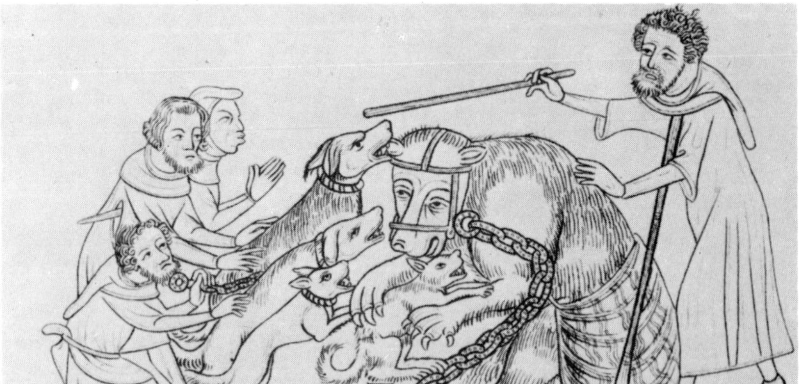

and during the thirteenth century the coinage was brought under direct government control.

Apart from the full purses carried by the rich on their travels, money was stored in strong chests and often placed for safety in the care of the religious houses. It was used for transactions in land, for paying taxes, for trading and buying luxury articles, but although we read that a horn blower in the royal household earned fourpence a day and his food, or that a master paid a penny for the weeding of three acres, it would be rash to attempt any calculation in terms of twentieth-century money. Lists of medieval retail prices show such items as "spectacles, 20*d*", or "one hat of russet, 6*d*", but at the same time sugar was a shilling a pound and salt, so necessary for preserving food as well as savouring it, was almost beyond the means of the poor.

The value of money has of course depreciated many times since the thirteenth century. In the first sixty years of the twentieth century alone it has depreciated by five times and the price of some articles may be fifty times as high today as in feudal times. But the law of supply and demand as well as the changing habits of society confuse the picture. Whatever the value, in modern terms, of the few pence received as wages or for the sale of goods or services in thirteenth-century England, they certainly would not buy the luxuries enjoyed only by the rich. For most of the community life was monotonous and hard.

To the villager, his land was all-important. His life was centred on his family and on the parish pump and the village inn where he met his friends, grumbled about the weather, joined in the deliberations of the village elders and kept abreast of the news. His newspaper was the mendicant friar or the pedlar, and stories no doubt grew more colourful on their travels. There too he would hear the gossip from the great house, and watch the arrival or departure of his lord or his lord's guests with their train of servants.

At the manor the rich enjoyed a high standard of living. Many of their houses were full of treasures and furnished with a certain degree of comfort, and although they were far from draught proof, with a huge log fire blazing in the great hall, fur-lined clothing, and the use of tapestries for screening, the worst winter cold could be kept at bay.

During the thirteenth-century clothes were becoming more elegant as the choice of materials widened, with English woollens among the finest in Europe. A lady of fashion could buy scarlet cloth from Lincolnshire or Yorkshire, coloured materials from Flanders, fine English worsteds, silks and linens from Italy, velvets and linens from France, rich furs from Scandinavia and the Baltic and jewellery from Asia. To display them, fashions grew more elaborate, with trailing sleeves, long pointed shoes and the introduction of pleating and colourful embroidery.

The wide choice of food enjoyed by richer households is even more astonishing. Bread and cakes were baked from fine flour, and cheesecake and gingerbread were well known. Fish was an important item, especially during Lent and other fast days. Herrings were salted in huge quantities and used to feed large households and to give to the poor, but Eleanor de Montfort's household accounts and other contemporary records mention mullet, plaice, flounders, mackerel, salmon, eels, conger, turbot, bream, pike, lampreys, porpoise, grampus (the tail and tongue were expensive luxuries), whale, lobsters and shrimps.

Fruits in wide variety were imported from the Mediterranean to supplement home grown fruit. Costly spices such as ginger, pepper, cloves, cinnamon, cardamom and capers, with herbs from the garden, probably helped to disguise the flavour of meat that had lost its freshness. Hunting, the prerogative of royal favourites, brought in venison and wild boar as well as game birds, hares and rabbits.

England still produced her own inferior sweet "bastard" wine (Domesday records thirty-eight vineyards), but her union with Gascony (also known as Guyenne) and her increasing export trade made it possible to introduce fine clarets from the area around Bordeaux in exchange for wool, cheese and hides. These wines were not yet ranked as important, but as Gascony came under the English crown through Henry II's marriage to

Eleanor of Aquitaine it was natural that their commercial ties should be close.

Rich and poor led their widely separated lives, and yet there were many links between them. No longer did they share a common danger from man's traditional enemy, the wolf, which was nearly extinct in England by the thirteenth century. It was not just that both waged a constant and relentless war against fleas, or that both lived in dread of leprosy and of the plagues that swept through the country leaving a trail of dead. Above all stood the universal custom of hospitality and charity which were generally observed. A wayfarer could find free lodging, and a beggar was given alms and food when he appealed to the lady of the manor.

An agricultural community tends to be conservative in outlook, slow to fight for progress or even to accept it. While village life changed almost imperceptibly, urban life was undergoing violent change. Radicals and reformers are mainly bred in towns. This was so in the thirteenth century just as it is today. During that time the townsman began to develop a sense of his own importance. The tradesman, instead of being a victim for plunder by the barons, compelled to live on his wits and flourish by guile, turned into a recognized and respectable citizen. Town markets increased in importance as they superseded the old cumbersome system of manorial rights, and as men united for their mutual protection and formulated a code of rules for their society, local authorities came into being. The towns produced the nucleus of a new, middle class. These were the men most eager to support a social revolution, and who were to emerge from the troubled years with a new status.

But life, even for the struggling peasant, had its lighter side. Man is by nature resilient and cheerful, and his natural inclination towards dancing and singing has helped him to endure many miseries and privations. The Church generally frowned upon dancing except at special occasions such as weddings, but no doubt many a round dance was performed on the village green, and even in the churchyard, while the musicians played a tune on a reed or a simple stringed instrument and the audience joined in a ballad that was passed from father to son but rarely committed to paper.

There were other delights too. Cock fighting was a popular sport and so were wrestling and ferreting. Sometimes a Punch and Judy show arrived on the village green, or games were played with bat and ball, precursor of village cricket. In its old form of stoolball this is still a popular game in the countryside around Lewes. And for winter evenings there were board games such as backgammon and chess, and the endless fascination of dice.

Minstrels were attached to some of the great households or wandered around the countryside spreading rumours and satirizing the foibles of their betters, always risking a ducking in the village pond if they gave offence. And there were the vagrant tumblers, jugglers and fools; the bear baiters, and troupes of performing dogs and monkeys. For the simple people, with neither books nor learning, when winter brought early nightfall and the mutton fat rushlight that served as a candle was beyond their means, the main amusements must have been gossip, storytelling and making love.

In the British Museum there is a manuscript which dates from between 1220 and 1240, giving the words and music of a remarkable song. Dr. Ernest Walker described it as "an extraordinary production, which combines beauty of sound and ingenuity of workmanship in a manner that is hardly realizable, were the date not certain, as possible in the thirteenth century".[6] As a composition it shows astonishing complexity, for it consists of a four-part canon combined with a Pes in two lower parts. This six-part counterpoint is expertly interwoven. The words are familiar:

Sumer is icumen in
Lhude sing, Cuccu;
Groweth sed and bloweth med
And springeth the wude nu;
Sing Cuccu . . .

The miracle of spring lifted the heart then as it does now, and I like to think that this gay and charming song conveys the lively, hopeful spirit of the age in which it was born. This, then, was the fascinating stage on which Simon de Montfort did battle royal against King Henry III.

II

"Magna Charter was therefore the chief cause of Democracy in England, and thus a *Good Thing* for everyone (except the Common People)."
(*1066 And All That.*)

THE UNHAPPY REIGN of King John ended in revolution and stalemate. Although *Magna Carta* appears, at this distance, to represent a real political advance, to the English citizens of the time it must have been a singular disappointment. Many charters had been issued before, and this one was called "great" only on account of its length. It was virtually a peace treaty, a legal contract, a technical concession to the barons wrung from the King by threats. It had little new to say, but it set out the terms of agreement between government and governed. During the reign of Henry III it was confirmed some thirty times, with various amendments and omissions. It was also on many occasions repudiated by both King and Pope. The laws and charters of France, Holland, Hungary and Spain were reflecting the same trends.

It was, however, an important document in two ways. This was the first time that the older, more powerful barons, the newer and lesser nobility, the towns (headed by London) with their growing mercantile importance, and the Church, had formed an active if temporary alliance. It was also remarkable for Clause 61 which provided, as it were, the teeth; the setting up of a council of twenty-five to enforce the terms was an early and brave attempt to impose some kind of parliamentary restraint upon the King.

The leader of this opposition movement was Stephen Langton, a friend and formerly a fellow student of Pope Innocent III and nominated by him to the See of Canterbury. King John was already in a state of disgrace and excommunication, but he was bold enough to refuse to accept the appointment. Langton remained abroad, waiting. In 1213 a papal bull was issued deposing John and offering the English throne to the King of France. Threatened by invasion, hated at home and despised abroad, the tyrannical King surrendered his kingdom and became a fief of the Pope, compelled to pay a tribute of a thousand marcs a year. For him, and for his son after him, the embracing arms of Rome, so dearly bought, were a shelter against the storm. For the country they were a bear's hug, squeezing out all the riches from clergy and people.

From the time of Langton's return in 1213 the strength of the opposition grew quickly, and in 1215 the King was compelled to sign the Charter. Having done so he at once repudiated it, and in this he was supported by the Pope who distrusted power in any hands other than his own. When the Council of Twenty-five invited Louis, son of the King of France (and later Louis VIII) to bring an army to England and attack John and his mercenaries, civil war broke out. One year later John suddenly died at Newark. The Archbishop of Canterbury was away in Rome and the Pope, through his legate, flung his powerful support behind the royalist party and against the French prince. Louis was defeated decisively at Lincoln and accepted good terms to leave the country. At once hasty plans were made at Gloucester for the coronation of John's elder son, Henry.

"Standing before the high altar, with Jocelin Bishop of Bath dictating the oath, he then swore in the presence of clergy and people, touching the holy gospels and the relics of many saints, that he would give honour, peace and reverence to God and His Holy Church and its ministers all the days of his life. Also he swore that he would show strict justice to the people committed to him, that he would destroy evil laws and unjust customs if there were any in his realm, and would observe the good and make everyone else observe them."[1]

With no archbishop present, and only a simple circlet to serve as a crown, the new King was crowned. He was a child of nine, brought from his nursery at Devizes to make these solemn vows. He was too young to learn from his father's disastrous mistakes or to profit from the guidance of the two great regents who ruled the country. One was Stephen Langton, and the other William Marshal Earl of Pembroke, another man of fearless integrity. With the help of Cardinal Gualo, the papal legate, they at once pronounced in favour of the Great Charter and set about a programme of reform.

England already had a competent and experienced civil service, and even during the upheavals of Henry's reign it continued to carry out the day to day work of government. The Norman and Plantagenet kings before John had mainly ruled *in absentia* and John was the first to style himself "King of England". Richard Coeur de Lion, for instance, spent barely six months in this country during the ten years of his reign, and it is surprising that he is remembered with such affection. Even Henry II was primarily a French prince and spent twice as long in France as in England.

The Angevin Empire, taking its name from Anjou and the capital town of Angers, comprised at least half of France, as well as England and southern and eastern Ireland. The domains included Normandy, Brittany and Gascony as well as Aquitaine, so that the western half of what we now call France, and a belt extending nearly to the eastern border, came under the same crown. Faced with the problem of running such widely separated domains Henry II, with his passion for law and order, introduced important legal reforms and built up a central government to run affairs in England in his absence through the offices of Justiciar and Exchequer. The justiciar was in effect the vice-regent and held authority over all matters, financial and judicial. The Court of Exchequer acted as auditors and accounts were settled by using counters on a chequered cloth, from which the name arose.

As each king in turn built up a stronger central government through his own household, and its work became more complex, it also became more costly. With no system of taxation as we know it today, and with no standing army to enforce foreign policy, it became increasingly difficult to finance the country's administration. During John's reign, when the crumbling

Angevin Empire was finally lost, the King was for the first time compelled to live in this backward corner of his realms instead of the civilized courts of France. This probably helped to kindle the beginnings of national pride that stirred his subjects. The Norman barons were slowly identifying themselves with their adopted country, and as their feudal power declined they demanded more say in the running of national affairs.

The young King Henry's minority hastened this process and gave impetus to the idea of the regular calling of Parliament. In the first years after the Conquest no representative assembly was possible. Only the King symbolized national unity, and he travelled from one stronghold to another dispensing justice, showing the flag and protecting his own interests as the feudal overlord. Even when the magnates met, vying with each other in magnificence, surrounded by their bodyguards and servants, their aim was propaganda rather than consultation. The Great Council assembled when the King willed it, but discussed only such matters as he ordained. They had no say in taxation or expenditure, no influence on foreign policy, and no rights beyond those of every vassal from his feudal lord.

As the Great Council evolved into a consultative body its primary function was to redress grievances and to advise the executive. When the professional civil servants met difficulties beyond their wits to solve, or with implications too dangerous to handle, they were glad to shelter behind this powerful body of the nobility. The barons, for their part, welcomed the chance to watch their own interests and keep a restraining hand on the executive. And so they encouraged the regular calling of what, from the 1240s, came to be known as "Parliament" or "*parlement*". The name was used officially after 1275, but it implied neither constitutional government nor popular representation.

Another less fortunate result of the period of regency was that the Pope increased his hold on the country. It was said that he regarded England as "an inexhaustible well of money" and he certainly plundered her without mercy. Her coffers had long been robbed by her indifferent Norman kings. Now she was the milch cow of the Curia. The Church of Rome, with its dreams of world domination, laid an oppressive burden on its subjects everywhere. In England the Pope could appoint his own nominees to vacant benefices, and bishoprics were a coin of favouritism and blackmail. Thus the English church suffered an infiltration of Italian and French clergy who cared little or nothing for the souls in their care. It is a remarkable feature of this period that this country produced so many courageous and incorruptible priests who took a leading part in the struggle against tyranny.

In 1219 William Marshal, Earl of Pembroke, died. He had guided the country in the name of the young King with firmness and wisdom, his limited outlook and his respect for the processes of law making him both strong and intelligible. On his death the power which he had wielded single-handed was divided between Pandulf the papal legate, Archbishop Stephen Langton and Hubert de Burgh the justiciar. Another faction competing for supremacy was the horde of foreign favourites led by Peter des Roches the Bishop of Winchester. When the young King began to play a more active rôle in national affairs and encouraged his alien friends and the papal legate to interfere in the work of reform, the justiciar found it impossible to fight on two fronts and keep control of a lawless country. He had already served two masters in a long and stormy career and he was a harsh administrator with little sympathy for the concept of national freedom. It was Stephen Langton who remained almost the sole champion of the principles laid down in the Great Charter, and with his death in 1228 went one of the hopes of resolving peacefully the conflict between monarch and people.

In 1223 there was serious threat of rebellion by Welsh and English forces in the border country and de Burgh, aiming to increase his own powers, obtained a Papal Bull declaring the young King to be of an age to rule. Henry's power was still to be subject to the Great Council, but his authority could be used to wrest the royal castles and the holders of the office of royal sheriff out of enemy hands. But both at home and in foreign affairs the forces ranged against the justiciar were too powerful. The King's day-dreams of restoring a French empire were already becoming too vivid and too dangerous, and no practical man could serve such a capricious master and at the same time govern England.

In 1234 when Henry took the reins of government into his own hands, the country began to understand the full extent of his ineptitude. There had already been signs of a weak and headstrong character. He had grandiose ideas of his own importance. With an almost touching faith in his own infallibility he was ready to rush into military enterprises for which he had neither the means nor the skill. Already he had clashed with the justiciar, rushing at him with drawn sword, because he was crossed in his wish to invade Poitou. When he got his way a year later the expedition met, like most of his campaigns, total disaster.

After the downfall of de Burgh the justiciarship was shorn of most of its powers and Henry was free to surround himself with his own favourites, most of whom were foreigners with an eye to the main chance. Roger of Wendover wrote angrily in his chronicle: "Judgment was then entrusted to the unjust, the laws to outlaws, peace to the turbulent and justice to wrongdoers."

The Church, too, was falling on evil days, and the satirical song-writers of the time were not afraid to express their views. "The clergy was once free and in high regard: none was more so. Now it is disgraced and downtrodden . . . I am afraid to say more." And again, "Weep, ye daughters of Sion, the bishops of the church at the present day are but remote imitators of Christ."[2]

Matthew Paris wrote in his Chronicle: "In these times the small fire of the faith began to grow exceeding chill, so that it was nigh well reduced to ashes, and scarce shewed a spark."

Henry lost no time in claiming that he had only confirmed *Magna Carta* in the ignorance of youth and under duress, and the Pope readily absolved him from his promises. But already he was in money difficulties, and opposition towards him was hardening. In 1232 the barons refused to grant him an aid for the war in Wales, and in the following year when he was in greater straits they disobeyed his summons to attend the Great Council, "partly because of the plots of the foreigners and partly because of the indignation that they had conceived against the King who had called in foreigners in contempt of these same barons."[1]

This resentment against aliens was a constant and growing grievance. Roger Bacon, the philosopher and scientist, warned the King publicly in a sermon "that he would never enjoy lasting peace till he removed Peter Bishop of Winchester and Peter of Rivaulx his kinsman from his councils". Recording the occasion, Matthew Paris goes on: "When others who were present protested likewise, the King coming to himself somewhat inclined his heart to reason, and when a certain witty clerk of the court, namely Roger Bacon, saw him thus softened, he said gaily and merrily but with a hint of blame, 'My lord King, what most harms and terrifies sailors at sea?' When the King answered, 'They who have their business in the great waters know,' the clerk said, 'My lord, I will tell you: rocks and stones (*petrae et rupes*). That is as though he said 'Peter des Roches' (*Petrus de Rupibus*), for this was the name and surname of the Bishop of Winchester.

"So the King bade the aforenamed magnates come to a conference at Westminster on 11 July, and there by their advice he would amend whatever he knew by right should be corrected. But when the said magnates heard that little by little many robbers were uniting in the kingdom at the King's invitation with horses and arms, seeing no signs of peace, and suspecting the inborn cunning of the Poitevins, they refrained from coming on the appointed day, but sent formal envoys to the King bidding him without delay turn out Peter Bishop of Winchester and the other Poitevins from his court. But if he did not, they themselves by the common counsel of the whole kingdom would drive him and his evil counsellors from the country and would take steps towards making a new king."[1]

The barons' message sounded uncompromising but their threats had not yet a great deal of weight behind them. Henry was a master of persuasion. It was easy to seduce the weak ones with flattery or the greedy ones with promises, and he was adept at dividing his enemies. He was also, without question, a man of real charm. Once again it was the Archbishop of Canterbury who tried to stiffen the opposition. This was Edmund Rich, or

Edmund of Abingdon, a saintly and ascetic man whose gentle character was out of tune with this coarse and violent age. He achieved a temporary success. Threatened with excommunication the King took the primate's advice and obeyed the barons.

"So, after a few days, understanding his own error and moved by penitence, he ordered Peter Bishop of Winchester to go to his diocese and turn his attention to the care of souls, and henceforth to meddle no more with the King's affairs . . . Besides, he expelled all the Poitevins from both his court and the custody of castles and sent them back to their own land."[1]

It is not surprising that the King enjoyed the company of his foreign courtiers. He was a man with wide interests and cultivated tastes, and as he saw one after another the lovely gothic cathedrals of northern France he dreamed of an England rich with such masterpieces. And so, whatever his faults as a king, as a patron of the arts he was sensitive, imaginative and generous. He was also theatrical, extravagant and ostentatious. Remembering his obligation to Rome he showered on the Church magnificent gifts which neither he nor his subjects could afford. His show of intense piety and his public acts of self-abasement had more than a hint of melodrama. Seeing in himself the descendant and natural heir of Saint Edward the Confessor, he devoted much of his life to the abbey at Westminster, built as a new shrine for the saint's bones and as a monument to his own artistic triumph.

It was and still is a masterpiece, sumptuous but graceful. W. R. Lethaby wrote: "The interior ever surprises me by its loveliness. The grace of the parts and their ordered disposition, the slender springing forms and the gaiety of the style, the fine materials and the romantic early monuments, are arresting beauties of a matchless whole."[3]

For its design, Henry probably turned to the cathedral at Amiens, and for inspiration to the Sainte Chapelle in Paris. Its furnishings were executed by the finest craftsmen in Europe and many of them were personal gifts of the King, though how he paid for them is another matter. He presented a gold-embroidered frontal for the great altar, encrusted with jewels and enamel work. Four women spent nearly four years working it, and it must have been a superb example of the famous *Opus Anglicanum.* He gave the great bells "of wonderful bigness"; four silver candlesticks for the shrine; a silver crown to bear the wax candles: a large cross for the nave; images worked in gold and set with sapphires, pearls, emeralds, rubies and garnets. The list of his gifts seems endless. Another was a banner of red samite with a dragon embroidered in gold, and this was later to be his personal standard on the battlefield.

The whole enterprise, which was the preoccupation of most of his waking hours and the centre of his dreams, filled most of his life. Matthew Paris tells us, "On Saturday, the vigil of Pentecost, in the year 1220, was begun the New Work of the chapel of the Blessed Virgin, of which the King laid the first stone." Henry was not yet thirteen.

He was much more than a nominal patron for he kept in close touch with the work, issuing orders, interviewing the craftsmen, taking wine with the master mason and studying the fabric accounts which are both detailed and accurate. From his home at the Palace across the road he watched the building rise. Lethaby wrote: "I want to think of it in its first fairness, when Henry III, in 1262, ordered pear trees to be planted in 'the herbary between the King's Chamber and the Church', evidently so that he might see it over a bank of blossom."[3]

Henry also took a leading part in the religious life of the abbey. He gave the principal relics, the stone with the imprint of Our Lord's feet at the Ascension, and the phial of the Holy Blood sent to him by the Patriarch of Jerusalem. This he carried in the procession of clergy, barefoot and humbly clad, through the dirty streets from Saint Paul's to the abbey and then "sat gloriously on his throne clad in a golden garment of the most precious brocade of Baghdad".

Matthew Paris was ordered to record this splendid scene. "And while the King sat thus on his royal throne he noticed the one who writes this and called me unto him, bidding me sit on the step below his throne, and asking, 'Hast thou observed all these things and engraved them upon thy heart?'

"I answered him, 'Yea, my lord, for it is truly a day of great splendour and worthy of remembrance.' "

In spite of the gathering political storm clouds the young Henry remained absorbed in his cultural interests. All his palaces and houses were constantly improved and restored, and the Liberate Rolls give some idea of his taste and of his astonishing attention to detail.

"The King to the guardians of the bishopric of Winchester, greeting. We bid you to cause to be made a house of fir running on six wheels, and have it roofed with lead. And cause the porch of the Queen's chapel in our castle at Winchester to be wainscoted and likewise the long passage from the same chapel to our chamber there . . . And cause a wall and a gate to be made before the doors of our kitchens there, and a herb-garden, and a wall on the side of our hall there, towards the south; and cause our well in the same castle to be repaired likewise, and four statues to be bought for the porch of the said hall, and a map of the world to be painted in the hall . . ."[4]

He employed the most famous artists of his day, many of them Italian, to paint scenes from the life of Edward the Confessor or from the Bible, or "pretty cherubims with cheerful and merry countenance". He is said to have favoured green for his walls, sometimes enlivened with silver stars, and frequently he introduced his favourite flower and emblem, the rose. It was to be his wife's badge too, and roses were painted on the walls of her chamber as well as growing in their gardens.

The artists and craftsmen, goldsmiths, embroiderers, stonemasons, wood-carvers and jewellers must have found Henry an imaginative master. "Command is given to Edward son of Odo, keeper of our works at Westminster, that he shall cause the fireplace in the Queen's chamber there to be made higher, and shall cause it to be painted. And he shall cause to be painted and portrayed on the said fireplace a figure of Winter, made the more like Winter by its sad countenance and other miserable attitudes of the body."[4]

Henry was not only a patron of the arts. He was interested in London's supply of piped water "for the poore to drink and the rich to dress their meate", and made money available for the purpose. He kept a menagerie at the Tower which included the first elephant seen in England. As the huge animal lumbered along the road from the coast to London, every village must have buzzed with excitement and surprise. The King of Norway gave him a bear, and the Emperor Frederick II added three leopards, in tribute to Henry's royal arms, a camel and some buffaloes.

"The King to the sheriffs of London, greeting. We bid you to find necessaries for our lion and his keeper while they are in the Tower of London, and this shall be reckoned to you at the Exchequer."[4]

"The King to the same, greeting. We bid you to cause William, keeper of our lion, to have 14*s.* which he spent on buying chains and other things for the use of the said lion, and this shall be reckoned to you at the Exchequer."[4]

Unfortunately the King's private and public expenditure became inextricably confused. Profligate with his own money and anyone else's he was reduced to every kind of expedient to make ends meet. Usually he rode the financial storms with some cunning and a poker-face, but occasionally the rocking of the boat made his "waxen heart" miss a beat. An immense bill came in for some work on Westminster Abbey, and he would have it "distinctly stated whether the repair of the King's houses was included in the sum of £28,127". But it was not, and he had to think up a fresh swindle to put his affairs in order.

Henry's appearance is well known from the bronze effigy in Westminster Abbey, made by William Torel in about 1291. It is one of the finest Gothic sculptures in England, and is probably a fair likeness of the man. Rishanger described him a "of middling height. He had a narrow forehead; one of his eyelids was half-closed and almost hid the dark of the pupil. Strong in physique, he was impulsive in action . . ."

"Impulsive" is too mild a word. He was a man of strong contrasts: rumbustious and unscrupulous yet chaste and pious. He had a weak man's obstinacy and a vain man's absurdity. Even his enemies held him in exasperated, almost affectionate contempt. It is not surprising that the stolid Norman barons were not to his liking. It was the urbane and fashionable Frenchmen who knew how to charm him. As each successive storm broke over his head and the cry "England for the English"

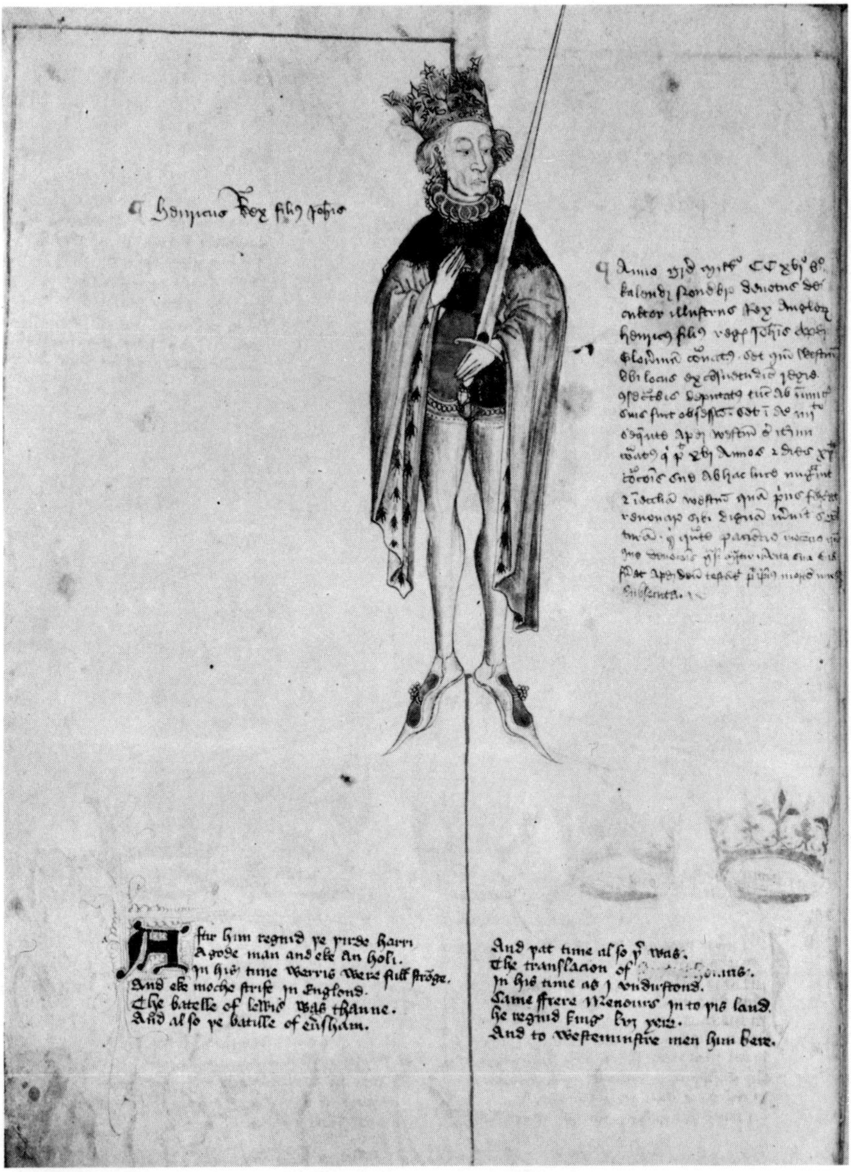

A posthumous portrait of Henry III (MS Cotton Julius E IV)

The verses describe the third Harry as a good and holy man. They also mention the strife in England during his reign and the coming of the Friars Minor

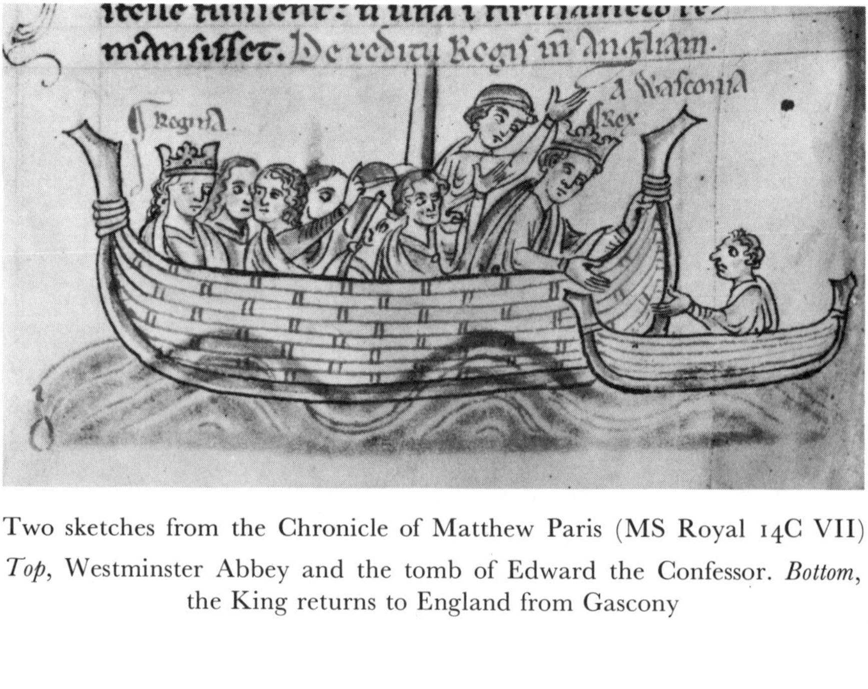

Two sketches from the Chronicle of Matthew Paris (MS Royal 14C VII)
Top, Westminster Abbey and the tomb of Edward the Confessor. *Bottom*, the King returns to England from Gascony

grew more ominous, he used every feint and stratagem in turn, blustering, bribing, wheedling, threatening, and if necessary confirming yet again, with grandiose display and an artful show of candour, the Great Charter.

He was certainly not one of England's great or able monarchs; but he had his qualities, and much can be forgiven of a man who loved art so passionately, and left his country so greatly enriched.

III

"Simon de Montfort, though only a Frenchman, was a Good Thing, and is very notable as being the only good Baron in history." (*1066 And All That.*)

AMONG THE HORDE of aliens who came to seek their fortune at the English court was a young French adventurer, Simon de Montfort. Like many another immigrant he became a great English patriot, but of the man himself, his personality, faults and foibles, not much is known. It is easy enough to peer across the dividing centuries and see Henry III as a whole man; to breathe into the dry bones of history and restore flesh and blood. But Simon de Montfort remains in the shadows, veiled by the patina of the years.

Plenty is known about his achievements, but it is a pity Shakespeare did not write *Henry III* and illumine his character, for he has never been painted "warts and all". Doubtless he considered it. Certainly de Montfort had much in common with Oliver Cromwell, whom Macaulay described as "the greatest prince that has ever ruled England". Both men were single-minded and constant, ambitious, tough, self-disciplined and God-fearing. It is impossible to guess whether Simon was as narrow and rigid in outlook, as uncompromisingly righteous, as coarse and as sensual as Cromwell. Probably not, for he enjoyed the friendship of many great scholars and churchmen of his day, men of enlightened and liberal views. Two outstanding monarchs, the Emperor Frederick II and Louis IX of France, recognized his qualities. Above all, he attracted to his cause not only men of his own rank and education, of both clergy and laity, but rich and poor, young and old of all classes. The merchants of London and their apprentices, students from Oxford, humble friars, and the common unprivileged people who were only just beginning to emerge from serfdom to find their own place in society looked to him as their leader.

At the time of his death many had deserted him. Jealousies and feuds had rent his party. Avarice and fear had seduced many to the royalist side. He said himself: "I have been in many lands and among many nations, pagan and Christian; but in no race have I ever found such faithlessness and deceit as I have met in England." But by his friends in the Church and by the humble people he was neither deserted nor forgotten.

One of Simon's most ardent champions, Paul Dunvan, in *A History of Lewes* (1795) wrote indignantly, ". . . yet calumny has added to the unauthentic catalogue of young Simon's faults that he was not an Englishman . . ."

Calumny is right. He was born of French parentage, and probably in France. His father was Simon, "the scourge of the Albigenses", a notorious and fanatical crusader whose cruelties were remarkable even in that harsh age. His mother, in spite of being blessed with "*filios multos et pulchros*" was an energetic crusader herself. There is considerable doubt about the younger Simon. Most authorities say that he was the youngest of their four sons, but others claim that he was the second or third. Again, he may have been born as early as the turn of the century, but the weight of evidence suggests that it was in 1208, one year after Henry III.

The de Montfort family took its name from a stronghold between the valleys of the Eure and the Seine known as Montfort l'Amaury in the south-east corner of Normandy, about thirty miles from Paris on the way to Chartres. The overgrown ruins of their ancient castle can still be seen there. The family also owned estates at Epernon, sixteen miles north-east of Chartres, and Evreux, one of the arondissements of the Eure. It is said that the climate there is mild, moist and foggy, which may have given Simon a foretaste of the rigours of his future home. Related by marriage to both the Norman and French royal houses, aggressive by nature and sturdy in physique, the de Montfort family fought and intrigued with each side in turn.

Very little is known about Simon's early life. There are stories of his having been taken on crusade by his mother while he was still a baby, and of his fighting beside his father as a young boy. There is no evidence to support it. Certainly he would be taught skill in arms as the most important training for life. He probably also received a sound education. His eldest brother Amauri, or Almeric, who later became Constable of France, was a pupil of Master Nicholas, one of the great mathematicians of his time. The nearby city of Chartres was a great centre of European culture and knowledge, and a family of such standing would move in educated circles.

There is no doubt at all about Simon's skill as a military commander. Such thoughtful planning of campaigns, attention to detail and enforcement of discipline were rare in an age of military ignorance. To his natural flair he added wide experience. His biographer, Prothero, described him as a great innovator in military engines, and Blaauw wrote in *The Barons' War:* "The castle of Kenilworth had been provided by de Montfort with warlike engines of defence not then known in England, for his engineering skill was repeatedly acknowledged by his contemporaries." The Master of the Armouries can find no evidence to suggest that de Montfort personally introduced any new engines of siege warfare, but there is no doubt that he was a master of the art of siege and was ready to improvise and experiment whenever occasion demanded it.

Simon's father inherited the earldom of Leicester from his mother, Amicia de Beaumont. She and her sister Margaret were co-heirs of their brother Robert FitzPernell, Earl of Leicester, and when he died Amicia inherited as her share of his titles and properties the Stewardship of England, the earldom of Leicester and lordship over the borough and lands of Leicester. Her son Simon, the famous crusader, was unable to claim his title and property. Relations between England and France were unfavourable, and King John assigned them to his royal favourites who administered them partly to the benefit of the royal purse but mainly to feather their own nests. In 1215 the earldom was granted to Ranulf, Earl of Chester.

Amauri, as the eldest, could claim in his turn to be the rightful heir when his father died, but as Constable of France he could not hope to be Steward of a hostile country.

Instead, as Simon himself recounts, he offered the whole inheritance to his young brother "providing that I could secure it; in return I released to him what I had in France. I went over to England and asked the lord King to restore to me my father's inheritance. He answered me that he could not do it, because he had given it to the Earl of Chester and his heirs. Whereupon I left without having found grace at his hands."

This brief visit took place in 1229 when Henry was busy with his foolish plan for an attack across the Channel. In the following year Simon met the Earl of Chester in Brittany. "He received my request in friendly fashion and, in the following August (1231) took me to England with him. He asked the King to receive my homage because, said he, I had more right than he to my father's inheritance; he then renounced everything that the King had given him, and the King of England received my homage."

After this act of generosity Simon was welcomed by the King with every mark of friendship. Henry was twenty-four and Simon probably one year younger. They could hardly have been less alike in character and ability, but the King would find much to admire in the Frenchman who could share his civilized tastes and also show the vigour and resolution that he lacked himself. But Simon's arrival was not popular with other members of the court. The English nobility were already smouldering with dislike of the alien favourites, and the aliens themselves were not anxious to divide their spoils with this arrogant stranger. Perhaps they also recognized and feared a man of such different calibre from themselves. The King waited discreetly for seven years before restoring to his friend the title and lands of Leicester and Simon spent much of that time abroad, fighting where opportunity offered and trying in vain to improve his fortunes by making a rich marriage.

His hopes were centred first on Mahaut, Countess of Boulogne, and then on Joan, Countess of Flanders. Both were wealthy widows and in each case marriage was refused by their guardians. Matters went so far with Joan of Flanders, who had been married twice, that there were rumours of this third one having already taken place. Queen Blanche, the mother of young King Louis IX and the Regent of France, had reason to distrust both the countess and Simon de Montfort. "The intriguing enemies of the King of France had secretly procured the marriage of the Countess of Flanders with Simon de Montfort, brother of Count Amauri. Simon was suspected at the court of France because of his English wealth and of the fealty which he had sworn to Henry III. And so he lost this marriage, just as he had lost that of the Countess of Boulogne."[1]

In England the breach between government and people was widening. Henry's abortive war with France landed him in money difficulties, and as unrest grew into violence the chief victims were the Italian clergy.

"In the same year (1232) almost everywhere in England the barns of the Romans were plundered by unknown and armed men, on good conditions and to the profit of many . . . The clerks took refuge in monasteries, but they did not dare to complain of the injuries done to them for they preferred to lose their property than be punished by an extreme sentence . . . When after a time the Pope heard what was happening, he was exceedingly angry, and sent bitter letters of reproof to the English king because he allowed such attacks to be made on ecclesiastical persons in his realm . . ."[2]

The King, always looking for a scapegoat, ". . . found on enquiry that the said trespasses were done by Hubert de Burgh during the time of his justiciarship and ordered him to be arrested and brought before him . . ."[2] De Burgh narrowly escaped with his life.

In 1235 Henry's sister Isabella was married to the Emperor Frederick II. This man, called by his contemporaries "the wonder of the world", was the most powerful monarch in Europe. He inherited from his mother the crowns of Sicily and Apulia, and was elected King of Germany and Emperor of the Holy Roman Empire, said by Voltaire to have been so called because it was neither an empire, Roman, nor holy. For more than eight centuries a succession of German princes claimed the powers and status of the former Roman emperors. Usually the title meant little, and although Frederick II held the state of Naples and other scattered parts of Italy, crowned himself

King of Jerusalem and carried on a harassing if futile struggle to thwart the papal dream of dominating Christendom, by the end of his life he ruled little more than a shadow empire. He was a brilliant man and an enlightened ruler, perhaps second only to Charlemagne in all the Middle Ages for his remarkable gifts. He was learned in many branches of knowledge, a linguist and a poet, a wise administrator and an original and liberal thinker. With his death in 1250 one of the brightest lights of Europe was extinguished.

In the following year Henry, now twenty-nine years old, married the talented and lovely Eleanor of Provence, sister of the Queen of France. Matthew Paris tells the story.

"For he had sent solemn and prudent men to Provence, to its Count Raymond, with letters expressing his great wish to marry the count's daughter, Eleanor. Now that count was a famous man, and a vigorous warrior, but because he was constantly fighting, nearly all his treasure had flown to the winds. He had married the daughter of Count Thomas of Savoy, now dead, sister to Amadeus the present count, a lady of wonderful beauty named Beatrice. She had borne to her husband, Count Raymond, very beautiful daughters, as was to be expected, and the King of France, Louis, had taken to wife the eldest, Margaret . . .

"Now the King of England by his messengers sought in marriage the youngest daughter, who was at this time twelve years of age and very fair to see . . . When they came to the French frontier, their passage was not only free but honourable, for the King of France, the Queen, sister of the bride that was to be, and Blanche, the French King's mother, escorted them. They embarked at Wissant, hastened across the sea, and reached Dover sooner than was expected. They landed safely and were on their way towards Canterbury when the King hastened to them and embraced the envoys. When he had seen and welcomed the maiden he married her at Canterbury. On 14 January the marriage ceremony was performed by Edmund, Archbishop of Canterbury, with the bishops who had accompanied the bride, and other magnates, nobles and prelates. On 19 January the King reached Westminster, and on the next day, a Sunday, with unheard-of and incomparable solemnity, Eleanor wore the crown and was crowned as Queen."

Paris goes on to tell us more of this splendid royal occasion. "There were assembled at the nuptial banquet such a host of nobility of both sexes, so many of the clergy, such crowds of the people, and such a variety of actors, that London with its capacious bosom could scarcely contain them. The whole city was therefore decorated with flags and banners, wreaths and hangings, candles and lamps, and with certain wonderful devices and extraordinary displays; all the streets were cleared of mud, dirt, sticks, and everything offensive. The citizens of London went out to meet the King and Queen in holiday attire and trappings, and vied with one another in trying the speed of their horses. On the same day when they set out from the City of Westminster, to perform the duties of butler to the King at the coronation, an office which belongs to them by ancient right, they proceeded thither dressed in silk garments, and with mantles of cloth of gold, and handsome tippets; they were mounted on costly steeds, which were ablaze with new bits and saddles, and were arranged in troops in order. They carried 360 cups of gold or silver, and the royal trumpeters went in front of them sounding their trumpets; so remarkable a novelty struck all who beheld it with astonishment."

On this occasion Simon de Montfort made his first public appearance as High Steward of England, when he "supplied the King with water in a basin to wash before dining".

Although Edmund Rich, the Archbishop of Canterbury, had persuaded the King to rid the country of most of the hated immigrants, after his marriage they returned in even greater numbers. Their leaders were the Queen's relatives, mainly Provençals: her mother, the strong-minded Beatrice; her brother Thomas, Count of Maurienne; her uncle, William of Champagne; another uncle, Peter of Savoy, whose house in the Strand was named after him and whose brother was the detested Boniface, later Archbishop of Canterbury. The King quickly discovered that he had married his wife's family as well, but he received them all with great pomp and a show of apparent delight. Apart from a state welcome with feasting and pageantry he lavishly showered on them lands, titles, offices, bishoprics, bounties of money and wardships. They in turn spread the good news to poorer relatives and hangers-on at home, and the invaders multiplied. They were also able to extend their influence further by bringing girls over from France to marry into the young English nobility.

Henry had foreign relatives of his own as well. His mother Isabella, widow of King John, had re-married, and three sons of this marriage were already firmly entrenched in England: William de Valence who was later made Earl of Pembroke; Aymer, who was bishop-elect of Winchester but never consecrated; and Guy de Lusignan. In the wake of these foreign parasites, pressed a greedy horde of Poitevins, Provençals and Savoyards whose power soon extended from the highest offices of state to the royal kitchens.

Cooks, of course, were people of some importance. Not only was cookery a highly developed art, but it called for a special degree of skill when ingredients were limited and costly. There was the danger of poisoning, deliberate or accidental. Henry, even when observing the Lenten fast most strictly, never neglected his palate.

"Order is given to the sheriff of Gloucester that since after lampreys all fish seem insipid to both the King and the Queen, the sheriff shall procure by purchase or otherwise as many lampreys as possible in his bailliwick, place them in bread and jelly, and send them to the King while he is at a distance from those parts by John of Dandon, the King's cook, who is being sent to him. When the King comes nearer, he shall send them to him fresh. And the King will make good any expense to which the Sheriff may be put in this connection when he comes to those parts. Witness the King at Canterbury on the fourth day of March."[3]

By 1238 Simon de Montfort was in high favour with the King, but the rest of the court still held aloof from this stiff-necked and opinionated man. When, suddenly and secretly, he married the King's sister, there was an immediate outcry. As Matthew Paris shows, it was a very different occasion from the last royal marriage.

"The ceremony was performed and Mass celebrated by Walter, chaplain of the royal chapel of Saint Stephen at Westminster, in the King's small chapel, which is in a corner of his chamber. The King in person gave away the bride to the said Simon Earl of Leicester, who received her gratefully, by reason of his disinterested love for her, her own beauty, the rich honours that were attached to her, and the distinguished and royal descent of the lady; for she was the legitimate daughter of a king and queen, and furthermore was sister of a king, an empress, and a queen; so that the offspring of so noble a lady would be a kingly race. Our lord the Pope too gave him a dispensation to marry her, as the subsequent narration will show."

Paris, with his usual astuteness, recognized all the worldly advantages of the match. How much they weighed with Simon de Montfort it is impossible to say, for if it was the bold stroke of an ambitious man it was a gamble that almost failed. His future hung in the balance.

Eleanor, who was now twenty-three, had been married in childhood to William Marshal Earl of Pembroke, son of the Regent. When she was suddenly widowed at the impressionable age of sixteen, she publicly took vows of chastity, and although she did not take the veil she wore the ring that symbolized her union with Christ. This most solemn and binding oath made marriage unthinkable, and it is difficult to understand how the King, with his obsessive piety and show of obedience to church discipline, came to countenance it. It was rumoured that he only did so because Simon had seduced his sister. The Pope had certainly not given a dispensation, as Matthew Paris believed, and the church leaders denounced the marriage at once. Archbishop Edmund Rich condemned it publicly, and a sense of outrage united in one party those groups traditionally at loggerheads, who now shared a common aim to rid the country, for all time, of the hated aliens.

Their leader was the King's brother Richard, Earl of Cornwall. Far shrewder and more practical than his brother he often tried to curb his worst follies and act as mediator between the king and the barons. He was also an avaricious money-grubber, and his profiteering soon made him one of the richest men in Europe. He took every advantage of his brother's ineptness. One of his dubious transactions gave him jurisdiction over all the Jews in the kingdom with extortionate powers over their money. In 1248 the coinage was so debased by the habit of "clipping" it round the edge that a proclamation was issued forbidding the circulation of money of less than lawful weight. Widespread hardship was caused by this measure, and it was Richard who issued the new coinage and took a considerable profit in payment of the King's debts to him.

It was this petty and unprincipled man who confronted his own brother with the threat of civil war. He was incensed by this surreptitious marriage, as Paris says, ". . . because the King had frequently sworn to take no important action without the advice of his natural subjects, and especially of the earl himself . . . In his rising Earl Richard was supported by Earl Gilbert Marshal and all the earls and barons of England, as well as by the citizens and the people generally, for they were confident and hopeful that Earl Richard would free the land from the miserable slavery to the Romans and other foreigners under which it groaned, and everyone from boys to old men constantly heaped blessings upon him . . ."

This sudden and surprising surge of antagonism drove the King to have second thoughts, and he promised to submit the whole matter to an impartial council. Simon, however, took matters into his own hands.

"But while the arrangements were incomplete, and the matter was still in suspense, Simon de Montfort humbled himself to Earl Richard, and through the agency of many mediators and certain presents, he obtained from Earl Richard the kiss of peace. This caused great annoyance to the other nobles, who had not been consulted as to the adoption of this course, though it was through their exertions that the matter had been carried thus far."

Paris goes on, "By these irregular proceedings the whole affair was, in a great measure, cut short, and did not take its full effect; but the misery of the kingdom was protracted and Earl Richard's fair fame clouded, and so it came to pass that he, who was believed to be a staff of strength, was thenceforth an object of suspicion."

When Richard defaulted the opposition collapsed. No other leader could weld so many factions into a single party. Paris tells how de Montfort got out of his difficulties.

"However, Simon de Montfort, perceiving that the hearts of the King and of Earl Richard, as well as of all the nobles, were estranged from him, and that the marriage which he had contracted with the sister of our lord the King was already in the eyes of many annulled, wasted away with excess of grief; and having seized a ship he set sail by stealth after extorting a large sum of money from every possible quarter; from one citizen of Leicester, Simon Curlevache, he wrung 500 marks. He then went to the court of Rome, hoping by means of his money to overreach it and obtain permission to enjoy his unlawful marriage."

How de Montfort raised so much money is a matter for conjecture. His estates at Leicester had been impoverished during the years of royal custody, and his wife had so far brought him nothing. There was no marriage-portion, and the claims she made on the Pembroke estates were being contested by the family. He had probably pledged his credit to the limit on all sides when he set off, armed with letters of recommendation from the King as well as peace-offerings, to gain the Pope's forgiveness. On the way he offered his services as a soldier to the Emperor Frederick, now at the height of his power, and backed by letters of commendation from him as well he reached Rome. His plea was successful. Pope Gregory IX, no doubt softened by Simon's gifts to the Curia, declared that the marriage was valid having been contracted *in faciem ecclesiae*, and ordered his legate to pronounce in the earl's favour. Matthew Paris, who like other strict churchmen of the day disapproved of this ruling, remarked cryptically, "Rome had designs too subtle for our understanding."

Simon lingered on in Italy, perhaps partly to let hostility at home simmer down, and also to help the Emperor Frederick at the disastrous Siege of Brescia. No doubt he gained more than mere military experience from his association with this idealistic and gifted man. When at last he reached England the King welcomed him with joy, but Simon hurried on to their castle at Kenilworth where Eleanor was expecting their first child. A son was born eleven months after their marriage and was named Henry after the king, who acted as godfather. Soon after this, at an official investiture, Simon was proclaimed Earl of Leicester.

There is no evidence that he made Leicester his home for any appreciable time, and his administration of the estates appears to have been harsh. In 1253 he granted the town a charter, with a stipulation which would not then be thought either exceptional or cruel: ". . . he concedes that for the good of his own soul and that of his ancestors and successor, no Jew or Jewess should ever reside there, either in his own time or that of his heirs to the end of the world."

But on another occasion his friend Robert Grosseteste, Bishop of Lincoln, wrote to him: "We have learned that you are thinking of punishing S., your burgess, with a severity disproportionate to his offence. Let not your severity be turned against him, or your justice be unappeased, but let pity mercifully exalt your judgment, so as to give an example of kindness instead of cruelty."

Little trace remains of the de Montfort family in Leicester now. The banqueting hall of the Norman castle is incorporated in the assize hall, and a mound and gateway are still standing, but it is other Earls of Leicester that are better remembered.

Simon also acquired Odiham Castle not far from Basingstoke in Hampshire, but Kenilworth was his main home. There Eleanor ran her household and brought up their children, and there Adam Marsh the Franciscan joined the household as tutor and chaplain. Robert Grosseteste, Walter de Cantelupe the Bishop of Worcester and other distinguished churchmen were frequent visitors. It was the background of their family life and the last refuge of their supporters. Built in about 1140 by Geoffrey de Clinton, Kenilworth Castle became in Simon's hands one of the strongest fortresses in the kingdom.

We can get a glimpse into their domestic life through Eleanor's household accounts at Odiham for some months of 1265. She ran their home in a style suitable to their rank, buying fine cloths of English wool and Italian linen for the family wardrobe. Her own underwear was of treated sheepskin. Like other wealthy housewives she imported wine, probably from Gascony, at about threepence a gallon, and precious and expensive spices for cooking. The servants drank beer which was brewed on the estate. There are regular entries of alms given to the poor.

These meticulous accounts, relating to her middle-age, give no sign of her earlier extravagance. Eleanor was a high-spirited girl, with something of her brother's love of luxury and finery and with a flash of his uncertain temper. Adam Marsh once wrote to her: "To fly into a temper destroys the peace of the household, and breaks the bonds which God willed to strengthen when he said 'let us make for man a companion like unto him'. In anger the heart palpitates, urges on the arm to strike, impels the tongue to slander, destroys the intelligence, engenders hatred between beings better made to love each other, and breaks the pact of friendship. Please God that this execrable taint do not throw your soul into the detestable ignominy of sin."

It is easy to imagine that there was friction between the frugal, serious-minded earl and his more worldly wife. Adam Marsh once condemned her frivolous extravagance. "Let not the asperity of my words astonish you. Yet why this excessive cult of your person, these enormous expenses and insensate taste for unnecessary ornaments which provoke the divine majesty?"

Simon, on the other hand, was almost an ascetic. ". . . his private attendants in his bedchamber reported of him, namely, that all day long and all night long he was clothed in hair-cloth . . . Furthermore, let us observe the nature of the moderation which dwelt in Simon the knight. You must observe that the character of moderation is this, that it takes neither too much food or drink nor too little, but always holds a middle course between the two . . . Now, Simon never exceeded the accustomed measure prescribed to him by his frugality, either in his eating or his drinking . . . So great was his temperance in his diet, so praiseworthy was his frugality in his clothing, that he did not exercise himself in great matters which were too high for him; but whilst he was with those of his own household he was contented with a russet garb; even when associated with the nobility of the land he seldom wore a scarlet dress, but most generally clothing of a blue or brown colour, possibly that they might the less suspect that his undergarments were of haircloth; for he was apprehensive that some such report had got abroad among men."[4]

Rishanger in his Chronicle also gives little more than a catalogue of virtues. "He was indeed a mighty man, and prudent, and circumspect; in the use of arms and experience of warfare, superior to all others of his time; commendably endowed with knowledge of letters; fond of hearing the offices of the church by day and night . . . He was moreover pleasant and witty in speech, and ever aimed at the reward of an admirable faith; on account of which he did not fear to undergo death, as shall be told hereafter. His constancy all men, even his enemies, admired. And the earl, like a second Joshua, worshipped justice as the very medicine of his soul."

Of his appearance we know little. His seal shows him on a galloping horse dressed for the chase. Beside him runs a greyhound, one of the oldest breeds of dog recorded and at that time a favourite hunting animal in royal circles. Quick brained, lithe and decisive, it would have been a suitable choice of emblem for this resilient soldier. The rider appears to be tall and clean-shaven, but nothing else can be learned from the stylized impression. Some experts have said that Simon is represented in one of the jewel-like clerestory windows of the cathedral at Chartres, showing a knight mounted and accoutred for battle with the de Montfort lion rampant on his shield. But as Bémont says, "Even if the earl's helm was open and not closed, we should not be able to discover the slightest personal characteristic . . . At the most we can say that he had no beard. Under these conditions any and every picture of him must be purely imaginary."[5]

Added to their differences in temperament, Simon and his wife had other difficulties. Unlike so many brides, Eleanor was a mature woman when she married him, and with her royal birth she would hardly feel subservient to her unpopular, foreign and impoverished husband. A clash of wills between such strong personalities seems inevitable, especially in the early days when Eleanor, after her years of cloistered widowhood, enjoyed worldly pleasures again.

In spite of this, and the storms that beat about them, their marriage never foundered. Eleanor remained loyal to her husband against her brothers King Henry and Richard of Cornwall and when most of the leading figures of her world were ranged against him. The traditional ties with Church and family were broken. The Pope, the Archbishop of Canterbury, the saintly King of France and the leading barons of England denounced the rebels, but she never faltered. She shared many rigours of Simon's life, guarded his castles, joined him on crusade and after his death went, mourning, into exile.

Perhaps not a little of the adulation heaped upon Simon de Montfort rightly belongs to her, for the observant Adam Marsh wrote to her: "If, however, through injudicious actions, themselves the produce of praiseworthy intentions, he has observed certain agreements less strictly than he should have done, if he has had recourse to excessive measures, it is for you, considering the fact that he has been manifestly driven to them by necessity, to display all your industry and tact in putting an end to these irritating disputes and in bringing him gently, by your sweetness and good advice, to conduct himself more prudently in the future."

Eleanor de Montfort

The Great Seal of
Henry III

Simon de Montfort

The Privy Seal of Richard
Earl of Cornwall,
King of the Romans

FOUR SEALS

A map of Britain by Matthew Paris (MS Cotton Claudius D VI)

IV

"Henry III was a confused kind of King . . ."
(*1066 And All That.*)

ENGLAND WAS already suffering from the unstable temper and sanguine obstinacy of the King. His heart was in the restoration and adornment of his palaces and the building of the great abbey at Westminster. He had little taste for the detailed routine of government and was content to let his royal favourites exercise and abuse his powers. Only the recurring need for money, or the dream of regaining an empire, stirred him to interfere in affairs of state.

In 1239 the Queen gave birth to a son who was named after his father's ancestor and hero, Saint Edward the Confessor.

"At Westminster on the night of the 16th of June a son was born to the King by Eleanor his Queen. All the magnates of the realm congratulated him, and the citizens of London in particular, since the child was born in London; they assembled troops of dancers with drums and timbrels, and brilliantly illuminated the streets at night. The Bishop of Carlisle initiated the infant, but the legate baptized him, although he was not a priest; Edmund Archbishop of Canterbury however confirmed him; at the King's wish he was called Edward. A great number of messengers were despatched to announce the news, and returned laden with splendid gifts. And in this matter the King cast a dark stain on his royal magnificence; for when the various messengers returned, the King inquired of them what each had received, and though the gifts they had brought were valuable, he commanded those who had received less to return their presents with scorn. Nor was his anger appeased till each had received satisfaction according to the pleasures of the messengers. Whereon a woman wittily remarked: 'God gave us this child, but the King sells him to us.' "[1]

Later that year Simon de Montfort had a taste of the King's dangerous and unpredictable humour. In August the earl and countess were to be among the guests at the churching of the Queen in Westminster Abbey. Paris tells how Henry, suddenly staging one of his freakish outbursts of rage, "burst out in anger upon him, and treating him as excommunicate forbade the pair to be present at the festival; as his abusive language continued, the earl and his wife took a boat, so as to return quickly to their quarters, but the King had them forcibly ejected. Weeping and groaning they returned to his presence, without being able to appease his wrath.

"Addressing himself to the earl, Henry cast these words in his face: 'You seduced my sister before the wedding; to avoid scandal I gave my consent, in my own despite. You went to Rome to secure that the vow she had taken should not prevent the marriage, and you corrupted the Curia in order to obtain that which was forbidden . . .' The earl was put to shame by these words, and at the close of day he embarked on the Thames in a little boat with his wife, who was pregnant, and a small retinue, and hastily going down to the sea coast immediately crossed the Straits."

There were probably complex reasons for Henry's attack on his former friend, and some of them continued to rankle for many years. Simon was in financial difficulty. His earldom, according to him, was little more than a liability, and it is true that much of the land had been mortgaged, the forests cut down and the revenues squandered. His marriage had so far proved a costly one, and he was in debt to Thomas of Savoy who had married his old love, Joan of Flanders. In his own account of the humiliating incident, Simon suggests that some of his debts were the King's liability rather than his own. Whatever the rights or wrongs of the matter, the King was not easily appeased, and it was Richard of Cornwall who interceded as peacemaker and saved Simon from imprisonment in the Tower.

Pope Gregory IX had been preaching a Crusade for some years, and this was not only an attractive enterprise to a keen soldier and a devout Christian; it was also the ideal escape for a soured and friendless man burdened with debts. Simon set off for Acre leaving his wife and their baby son Henry at Brindisi. Little is known about his exploits in the Holy Land but evidently he gave a good account of himself, for in June 1241 the barons, knights and citizens of Jerusalem sent a petition to the Emperor Frederick praying that the earl might be appointed regent until their young King Conrad came of age. Simon refused this invitation, and faithful to his oath of fealty placed himself once more at the service of King Henry. First, however, he named his price.

As Richard of Cornwall and many of the great barons were also away on crusade, the King was free to commit his blunders without restraint. Spurred on by his ambitious and headstrong mother he decided to renew his war with France, and having landed at Royan at the mouth of the Garonne, he called upon all his subjects in Gascony or elsewhere in the country to join him. Simon, who was now with the Duke of Burgundy, reminded the King of his injustices and grievances and demanded repayment of the money which had been levied from the Leicester lands to pay Thomas of Savoy, with a hundred marks in addition. The King was conciliatory and the bargain was made.

The campaign quickly ended in disaster. Heavily outnumbered, the King withdrew to Bordeaux and settled down to enjoy Christmas and the winter months before renewing the struggle in the spring. But when it came his resources, like his army, were exhausted and he was forced to agree to a five years' truce with the French King.

The Earl of Leicester was not yet as much at home in England as in France. There he had connections in many of the ruling houses, and these alliances were to prove useful to him later. He also had bitter enemies, some remembering the atrocities of his father and others eager by any wiles to upset the delicate and unpredictable relationship between Simon and King Henry. In this they failed. At the end of 1243, when Henry and Simon were both back in England, they appeared to be on the most cordial and intimate terms. Henry's moods were always as changeable as English weather, but the bitter squabble between the two men had left its mark. They could never again be on quite the same friendly footing, and Simon could no longer wholly trust his fickle master.

In England these were years of uneasy peace, for she was like a ship without a captain or rudder. When Richard of Cornwall left for the Holy Land there was no one to take his place as effective leader of that element both in the Church and the English nobility which tried to restrain the King's agents.

"Earl Richard and the other crusading nobles who were there present, bade farewell to all assembled there, for they were ready to start on their journey to Jerusalem. And when the prelates saw this, they all burst into tears and said to Earl Richard, 'Why, earl, dost thou, our only hope after the King, abandon us? To whom dost thou leave us in our desolation? In thy absence will greedy foreigners attack us.' Then the earl replied in tears to the Archbishop of Canterbury on behalf of them all: 'My lord and father, verily though I had not taken the cross, yet would I depart and absent myself, that I might not behold the evils of our nation, and the desolation of the realm, which men think I have power to prevent, though I have not.' "[1]

The state of the country was certainly pitiful. The Pope's demands were more and more oppressive. At one time he ordered that the next three hundred benefices to fall vacant should be filled by Italian priests, and so removed from the Church the power of free election which she prized so highly.

The Archbishop of Canterbury, Edmund Rich, went into voluntary exile "seeing that the church of England was daily trampled on more and more, and robbed of its temporal goods and spoiled of its liberties, was overcome with weariness, for that he lived to behold evils upon earth; and on reproving the King for allowing it, he obtained nothing but evasive answers." Shortly after, he died. "And so, worn out by fasting and grown weak through grief, with his body consumed, shrunk, and enfeebled, he fell seriously ill. By the advice of his physicians he had himself carried to Soissy for the sake of the better air. There, after a short time of suffering from dysentery, he was freed from the bondage of the flesh, and, bidding farewell to a worthless generation, went the way of all flesh. His spirit happily exchanged the exile of this life for the heavenly country."[1]

Some dispute arose about his successor, but at the King's insistence "the monks of Canterbury, finding that the Pope and the King indulged them by turns and mutually assented to each other's requests, after invoking the favour of the Holy Spirit and the King, chose as shepherd of their souls Boniface the elect of Bellay, a man who was unknown to them and, as was asserted, was, in knowledge, morals, and age, unfitted for so high a dignity, when compared with his predecessors, the archbishops of Canterbury."[1]

Matthew Paris later had second thoughts about the wisdom of this candid entry. Perhaps he feared that a royal eye might see it, for he erased it and substituted ". . . chose as shepherd of their souls Boniface the elect of Bellay, a man of lofty stature and handsome figure, and uncle of the Lady Eleanor, the illustrious Queen of England, though utterly unknown to the aforesaid monks."

In 1242 the King was in trouble again. Opposition had stiffened, and the earls, barons and bishops who assembled at his summons were resolved, under oath, not to weaken in the face of his demands. "For they all well knew that the Count de la Marche, who was urgently pressing the King to cross the sea with all the treasure he could scrape together, cared nothing for the military force of the English, and would set little value on the knighthood, strength and loyalty of the kingdom, for he regarded the king as a huckster, whose money was all he wanted to get." The unscrupulous count was Henry's stepfather, a man who flourished by chicanery and fraud.

When the King was confronted with a list of grievances and refused the aid he sought, he practised the devious art of playing one enemy off against another. At this he was a master, and even Robert Grosseteste, the outstanding churchman of the time, of forceful and intrepid character, could not hold the opposition together. It was not only the King they had to resist. The struggle between the papacy and the Emperor Frederick was reaching its climax. All the civilized world was embroiled in it, and Rome was using every device to exploit and subjugate the restless Church in England.

The song writers of the time voiced the unhappiness of the people. "Everybody has a right to satirize the world's vices; for now I see many in the world err, despise what is good, love what is bad, and spontaneously turn away to evil." Another wrote: "The King and the Pope think of nothing else but how they may take from the clergy their gold and their silver."[2]

Not all the King's demands were reasonable. No government can function without steady revenues, and as the country developed and a stronger central administration replaced the weakening feudal system expenses naturally rose. But the King's personal extravagance, his lavish generosity to his own favourites and his squandering on artistic pursuits were not at all popular with the barons or the prelates, and every military exploit was an expensive failure. In 1242 he not only waged his hopeless attack on France, but there was a disaster at sea as well.

"When autumn was coming on, the King of the French issued a harsh order that the persons of English merchants trafficking in his kingdom should be seized, which was very unbecoming; by so doing he inflicted a heavy wound on the ancient reputation of Gaul, which once offered an asylum and protection to all refugees and even to exiles, especially if they were peaceable, and it was for this reason that it first obtained the name of France in the vulgar tongue. When this disgraceful wantonness came to the ears and heart of the King of England, he gave a like order that all French merchants who were in England should suffer a well-deserved retribution."[1]

The little fleet that set out was scattered by storms, and "by this unhappy chance, the King incurred a great and ireparable loss of powerful and prudent men, arms, and provisions of corn which he had collected from the archbishopric of Canterbury and other bishoprics, together with a considerable sum of money which he had got together from all quarters."[1]

There was a further weakening of the links between France and England in 1244 when "The King of the French assembled at Paris all dwellers beyond the sea who had estates in England

and thus addressed them: 'Whatever inhabitant of my realm has estates in England, seeing that he cannot fitly serve two masters, must completely and irrevocably attach himself to me or to the King of England.' For which cause some who had estates and revenues in England abandoned them and devoted themselves to their French properties, and others did the reverse. And when the King of England was informed of this he directed that all natives of the realm of France, and especially Normans, should be disseized of the land which they held in England".[1]

In 1244 Henry summoned all the barons who owed him military service to meet at Newcastle so that he might threaten aggression against Scotland. The King of Scotland met him there, "a good, just, pious, and generous man, deservedly beloved by all the English as well as by his own people. He had with him a very numerous and powerful force, consisting of a thousand knights sufficiently well mounted, though not on Spanish, Italian, or other costly horses, and properly equipped in mail and linen accoutrements, and also about a hundred thousand foot, who were all of one mind, and who, having made confession and being encouraged by the assurance of their preachers that they would fight in a just cause for their country, felt little fear of death."[1]

This show of strength on the part of Alexander II, and the pressure brought to bear on Henry by Richard of Cornwall and the other barons, had the desired effect, and peace terms were agreed.

The wiser among the King's counsellors were waging a running fight against his rashness and extravagance. Several times he tried to raise money on the pretext that he was going on crusade. When they were adamant, he would play them off against each other, and if they brought a list of complaints he would bring out the Great Charter for another solemn affirmation. Occasionally he put on a convincing show of penitence.

"When the lord King heard these complaints he at once blushed with shame, for he knew the truth of them. And he gave his word therefore that all these things should truly be set right, for he hoped by this show of false meekness to sway the hearts of all men towards his own desires. When those who were assembled, quite ensnared by these promises, were agreed, they said to him, 'This shall be done quickly, and we will bear ourselves in patience; and as the lord King bears himself toward us, so shall we bear with him in all things.' In this way were all things to wait until two weeks after the Nativity of Saint John the Baptist. Meanwhile the lord King, stubborn in his spirit towards those around him who were jealous of their own power, and made impatient towards his friends, hardly disturbed himself in amending those evils as he had sworn to his liege subjects."[1]

The name of Simon de Montfort was occurring more frequently among the signatories to various state documents, but there is no evidence that he had any real taste for domestic politics. Nor does it appear that he had at this stage any ambition to rule England. When he was in the country he took his part in the deliberations of the Great Council, and as a man of forceful character he undoubtedly made himself heard, but a great part of his life was spent abroad. In 1248 he resolved to go on crusade once more.

"At this time Simon Earl of Leicester took the cross, that he might win absolution from his sins and gain admission to heaven. For, on reflection, he was in great alarm about the marriage he had contracted with his wife, who had previously taken a vow of chastity before Saint Edmund Archbishop of Canterbury. The countess, too, influenced, it is believed, by the same spirit, when she saw her husband wearing the cross, flew with all speed to assume it also. The knights and many others of their household took the cross to obtain the reward of eternal salvation."[1]

Instead of going to Palestine he was sent to Gascony, almost the only remaining English possession in France and a constant source of trouble. Just as in England the landowners were plundering the merchants, and while the feudal lords wanted unlimited power in their own hands, the mercantile classes needed protection and peaceful relations with neighbouring states if they were to carry on successful trading. In this weak and divided state Gascony was a prey for her covetous neighbours, and marauders from Navarre invaded the fertile valleys while Aragon and Castile claimed legal rights of interference. Henry had made sporadic attempts to reduce it to order, and failed. Now he invited the Earl of Leicester to go out as viceroy and quell the turbulent province once and for all. After long deliberation Simon agreed, but he stipulated that his term of office should be seven years and that the King should provide fifty knights a year and two thousand marks.

On these terms he left for Gascony in the summer of 1248 leaving his children in the care of their tutor, Adam Marsh. For a year he was successful in restoring order. He captured the chief troublemaker, Gaston de Bearn, "a great talker like all Normans", and established a temporary state of peace. At Christmas he joined the royal party at Westminster where he was treated as a hero. But before the year was out his enemies had begun their sinister work. While rebellion broke out again in Gascony, de Bearn's friends whispered into the ear of the gullible king. This dangerous and treacherous man was released, and stories of Simon's excessive harshness and extortionate taxation were circulated in the English court.

In January 1251 "on the day of the Epiphany Simon Earl of Leicester suddenly returned from Gascony in inglorious haste, accompanied by only three squires, and with his horses worn out with hunger and work. On arriving in London, where he found the King, he urgently demanded effectual assistance from him both in men and money, for the purpose of crushing the insolence of the Gascons who were in rebellion against him."[1]

When he had pleaded his cause the King, "touched with pity for the earl's trouble, replied by way of consolation: 'By God's head, thou speakest truth, sir earl! And since thou servest me so doughtily I will not deny thee effectual aid. But loud cries of complaint reach me that thou hast improperly thrown into prison or even put to death men who came to thee in peace, or whom thou hadst thyself summoned.' This the earl positively denied, answering: 'My lord, their treachery which thou knowest and hast experienced makes them unworthy of belief.' "[1]

Henry gave Simon a grant, and after squeezing what money

he could out of his own estates the earl returned to Gascony. Again the Gascons revolted and many came to whisper to the King, who was only too ready to listen, about the tyrannical behaviour of his viceroy. Royal commissioners were sent out to investigate the charges and brought back reports of the earl's cruelties. The King, as usual, watched the barons take sides and waited to see which was the stronger. There was great bitterness, while ". . . by shuffling speeches either side provoked the other to angry quarrelling."[1]

Simon, however, was far from friendless, as Adam Marsh explained in a letter to Grosseteste. "Moreover, the said earl in the meantime frequently endured reproaches and insults from the lord King in front of many great people, with immoderate shoutings, but through all he observed toward both his lord and his adversaries the forbearance of the humble together with the generosity of the great minded . . . Very few beyond the Bishop of Worcester, Peter of Savoy and Peter de Montfort were faithful enough to defend him in the midst of such revilings and discord, but when the priests who were present, the lord Earl of Cornwall and the other brothers of the lord King, the leading men of his council and the barons of the realm publicly in a remarkable laudation extolled the Earl of Leicester's magnificent courage, undefiled loyalty, victorious activity and just intention, they did not omit to promise help also and counsel to preserve the said earl from peril, loss and shame. And I also, such as I am, encouraged some of the greater of these."[3]

Matthew Paris described the bitter quarrel that broke out between the King and the earl. "At this the earl was very wrath, and rising openly declared that the King was a manifest liar, and that were it not for the shelter of his royal name and dignity, it would have been an evil hour in which he made such a speech. The King, almost beside himself with rage, would have at once ordered his arrest, had he not felt certain that the magnates would never allow it.

"The earl continued, 'Who could believe thou art a Christian? Hast thou ever confessed?'

" 'Yea,' said the King.

" 'What avails confession without repentance and atonement?' replied the earl . . .

"The King, blazing into a yet greater rage, retorted: 'I never repented of ought so much as I now repent me that I ever allowed thee to enter England, or to hold any land or honour in that country where thou hast fattened so as to kick against me.'

"Their friends then interrupted the dispute and so they were divided."

The men were not reconciled. In the summer of 1252 when Simon returned to Gascony the King taunted him: "Return to Gascony, that thou, who art so fond and such a fomenter of wars, mayst there find enough of them, and bring back with thee therefrom thy merited reward, as did thy father."

It is interesting that Simon continued his thankless work in spite of such provocation. He was not a mild man, and however just and moderate he may have been before, Matthew Paris hints that he showed little mercy now. "So, more greedy than bloodsuckers, they followed the steps of the earl, who was burning with eagerness to take vengeance for the defamation of his character."[1]

His loyalty, however, is without question. In November 1252 Blanche of Castile, who had so long served France as Queen Regent, died. Her son King Louis IX was away on crusade. When the French nobility offered Simon the office of Seneschal, or High Steward, he refused to serve two masters and remained faithful to his adopted country and its king.

While Simon was busy in Gascony King Henry pursued his reckless and changeable course. His money troubles were chronic and humiliating. Paris wrote: "Whilst the King, with open mouth, was thus greedily gaping after money, he happened, about the feast of Saint Hilary, to go to Huntingdon; there he sent for the Abbot of Ramsey and, addressing him privately, said, 'My friend, I earnestly beg you to afford me a hundred pounds; for I am in want and must have them without delay.'

"The abbot, as he could not honourably do otherwise, replied, 'I have sometimes given, but I have never lent to you, nor will I now.' And he at once borrowed that sum at heavy interest from the Caursines, in order that he might supply his beggar-king."[1]

At another time he tried to put matters straight by economy. "The King, disgracefully leaving the footsteps of his father, ordered the expenses of his court and the pleasures of ordinary hospitality to be lessened to such a degree as to bring on him the charge of inexcusable avarice. He also ordered the bounty of his usual alms, and the number of tapers in his church to be cut down. However, he wisely freed himself from the entanglement of the debts which he owed to many merchants, which was praiseworthy."[1]

And another time, "At Christmas the King, perhaps in anxiety and saving for his pilgrimage gave no presents to his knights or household, although all his predecessors had been accustomed to give royal garments and costly jewels. The usual richness and hospitality of the royal table was also diminished, and his usual shame was set aside. He sought his lodgings and his meals with abbots, priors, clerks and men of low degree, staying with them and asking for gifts. He was no longer considered a courteous host who did not, besides showing the King and his household splendid hospitality, honour him, the Queen, Sir Edward and the several courtiers of dignity with noble and valuable presents; nay, the Queen herself did not blush to ask for them, not as a favour but as her due . . . Nor did the courtiers and royal household appreciate any gifts but rich and costly ones, as for instance desirable palfreys, gold and silver cups, necklaces with choice jewels, and imperial girdles and the like. So the King's court became like to that of Rome, sitting or rather prostituting itself like a harlot for gain."[1]

The King's essays in statecraft usually ended in trouble. Without consulting his viceroy he suddenly conferred the commune of Gascony on his son Edward. "This was very acceptable to the Gascons, and they at once did homage and swore fealty to Edward, who made them some noble presents of gold, silver, necklaces, belts and silk clothes, and promised them yet greater gifts."[1]

The Gascon emissaries left Westminster in high spirits, boasting that Simon "would either be cut to pieces or driven an exile from his country". They were empty threats, and Simon had little difficulty in defeating them. By now he must have been one of the most experienced commanders in Europe, and he was also noted for his personal courage and skill. Matthew Paris describes how he rescued a captured friend: "The earl, eager to rescue the knight, hardly waiting for his own troops, but, taking the messenger as a guide, flew off swifter than the whirlwind, and spared not his horse's flanks. The moment he came up with the enemy, his lightning sword drank the blood of many of them; by his prowess he freed the prisoners and cut and broke their chains . . ."[1]

While Simon struggled to keep order in Gascony matters in England went from bad to worse. Henry's royal relatives did much to increase public resentment. Boniface, the Queen's uncle, was a tyrannical and greedy Archbishop of Canterbury. William de Valence, the King's half-brother, insolently went poaching in the grounds of the Bishop of Ely at Hatfield. When the hunting was over he broke into the house and made free with the wine, leaving the casks unbunged and the wine running to waste. When Guy de Lusignan, his youngest half-brother, left England Matthew Paris said that the King "filled his saddlebags with such a weight of new money that Guy had to increase the number of his horses".

The citizens of London complained of "the violence and madness of the King, who, however, proved harsh and inexorable. So in great excitement they went to Earl Richard, the Earl of Leicester and other nobles of the realm, with sorrowful complaints of how the King had not blushed to violate the charters granted them by his predecessors . . ." From the north came stories of the vicious enforcement of the Forest Laws by one of the royal bailiffs who showed "cunning, wantonness and violence in the collection of money".[1]

All over the country there were rumours of oppression that fanned smouldering resentment into flames. In 1253 the barons assembled in London after Easter "to treat with the King concerning the important business of the realm", and the representatives of the Church were also there in strength. All of them were in ugly mood. When the King asked for an aid, this time for a pilgrimage, he met stiff opposition. Instead of his usual line of conciliation and cunning, Henry indulged in a little sarcasm and brazenly reminded the Council that there are two sides to the patronage coin.

" 'It is true, and I grieve for it, and repent me greatly for having so acted. We ought therefore to arrange forthwith for the remedying of what has been done, and to prevent its occurrence in the future. And in this you should be my coadjutors; for remember it is I who advanced Boniface of Canterbury here to this high dignity, and thee, William of Salisbury, who art the writer of my briefs, I raised from the lowest position: and thee Silvester of Carlisle, who wert long a petty clerk in my chancery, how have I raised thee over the heads of many reverend men to be a bishop? . . . And I being justified and chastened by such an example will take care for the future to promote no man who is not worthy.'

"To this courteous and satirical rebuke they replied 'Lord King, we make no mention of the past, but direct our speech to the future'."

The King's "pious design" of a pilgrimage was an obvious ruse but it was difficult to oppose. It appealed to the mass of his subjects, and to deny him an aid meant challenging the Pope as well as Henry himself. If money were not forthcoming from the tithes he demanded, it would be extorted by other and more oppressive means. The clergy wavered, and it was Grosseteste who persuaded them to stand their ground. He was an old man now, frail in body and despairing of success, described by the Pope as an 'old dotard'. But the fire of his courage was not yet quenched. He still dared to defy the Pope, and he was protected by the admiration of leading churchmen throughout Christendom. According to Matthew Paris the cardinals said of him, "We cannot condemn him. He is Catholic, nay most saintly, more religious, more holy, of greater excellence than we are, and so men believe that he has no superior among all the bishops, nor yet any equal.'

After fifteen days of argument a compromise was reached. The King was to have his aid, but the Great Council would exercise some control over the spending of it and the Great Charter was to be reaffirmed.

Henry entered wholeheartedly into the dramatic and moving ceremony in which the Archbishop of Canterbury, with the bishops in their pontifical robes and with candles lighted, excommunicated any who transgressed against the charters of the common liberties of England.

"During the reading of the above sentence the King had held his hand to his breast with a calm and cheerful countenance; and when at the end they threw down their candles and each and all exclaimed, 'So let all who incur this sentence be extinguished and stink in hell,' the King himself said, 'All these will I faithfully observe unimpaired, as I am a man, a Christian, a knight and a crowned and anointed king. So help me God'."[1]

This piece of arrant humbug did not keep the barons and prelates quiescent for long, for in 1255 Henry committed another of his major blunders. Frederick II had died in 1250 and while the royal houses of Europe shared out nominal sovereignty over his empire, the Pope hoped to restore Sicily to the papal dominions. For a year he carried on negotiations with one prince or another, hoping to get the best of all worlds by selling a meaningless title for a high price. Richard of Cornwall was wise enough to refuse the dangled prize.

"Then the Pope, finding that his hints had no effect upon the earl, added 'We do not care for an alliance with him, or to have anything in common with him.' So when the Pope was satisfied that he had spread his net in vain in the sight of the birds, he sent secret messengers to our lord the King of England, to work on his simplicity, since he knew that he was easy of belief and prone to his own loss, and offered to grant him the kingdom of Sicily and Apulia, and to give him such assistance in getting possession of it as he could without loss to himself."

Next the Pope wrote to King Henry. "The royal race of England, which we view with special affection and the distinction of our intimate love, we wish to exalt above the other kings and princes of the world, and we have sent as legate of the Apostolic See our notary who is as devoted to the honour and advantage of that people as to his own, to those regions, with the special object of enriching and exalting that same nation by conferring upon it the kingdom of Sicily, which surpasses in riches and charm all other kingdoms of the world . . ."[4]

The barons were obstinately opposed to the idea, which was clearly to be an expensive piece of tomfoolery. The clergy also feared that by this means the Pope would strengthen still further his hold upon the country.

"The King, however, was so delighted with the Pope's shadowy promise, and his heart was so puffed up with vain joy, that his exultation showed itself in voice, manner and laugh, and he openly called his son Edmund King of Sicily, firmly believing that the agreement about the kingdom was already concluded."[1]

In fact, it was not a gift at all. Henry was only being invited to raise an army and to stand surety for papal debts amounting to something like three times his gross annual revenue. The only reward for success would be that Edmund would rule Sicily and Naples as the Pope's vassal. The price of failure was Henry's greatest dread: excommunication.

When it was known that Henry had been too stupid to resist the Pope's blandishments a storm broke over his head. The papal army was heavily defeated and the King had to face the threats of Rome on the one hand and the angry barons on the other. He had nowhere to turn for help or sympathy. The Sicilian Adventure from his point of view was an unmitigated disaster.

Even when he presented the young prince to the Great Council in all the magnificence of his kingly robes and crown, they were unmoved. But it is easy to guess why Henry himself had such enthusiasm for the scheme. Foreign connections and royal pageantry held great attraction for him, and as he had inherited only the fragment of a former empire he was glad to extend his dominions by any means. He had no ambition to impose new systems of government or codes of law, nor was he interested in money for money's sake. He was a man who liked to "cut a dash", and perhaps he dreamed of becoming Europe's brightest star, flashing brilliance as he travelled from one of his family kingdoms to another.

Right, a typical marginal sketch from the Chronicle of John of Oxonede (MS Cotton Nero D II)

Henry III and his family tree from Peter Langtoft's Chronicle (MS Royal 20 A II)

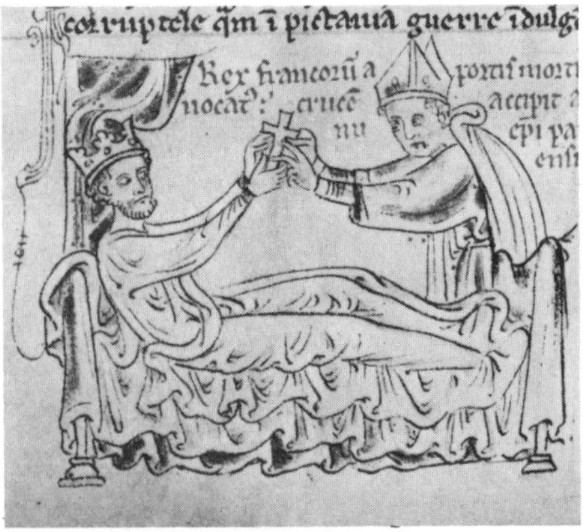

Three illustrations from the Chronicle of Matthew Paris (MS Royal 14C VII)

Top left, a Council is held in London. *Top right*, the King of France, near to death, receives the cross from the Bishop of Paris. *Bottom*, Matthew Paris on his deathbed

He had already married his eldest son Edward to Eleanor of Castile. "At this time Edward was sent with great pomp and state to Alfonso King of Spain, where he was received with honour and reverence, and espoused the King's young sister Eleanor at Burgos; he also received the honour of knighthood at the hands of the King, who was well pleased at the youth's handsome appearance and bearing. Edward then returned with his bride to his father and was received with great rejoicing, as though he had been an angel from God . . . Then the King of the English bestowed on Edward and his wife, Gascony, Ireland, Wales, Bristol, Stamford, and Grantham, so that he himself seemed to be but half a king."[1]

In 1257, to Henry's delight, his brother Richard of Cornwall was elected King of Almaine, or King of the Romans. The Holy Roman Empire was at this time almost a myth, but with some expense and effort he might have established his powers over the kingdoms of Germany. Instead during fifteen years' reign he made only four visits of a few months each to his country, and the feudal barons built up immense power unchecked.

Richard was easily persuaded to accept the title. "The King and his brothers, particularly the elect of Winchester, eagerly encouraged him, declaring that the honour would exalt the whole English nation for ever. Thereon the earl, inspired with many feelings and roused to good hopes, said with a free and eager voice, 'I, trusting in the mercy of God, though I am incompetent and unworthy, gratefully accept this honour and burden, conferred on me as I hope by heaven, and this I do that I may not be called timid and weak-hearted . . . If I do this from ambition or courteousness, may I be consumed by hell-fire, and die by a sudden death before leaving this chapel . . .' This speech drew tears from many, and caused great joy to the German envoys, who had been doubtful about obtaining his consent, but now being assured of his goodwill and favour, they returned home in joy to make their report to the magnates who had sent them, within twenty days of Christmas."[1]

Surprisingly, Richard left the chapel alive, but while tears of joy flowed at Westminster there were tears of grief in the rest of

England. There were disasters on all sides. An expedition was sent against the Welsh, who were again making trouble in the border country. Wisely, the Welsh adopted a scorched earth policy, sent their wives and sheep into the mountainous country around Snowdon, and destroyed every bridge and ford and laid waste to any crop that could help or support the invading army.

Matthew Paris wrote unhappily: "Shame to the wretched English, who are trampled under foot by every foreigner and do not blush at suffering the ancient liberties of their realm to be extinguished, nor model themselves on the pattern of the Welsh . . . O England! Justly art thou reckoned the handmaid of nations, and the last of them in rank. What thy inhabitants produce, strangers plunder and carry away."

Matters were made worse by a bad harvest in 1257 followed by a severe winter. The result was famine. It was said that in London alone 15,000 died, and even if this was an exaggeration there is no doubt that the whole country suffered hunger, misery and shame. When corn was imported from Germany to feed the starving people the King seized it to sell for his own profit at famine prices.

In April the summons went out to the Great Council, but roads were still nearly impassable and the barons, after struggling into London through a quagmire of mud, peremptorily refused the large sum of money which the King needed to pay for his absurd Sicilian exploit. After a whole month of fruitless and acrimonious argument they dispersed, to meet again at Oxford in June.

Through all the suffering and misery shone one ray of hope. At last the King was genuinely frightened. He had wriggled out of all his previous escapades by double dealing and taking advantage of the inherent loyalty to the Crown. But now he was ready to sacrifice his absolute power as king if in return he could meet the Pope's demands and save his soul. This was the moment for the radical party to produce an effective plan of reform. A century before, John of Salisbury had laid down the principles of good government and his ideas had been developed by such great Franciscans as Grosseteste, Adam Marsh and Roger Bacon. So in the four weeks before Parliament met again the leaders of the barons and clergy hammered out together the terms to be imposed on the King.

The "Mad Parliament" of June 1258 was of a most unusual character. It was no more a "parliament" as we know it today than the ones that had gone before, but it marked the end of the years of dissension and half-hearted resolve, and the beginning of a genuine determination to reform the system of government. It was a point of no return. Unless the King offered something better than promises, civil war was inevitable.

Instead of the usual twenty or thirty representative barons and their retinues, at least a hundred assembled in Oxford. The streets of the little university town must have been choked with people, and one contemporary estimate put the number as high as 60,000.

They were in full armour, "cloaking their coming in such guise, under the pretence that they might thus show their readiness to set out with their united forces against the King's enemies in Wales."[1] In fact, fearing that rebellion might break out and the King send abroad for help, they had already taken the precaution of guarding the seaports.

The King can have been under no illusion. This time the opposition meant business. Their leaders met at the house of the Friars Preachers where, "after renewing their league and reiterating their oath, they confirmed the design which they had conceived, that neither for life, death, or holdings, for hatred or for love, or for any cause whatever, would they be bent or weakened in their intent to regain praiseworthy laws, and to cleanse from foreigners this kingdom which is the native land of men of noble birth, and of their ancestors."[1]

It would be interesting to know the identity of the men who met at the Dominican Friary. Simon de Montfort was almost certainly one, but his two closest friends and advisers were absent. Adam Marsh had died the year before, and Robert Grosseteste, surely one of the architects of the plan for reform, had died in 1253.

"So the saintly Robert II, bishop of Lincoln, passed away from the exile of this world, which he never loved, at his manor of Buckden, on the night of Saint Denis's day; he had been an open rebuker of Pope and King, the corrector of bishops, the reformer of monks, the instructor of the clergy, the support of scholars, the preacher of the people, the persecutor of the incontinent, a careful reader of the scriptures, the hammer of the Romans whom he despised. At the table of bodily food he was liberal, plentiful, courteous, cheerful, affable; at the table of spiritual food devout, tearful, penitent; as a prelate, sedulous, venerable, indefatigable."[1]

There is some doubt whether de Montfort was an enthusiast for the new constitution, and according to the Lanercost Chronicle there was even difficulty in persuading him to accept it. It may be that he thought the reforms did not go far enough and that the power of the new government would still be too narrowly based. He may have been disappointed to find that personal ambition loomed largely in the minds of his colleagues. Whether this is so or not, having taken the oath to observe them he always regarded the Provisions of Oxford as an essential constitutional foundation for more far-reaching reforms.

Simon's strongest collaborator was probably Richard Earl of Gloucester, a violent and changeable man who had a powerful voice in state affairs. These two men, with Humphrey de Bohun the Earl of Hereford, Roger Bigod the Earl Marshal, Roger de Mortimer, Peter de Montfort who was a faithful friend to Simon and possibly a distant kinsman, and Simon's devoted supporter Walter de Cantelupe, Bishop of Worcester, were busy for a month drawing up the Provisions of Oxford that were to reform the state.

The King readily took the oath that he would observe them but his promises were like piecrusts and he just as readily broke them. After him Prince Edward took the oath with reluctance, and Prince Henry of Almaine, son of Richard of Cornwall (who was busy abroad in his new position as King of Almaine) pleaded that he was too young to swear. Simon de Montfort took the oath "never under any pretence to break the pledge he was solemnly contracting, whatever others might do".[5] To demonstrate his good faith he fulfilled one of the provisions which stated that castles of the state should be put into the hands of Englishmen. Having surrendered his castles at Kenilworth and Odiham he called upon William de Valence "who was blustering more than the others" to do the same.

"Then were the Poitevins in no small fear, not knowing what to do, for if they betook themselves to any castle for concealment they would be closely besieged, and in lack of any means of defence would be starved out. For even if the nobles did not do so, the whole community of the people at large would besiege them, and utterly destroy their castles. So they suddenly and secretly took to flight, while dinner was being prepared . . . As they fled they frequently looked back, and made some of their attendants ascend lofty towers to see if the barons were pursuing them. In their panic they did not spare the spur till they reached Winchester and the sheltering wings of the bishop elect, in whom all their hopes reposed . . ."[1]

Even there they were not safe. The barons were inexorable, and apart from Archbishop Boniface and Peter of Savoy most of the aliens went into exile. The royalist cause was left with only one brave champion outside the King's family and eventually he, the Earl de Warenne, had to add his pledge to the rest.

V

"And the whole reign was rapidly becoming less and less memorable . . ." (*1066 And All That.*)

THE PROVISIONS of Oxford represent the next real step in political development after 1215. But whereas *Magna Carta* was primarily a legal document setting out terms of contract, the Provisions of Oxford marked the determination of both barons and clergy to have a regular say in how the country was governed. Power was still to lie with a small ruling class and only lip service was paid to the rights of the community at large. The feudal system remained in force. And yet this was at the same time a genuine effort to alter the balance of power between the populace and the increasingly arbitrary central government, and it showed a considerable advance in political thinking. It was an early and primitive attempt at a system of constitutional monarchy. No wonder such an unseasonable plant withered in unprepared ground.

The Earls of Leicester and Gloucester shared the leadership of the barons, but they were uneasy partners. The names most in the forefront of the reforming clergy were those of John de Exon, Bishop of Winchester; Walter de Cantelupe, Bishop of Worcester; and Stephen de Berksted, Bishop of Chichester. Another man who played an important part in the new administration was Hugh Bigod, whose strong character and wide experience fitted him for the office of justiciar.

It seems surprising at first sight that the barons did not take greater advantage of their strength and the King's desperate situation. In fact, they were not seeking to make a permanent change in the form of government. The King had brought the country to a state of near-ruin and the barons hoped that by taking power into their own hands for a period limited to twelve years they could restore England's fortunes, reform the administration and make a clean sweep of the great horde of aliens. The forms of oath, the Provisions themselves and the names of the men appointed by each side to serve as counsellors are given in the Appendix on page 253.

The Provisions first set out the rules for holding county courts, and the presentation of plaints through 'four discreet and lawful knights' elected in each shire. Then followed the names of twelve men elected by each side, following the pattern of *Magna Carta*, forming a commission of twenty-four. Four of their number, two from each side, were chosen to be "electors" whose duty it was to appoint a council of fifteen as a permanent advisory body to the King. Twelve men were elected by the barons "to treat at the three parliaments by year with the King's council" and twenty-four were "appointed by the commonalty to treat of aid to the King". In this context "commonalty" probably referred to the lesser barons, or knights of the shires, but certainly not to the ordinary citizens.

The system was unfortunately too cumbersome and complex, and many names occur on more than one list. It appears to have been an attempt to form an elected "Cabinet" or royal council of fifteen, a committee of twelve representatives to help them, a council of twenty-four chosen by the barons and the twenty-four commissioners, half representing each side. It is not easy to understand or separate the functions of each council, but it is clear that there was a real attempt to surround the King with men to advise and restrain him even while Parliament was not sitting.

Separate oaths were sworn by the commonalty, the twenty-four commissioners, the chief justice of England, and the chancellor of England. The guardians of the king's castles swore that they would keep them only for the use of the King and his heirs and surrender them to no one else, for a period of twelve years.

The first of the promised reforms was "that the state of the Holy Church be amended". The next stated that the chief justice was to be appointed for one year only; that his powers were to be defined, and that he must "answer concerning his time before the King and his council and before him who shall follow him". The same should apply to the treasurer and the officials of the exchequer, and to the chancellor.[1]

The law of the land was in future to be properly observed, and the chief justice was "to amend the wrongs done by all other justices and bailiffs, and earls, and all other people . . ." The bribing of justices was to cease "unless it be presents of bread and wine, and such things, to wit, meat and drink, as have been used to be brought to the tables of the chief men for the day".

"Let there be provided as sheriffs, loyal people, and substantial men and land tenants; so that in each county there be a vavasour of the same county as sheriff, to treat the people of the county well, loyally and rightfully. And that he take no fee, and that he be sheriff only for a year together; and that in the year he give up his accounts at the exchequer, and answer for his time . . ."

Good escheators were to be appointed who should "take nothing of the effects of the dead, of such lands as ought to be in the King's hand".

"Be it remembered to amend the exchange of London, and the city of London, and all the other cities of the King which have gone to shame and destruction by the tallages and other oppressions."

The royal household was to be "amended", and, finally, three parliaments were to be held each year: one at the "octave of Saint Michael, the second the morrow of Candlemas, the third the first day of June . . ."

The clause relating to sheriffs has a modern ring. Today's High Sheriff usually fulfils the requirements laid down in the Provisions, but whereas once, as G. M. Trevelyan wrote in his *History of England*, the sheriffdom was "the chief pillar of the medieval English monarchy", now it is mainly a ceremonial office. It is still the High Sheriff's duty to execute writs including the writ to hold a parliamentary election, and in County constituencies he serves as the Returning Officer, but he no longer acts in the King's name as judge, tax collector, and military organizer. It is not surprising that through all the years of civil strife both the royalists and the barons struggled to keep authority in each county through these powerful men. The attempt to control their appointment and restrict the office to men with local interests and loyalty did not succeed for long. The privileges were too highly coveted, and proved a useful incentive or reward for faithful supporters.

The aims of the reformers sound moderate and sensible, but the machinery for enforcing the Provisions was not only too complex. It was also too narrowly based. No new class of citizen was to join in the deliberations of Parliament, and although the barons were groping for some sort of representative system the habits of feudalism died hard. However, government by discussion is an essential part of democracy, and this now took a hesitant stride forward. So, too, even if born of necessity and self-interest, did recognition of the need for informed public opinion if the work of reform was to have popular support.

The sheriffs were ordered "to have the charter written in English and sealed with the King's great seal, and that many times in the year it should be read in the presence of the county, so that what was therein contained should come to the notice of all".[2] In a real attempt to communicate with all the people both *Magna Carta* and the Oxford Statutes were read publicly throughout England and Ireland in English, French and Latin, and the royal circular letter to each county is the earliest state paper that has survived in the English language. Having pledged himself to obey and enforce the Oxford Statutes, the King declared:

> "Widnesse usselven aet Lunden thane egtetenthe day on the monthe of October in the two fowertigthe year of ure cruninge; and this wes idon aetforen ure isworne redesmen" (here follow the names of the councillors). "Aetforen othre moge, and al on the ilche worden is isend in to aurihce othre shcire over al thare Kuneriche on Engleneloande ek in tel Irelonde."

At the same time the barons addressed a letter to the Pope, explaining their conduct and complaining of "the ruinous disorders, the distress, and the decay of learning to which the introduction of so many Italians into English benefices, and the infatuation of the King, by denying justice against his favourites, has brought the country". They also urged the Pope to dismiss the King's half-brother Aymer, at present in exile, from his position as Bishop-elect of Winchester, declaring him to be an evil influence on the King and on Prince Edward. The Pope left their complaints unanswered for two years.

The new government embarked on its programme of reform with energy, but it was largely due to the choice of Hugh Bigod as justiciar that it even partially succeeded. Reform was in the air. There was a ruthless drive against undesirable aliens and corrupt officials, and a conscientious attempt to redress the grievances of even the humblest citizens. The justiciar, who was no respecter of persons, travelled the country himself hearing cases and cutting to a minimum the delays of legal procedure. Even so, the courts were overwhelmed with work. Four knights were appointed in each shire to hear complaints in the name of the King, and in the Provisions of Westminster in October 1259 much of the power and lucrative business of the feudal courts was transferred to the royal courts. These Provisions also amended the laws of inheritance and the granting of lands, restricted the rights of feudal lords over their military tenants and brought the clergy under the jurisdiction of the royal courts instead of the ecclesiastical courts, for certain offences. They laid down once more that only Englishmen could hold offices of state and control royal castles. These Provisions were later to be embodied in the Statute of Marlborough in 1267.

It is clear that there was now a third contestant for power. When their eyes were no longer dazzled by the blaze of reforming zeal the feudal lords saw only too clearly that their own authority and privileges were at stake. They were no longer sure that they had chosen the winning side. It was the "bachelors", the new rising class of knights and gentry who with Prince Edward as their titular head challenged the absolute power of the feudal barons. These were the men with local interests and some experience of responsibility in local government. With townsmen of similar standing they were to form the nucleus of a strong middle class, and their influence is clear in the Provisions of Westminster.

The King had two advantages. Not only were his enemies divided, but many of the greater barons soon scrambled back to the safety of royal favour. Hugh Bigod, an enthusiast for reform but not for rebellion, was among them. By the time the government fell from power many progressive measures in judicial and administrative fields had been passed into law. At the same time the country's foreign relations looked much healthier. England could not afford imperial ambitions either by war or purchase, and there was general rejoicing when the King's councillors opened negotiations for peace with France and repudiated the unhappy bargain for the crown of Sicily.

By 1260 the baronial party had lost much of its cohesion as well as popular support. Royalist emotion was stirring again, and even the reformers themselves were monarchists at heart. After the severe famine in 1258 there promised to be a fine harvest in 1259 but it was destroyed by floods. Again corn had to be imported at high prices. Many people, including the Bishop of London, died of plague. Such suffering, even if it sprang from an act of God, was borne more easily under the hand of their traditional ruler the King.

It is easy seven hundred years later to criticize de Montfort and his colleagues for failing to maintain the reforming enthusiasm of their party. They were hampered by an almost total lack of political experience which the professional civil servants possibly did as little as possible to make good. The inevitable jealousies and feuds soon divided them again. Basically it was still "every man for himself". The reformers did not cling to one coherent policy, nor belong to one disciplined party. Simon de Montfort, tough soldier and firm commander though he was, had shown little sign of the political flair and sureness of touch that were needed now.

It is interesting to speculate whether at any time he had designs upon the English throne for himself or his heirs. His marriage was thought by many people to be directed to that end. His readiness to lead the anti-royalist element could be interpreted as the ambition of a despot, and his enemies, then and ever since, have accused him of it. Yet this picture does not accord with what we know of the man or of the quality and ideals of his friends. It is difficult to believe that Walter de Cantelupe, who worked untiringly for a peaceful settlement, would have a high regard for a man animated by such dishonourable motives. To him the King, whatever his shortcomings, ruled by the will of God.

Whatever the truth may be, the King himself certainly feared and distrusted Simon. "The fears and anxieties of the barons were increased by the coming of the month of July with its pestilence-bearing lion and scorching dog-star, whose deadly barking usually disturbs the atmosphere. More than all else were they alarmed at the fickleness and inscrutable duplicity of the King, which they discovered from a certain ominous speech.

"One day he had left his palace at Westminster and gone down the Thames in a boat to take his dinner out of doors, when the sky clouded over and a thunderstorm came on, attended with lightning and heavy rain. Now the King feared a storm of this kind more than any, so he directed them to land him at once; and the boat was opposite to the stately palace of the Bishop of Durham, where the Earl of Leicester was then staying.

"On knowing of his arrival the earl goes gladly to meet him, and greeting him with respect as was proper, says by way of consolation: 'What is it that you fear? The storm is now passed.'

"To this the King, not in jest but seriously, answered with a severe look, 'The thunder and lightning I fear beyond measure, but by the Head of God, I fear thee more than all the thunder and lightning in the world.'

'The earl gently replied, 'My lord, it is unjust and incredible that you should fear me your firm friend, who am ever faithful to you and yours, and to the kingdom of England; it is your enemies, your destroyers, and false flatterers that you ought to fear.' "[4]

Simon de Montfort did not only clash with the King. He and Richard de Clare, Earl of Gloucester, had worked in uneasy harness together over the years, for they were quite different in temperament. Where Simon was practical, outspoken and opinionated, a man of action and physical courage, Richard was more intellectual and devious, more diplomatic, full of dark corners; perhaps a bit of a "barrack room lawyer", and for all his love of tournaments, not a successful soldier.

As the first ardent enthusiasm for the new government began to cool the Earl of Gloucester prevaricated. A heated quarrel broke out between the two men, and de Montfort told Gloucester: " 'I care not to live or hold converse with men so fickle and false as thee. For we have made a promise and oath to one another in these matters whereof we are treating. And as for thee, my lord Earl of Gloucester, the more thou dost excel all men in rank, the more art thou bound by wholesome statutes', and with this he shortly left England."[4]

The reforming party was torn by these dissensions and by the desertion of large numbers. A contemporary song-writer mourned the state of the country:

"Lament with weeping, O England, full as thou now art with matter of grief, in sadness thou beholdest sorrowful things, languishing in sorrow . . . Very many have pledged themselves to preserve thee in safety, but now they have too much neglected their promise; for many desert, who have it in their power to help; and some slink away over the sea. Hence the rest begin to quarrel, and to go over to different sides; while things which disagree in this matter will not be reconciled, and what has been begun is left unfinished . . . Earl Simon de Montfort, a strong man and a bold, fight now for thy country, and be the leader of the band; neither let threats scare thee, nor the fear of death; defend the state and thy own fortune . . ."[5]

IN FACT Simon de Montfort still had heavy commitments abroad, and his preoccupation with foreign affairs overshadowed his interest in domestic policy. He was busy negotiating the peace treaty with France which was to end half a century of hostilities. The truce of 1243 had several times been extended, and although the King had been sorely tempted to make another pounce on his old enemies while Louis IX was away on crusade, the Pope firmly vetoed the idea. Henry was also in some financial embarrassment again, and he hoped that by ceding certain territorial rights in France he might raise sufficient money and military reinforcements for his struggle against the barons.

The following extracts are from a French poem which may well date from this time. They lose something in translation because of the coarse word-play of the original, but they convey Henry's bravado and incurable optimism and the rashness of his friends.

"Now May is come, with roses in full bloom,
With weather fair, and singing nightingales,
Fields decked in green, and gardens full of flowers,
And I have found, deep-buried in my heart,
A tale which I will tell of my good lord,
Of England's King, and of his men of war.
A valiant knight was he, both bold and true.

Of Edward too, his fair-haired son, I wish
New stories to relate, and of the stately
King of France, the Lord who Normandy took
Unlawfully; false Fortune frowned that day . . .

My lords, I crave your hearing, for my tale
No laughing matter is; all men should cry
Aloud the news I bring fresh to your ears.
The other day in London there did meet
A great assembly, both of best and worst,
No living baron was, but he did come
To this debate. Such things were uttered there
That truly I believe the King of France
May quail in fear for all those lands he holds
In spite of English rights . . .

The Englishmen were eager for a fight.
Such was their mood, that should a Frenchman dare
Challenge their right, such fear would they inspire
With sword and greyhound, that no more would he
Against them bravely raise his hostile voice.

There stood some way apart England's good King,
With Richard his own brother, both enraged
As angry leopards. Deeply sighed he there,
And bitterly cried out within himself:

'O God! How can it be that I again
Shall have my share of Normandy?' To him,
'Despair you not,' the Earl of Gloucester said.
'Still may you do it. We may win again.
If God protects, I pray my back, my feet,
And my right arm, you, Sire, will once more be
Sole ruler, and in Paris, master, king.' . . .

De Montfort listened to these speeches, then
Sprang to his feet, a plain man he, and said,
'My lord of England, by the Holy Lamb
Leave well alone. The Frenchmen are not soft.
If you attack, they'll sure defend themselves.
They'll burn your tents to ashes, and no man,
No, not the bravest, will stand firm, unmoved.
The captured at their hands will suffer much.'

Cried Roger Bigod, 'Do I hear aright?
Does Simon think the King a senseless fool?
Beware! For if you say another word
You'll do yourself no favour, this I swear!'

'Sir Roger,' said the King, 'For God's sake, peace!
Calm down. Let's not be angry with this wretch.
Nothing care I for all the French there are.
My wish I'll have, no matter what befalls.
I know that Paris will be mine for sure,
I'll even set on fire the very Seine,
I'll burn their mills—they'll rue the sorry day
When there's no bread to eat for one whole week.
By God's five wounds! How great that city is!
A chapel I have seen within its walls
Which I have long desired. I'll have it brought
To London in a cart to Saint Amont,
Just as it stands, to have it for my own . . .' "[1]

THE TREATY OF PARIS was ratified on 4 December 1259, when Henry, surrounded by the highest nobles of England and France, knelt before Louis of France and made the oath of fealty and liege homage. His sister Eleanor de Montfort also surrendered her claims to her father's heritage, and Simon de Montfort relinquished any claim to his family possessions in France. Henry also "resigned fully and freely all lands then in the hands of the King of France. And thenceforward he shortened his title, calling himself no more Duke of Normandy or Count of Anjou".[4] In return, Louis undertook to pay by six yearly instalments the sum necessary to maintain five hundred knights, but this money was to be used only "for the service of God, the Church, or the welfare of England".

The day ended in splendid festivities, and Henry, delighted with his bargain, remained in France for a few weeks more to arrange a marriage for his second daughter.

One incident in 1259 probably passed almost unnoticed: the death of Matthew Paris. He died during the summer at the monastery at Saint Albans where most of his life had been spent. He remained remarkably independent in spite of royal patronage, and although he had strong convictions and warm sympathies he left a fair and critical history of his times. He said himself, "The case of historical writers is hard, for if they tell the truth they provoke men, and if they write what is false they offend God."

There is no doubt that he knew the King well and was not afraid to speak his mind. He described how the King spent a week at the monastery in 1258, "and since I who write these things was constantly beside the King, at table, in his court and in his chamber, he guided my pen with energy and friendliness . . . So, at that time, the writer of these words addressed the lord king, 'My lord, in God's name keep the Church from harm, which even now stumbleth to her downfall.'

"The King answered, 'Nay, in the name of God, and above all things not in mine own time.' "

His colleagues must have sadly missed his sense of fun, his enthusiasms and his often sardonic wit. The work which Matthew Paris took over from Roger of Wendover was now carried on by other hands, mainly those of William of Rishanger.

RELATIONS BETWEEN King Henry and Simon de Montfort grew steadily worse. There were two fields of disagreement: one centred round national political issues; the other was personal, involving complex arguments between Henry and his sister Eleanor, and between Henry and Simon, about her marriage portion and her title to certain lands. All these matters were from time to time presented for arbitration to Louis IX of France. They became so indissolubly confused that it is difficult to decide where personal disputes ended and national differences began. James Ramsay wrote in *The Dawn of the Constitution*, "The critical epoch 1258–61 seems a time of confusion, hard to follow. It was no doubt a time of great fluctuations in public opinion. But in reality the successive oscillations in the ascendance of the parties are perfectly intelligible, and due to the struggle between constitutional instinct and a demand for just rights, on the one hand, and innate loyalty and regard for royal authority on the other."

While Henry and the de Montforts stayed on in France to argue their rights, the barons in England demanded that Parliament should be called. The King refused on the grounds that "innovations" might be made in his absence. In February 1260 Simon and his wife left Paris for London, and three weeks later the defiant barons assembled.

The government was beginning to totter. Hugh Bigod resigned the justiciarship and his place was taken by de Montfort's supporter, Hugh le Despenser, but the Earl of Gloucester and other leading barons were now ready to side with the King, and the reforming party gained little strength from their new adherents. Among them was Prince Edward, who never openly deserted his father but for a time showed sympathetic leanings towards the radicals. It was natural that such a spirited young man should find little to admire in his father and much to respect in his uncle. Edward, Henry of Almaine and Simon de Montfort's sons had grown up together as cousins and friends. The cause of the rebels promised excitement and danger which attracted young men and the restless mood of the country unsettled them. The King had some reason to fear that his son and his brother-in-law were conspiring against him. When he returned to England at the end of April he lodged in the bishop's palace at Saint Paul's and ordered the gates of the city to be closely guarded.

In fact, the tide was now running in the King's favour, for the country no longer trusted the instrument it had so recently created. The Cinque Ports were back in royalist hands, and the Pope had sent letters absolving Henry and all his subjects from the oath they had sworn, adding "that the sanctity of an oath, by which faith and truth should be confirmed, ought not to be made the strengthening bond of wickedness and perfidy".[7]

The shock of this decision temporarily united the opposition of barons and clergy. Gloucester and Leicester forgot their differences, and Walter de Cantelupe the Bishop of Worcester made a public protest against the breaking of the oath. An agreement between both parties to ask King Louis to mediate on the disputed points came to nothing.

The King, having replaced the justiciar by Philip Basset, a member of his own household, ". . . shut himself in the Tower, broke open the fastenings of the treasure therein stored of old and consumed it. Moreover, he collected workmen who repaired the said Tower and greatly strengthened it in suitable places. Further he commanded the city of London to be guarded all round with bolts and bars, and having assembled all in the city, from twelve years old and upwards, he made them swear to preserve their allegiance to him, a herald at the same time proclaiming that those who would fight for the King should come forward at once and should be supported at his expense. When they heard this, the barons assembled from all quarters with great hosts of soldiers, and were billetted outside the walls, lodging within the city being straitly denied them."[8]

While the King lived in this state of voluntary siege, the Queen was busy across the Channel drumming up support. She had taken the crown jewels to her sister the Queen of France, perhaps for their greater safety, but also as surety for men and money. As well as the crowns and garlands were many gold girdles, clasps and combs, an alphabet, two hundred and eight jewelled rings and two golden peacocks which poured sweet waters from their beaks.

Simon de Montfort was also in France. Prothero suggested that at this time he and the King were like two independent princes, each working to gain allies while the other was absent.

Simon had many friends in France whose support would strengthen his hand. He also wanted to plead his case before King Louis in his personal quarrels with Henry. The litigation between Simon and Eleanor de Montfort on one side and the King on the other had dragged on with sporadic attempts by the French King and his wife to arbitrate. It was not honour that was at stake, but money, and as money would buy an army both sides were anxious for a favourable settlement.

There was probably another reason for Simon's absence from England for as long as eighteen months: that he was not content to remain there as leader of an almost non-existent party. Disillusioned, resentful and, after all, a Frenchman by blood, he may well have decided to shake the dust of England from his feet and extricate himself from the conflict between Englishmen who demanded justice but would not keep faith. There is no reason to think that he played any active part in leading the reforming party from France, or that he delegated his powers to any one man. In the meantime, the country drifted to the edge of civil war.

Prince Edward, whatever his innermost sympathies, now firmly supported his father. Henry wrote to him: "This is no time for laziness and boyish wantonness . . . I am getting old, you are in the flower of your young manhood." It was true, for Edward was developing from an impulsive, hot-tempered young man, quick to resent injustice and eager to display his virtuosity in a fight, into a mature and high-principled man who would become a great king. He had yet to learn bitter lessons from his own mistakes, but all the signs of growing stability were there.

Richard Earl of Gloucester died, as a stalwart royalist, but his son Gilbert de Clare, a young man of nineteen, threw himself ardently into the baronial cause. There were many others like him, among them Henry of Almaine, John de Warenne Earl of Surrey, Robert de Ferrers Earl of Derby, Roger de Clifford, Roger de Leyburne, John Giffard, Nicholas Segrave and Geoffrey Lucy. These men, with a number of bishops, and Peter de Montfort who was an old friend, kept alive the spirit of rebellion, and when Simon de Montfort returned they placed themselves under his leadership. Thomas Wyke, an Augustinian monk of Osney, cynically described de Montfort as "moulding the barons with his own deep-cut impression, especially the younger ones, who, being ductile as soft wax, followed him not from any love of justice, but from greediness of gain". It is difficult to believe that among them all there was no spirit of genuine idealism too.

The country was dangerously sick. Disturbances between the Welsh and the border barons became an excuse for the two parties to skirmish against each other. Through the summer months of 1263 the baronial army marched from one stronghold to another leaving a trail of havoc and bloodshed. All the restless, high-spirited young men streamed out to follow them, as well as a motley collection of middle-aged bishops, humble friars, students from Oxford, citizens of London and other towns, and the usual proportion of wastrels and hooligans.

Rishanger described the country's misery. "The whole of that year, with five months and two weeks besides, trembled with the horrors of war; and as every one strove to defend his castles, they ravaged the whole neighbourhood, laying waste the fields, carrying off the cattle for the defence of the castles, and spared neither churches nor cemeteries. Moreover, the houses of the poor rustics were rummaged and plundered, even to the straw of the beds. Although the earl had given commandment that no one, on pain of decapitation, should presume to enter a sacred edifice or a cemetery for the purpose of plunder, or lay violent hands on religious or their servants, he gained nothing by this provision. For no bishops or abbots or any religious could go from town to town without being plundered by highwaymen."[8]

Simon's army must have been little more than an undisciplined mob. But his own role is difficult to define, for he neither appears as an active peacemaker nor a determined rebel. During the critical years since 1258 he had spent almost half the time in France, and it is impossible to guess whether he was helplessly letting things drift beyond his control, or deliberately encouraging sedition for national or personal ends.

By the end of June the baronial army had marched from

Gloucestershire and the border country through Reading, Guildford and Reigate, and were pressing rapidly towards Dover.

The importance of the Cinque Ports can hardly be exaggerated. The original five were Dover, Hastings, Hythe, Romney and Sandwich. Richard I added Rye and Winchelsea, and these seven ports formed a recognized corporate group. During the twelfth and thirteenth centuries they were granted certain privileges under charter, with exemption from many taxes and the right to set up a form of local government. In return they were bound to provide the country's coastal defence, and so until the growth of the navy in Tudor times they served as England's front line of defence. They were vital to trade as well as safety, and the wardenship of Dover Castle was a responsible and often dangerous office. Now, with civil war rending England and the possibility of foreign mercenaries coming to swell the rival armies, each side coveted the support of these small towns in Kent and Sussex. Their sympathies in general were with the baronial side, for they shared the universal hatred of the French and resented the King's meddling in commerce. So although Dover Castle did not yield to a baronial attack, it equally resisted every demand of the royalists.

London was subjected to another act of plunder. "The King went with the Queen to the Tower of London, while the Lord Edward remained in Clerkenwell hospital. Since they lacked money in their coffers and no one in London would give them a halfpenny on credit, and as the Lord Edward did not want to disgrace himself, joined by Robert Walerand and many others he went . . . to the New Temple when the gates were closed. When at his request the keys had been handed over to him, he said that he wanted to see the jewels belonging to the Queen his mother. The warden was summoned, and he fraudulently entered the Temple treasury with his men. Then with iron hammers which they had brought with them they broke open certain of the chests there and took much money, up to the sum of a thousand pounds, and had it carried away. At this outrage the citizens of London rose in rebellion against him and others of the king's council staying in the city . . ."[9]

Bitternesss was being stored up on both sides. "In the same year on Saint Mildred's day the Queen came out of the Tower to the Thames, and wishing to go to Windsor went by boat to London Bridge. There the Londoners assaulted her and her people shamefully with base and foul words and even with stones, so that she was with difficulty freed by the mayor of London, and was compelled of necessity to return to the Tower. The King did not let her enter, but she was conducted in safety to Saint Paul's by the mayor and was lodged in the bishop's house."[9]

It is said that Prince Edward swore to avenge this insult to his mother. The Queen and her younger son Edmund escaped once more to France.

A temporary peace was patched up between the frightened King and the disorderly rebels with some promise of success, for Philip Bassett was again replaced as justiciar by Hugh le Despenser from the baronial side and a writ was issued "to be read in the Gildhall, which said that the dissension between the King and the barons was ended . . ." It lasted only during the busy weeks of harvesting. Neither side can have been under any illusions: it was no more than the lull before the real storm. Yet even now war might have been averted. The Church longed only for peace. The rebellious barons, believing quite simply that Henry was "king by the grace of God" could never wholly forget their allegiance to him both as king and feudal lord. If Simon de Montfort had been more ready to compromise or more firmly in control of his supporters, the King less irresponsible and shifty, and if personal relations between the two men had been better the drift to war might still have been stopped.

That neither protagonist really wanted a full scale military trial of strength, and that neither was planning for it even at this stage, is pretty clear, and this is emphasised by two genuine efforts to get the French King to help them find a compromise.

Parliament met in September and heard complaints about the violence and pillaging of the baronial army. When it dispersed, the King, with Simon de Montfort, Peter de Montfort and supporters from both sides crossed to Boulogne to seek

King Louis' help in finding a reconciliation. Instead a violent quarrel broke out between de Montfort and King Henry and the whole party returned to England in a state of menacing calm. The truce was over. Simon withdrew to Kenilworth while the King and his court kept on the move, staying at Oxford, Winchester and Rochester. In December he reached Dover with a formidable army and demanded entry to the castle. The warden was away but his son John de Grey refused to admit him except as a peaceful visitor without armed attendants.

On his way back to Windsor the King tried to take Simon in an ambush at Southwark by hemming him in between the river and the city gates. "When the earl saw that he had far fewer men than the King so that he could in no way resist, he wished to enter the city, but the gates were shut and he could not. The earl considered this and armed himself and his men, and in the name of God he fastened crosses on both the back and the breast of himself and the others. Meanwhile, confessing their sins, they all took the Sacrament, and made ready to await the onslaught of their enemies and to struggle against them for the sake of truth. But when it was known in the city that the earl was shut out, the community at once broke open the gates, and the earl and his men entered. The other party fell into violent confusion when they heard this."[9]

It was stalemate. Only outright war or determined mediation could resolve it. With universal relief, on December 13 1263 letters were sealed in London and sent to King Louis asking him to arbitrate once more. Each side stated its case and swore to abide by his decision.

The barons set out their grievances at length. Four documents in the *Archives Nationales* in Paris, all written in the same hand, list the "*Gravamina quibus terra Angliae opprimebatur et super quibus necesse fuit statum eiusdem reformare*". In spite of constant reiteration, and the familiarity of the complaints, they clearly reveal the embitterment against the King and, more especially, against his foreign friends and counsellors.

The fourth document has only in recent years been recognized as one of the baronial letters of complaint.[10] It covers the main arguments, ecclesiastical, financial and judicial. As usual it mentions first the violation of the charters and the King's interference with the free elections of the Church. Then "the wards and escheats of possessions" which fell into the King's hands were being ruined by the sale of land and by total neglect.

Since the arrival of foreigners "whom the King called to his council, rejecting native citizens", no man could obtain justice. "For those who should have pronounced judgment dared not do so, for they were placed in office by these men, and were protected by them, so that they acquitted them either because they were bondsmen or because they were afraid of losing their positions . . ." These same foreigners and their bailiffs were demanding service from their tenants to which they had no right.

The King and his courtiers were interfering with the "established right and custom of the country that merchants from any country and merchandize of any kind should be able to come to England without hindrance, and free from unlawful attack". They were taking wine and cloth and other goods without payment and so driving merchants to find markets elsewhere.

There were general complaints of oppression and extortion against the sheriffs and bailiffs, and against the foreigners, and they were accused of keeping for themselves revenues due to the exchequer.

Finally, the Church had been sorely robbed on the pretext that the King and many nobles of the kingdom "had taken the cross, by his will, but against the hopes of all the people, in order to change those living in Saracen kingdoms, enemies of the cross of Christ, into brothers of the same Christian faith . . . From this robbery many thousands of marks were collected to the great loss of the churches and the community as a whole, but they were paid in vain, for all came to nothing, so that the Holy Land, to save which they had all so valiantly put on their swords, profited nothing, and neither did the ridiculous acceptance of Sicily help in any way . . ."

Louis IX was well fitted to act as arbiter. Like Henry III he succeeded to his father's throne as a child, but there the resemblance between the two men ended. This intelligent and versatile king devoted much of his reign, like Henry II of England, to drawing up a code of law for his country and establishing courts of justice. He was responsible for the Pragmatic Sanction which provided a workable relationship between the French Church and the papacy. He was a dedicated crusader, a patron of learning and a pious churchman. He was also a firm upholder of absolute monarchy who conscientiously shouldered the burdens and responsibilities of the crown.

This was the man, the great Saint Louis, whom royalists and anti-royalists trusted to act as mediator. Simon de Montfort knew him well, and these two forceful men respected each other. King Henry was his brother-in-law and fellow-king. Each apparently believed that he would find the arbitration acceptable, though some of de Montfort's supporters voiced their doubts about Louis' impartiality.

On 23 January 1264, in a deed known as the Mise of Amiens, Louis gave his verdict. "We, in the name of the Father, the Son, and the Holy Ghost, annul and make void the Oxford Statutes and all regulations depending on them, more especially inasmuch as the Pope has already annulled them."[11]

Louis ordered the barons to forfeit all castles to the King. He declared that the King should freely appoint all officials of his kingdom and his household and that "it is lawful for an alien to remain securely in the said kingdom, and that the said king can call to his council the aliens who seem to him useful and faithful . . ." He then added a saving clause:

"But it is neither our desire nor intention to detract by this ordinance from royal privileges, charters, rights, statutes nor any admirable customs of the realm of England established before the said time. We declare further that the said King shall show to the said barons tolerance, setting aside his wrath arising from these complaints, likewise the barons towards him, nor henceforth shall any suffer harshness nor be injured by reason of these matters."[11]

It is a pity Matthew Paris did not live long enough to record the reaction of the barons. They were enraged and bewildered. Historians have been at pains to explain why Louis made no attempt to find a just compromise but dismissed the barons' grievances out of hand. There is no doubt that the Pope wished, and perhaps ordered him to find in the King's favour. The crown of Sicily, once coveted by Henry for his son Edmund, had now been offered to Louis's brother, Charles of Anjou. Perhaps Queen Eleanor and her relatives and friends had pleaded the royal case successfully.

Louis was not a man to be swayed easily by such considerations, but for other reasons no other verdict was likely. Ruling firmly and wisely himself he believed that a king, empowered to choose his ministers and advisers, provided the only conceivable form of government. The idea of limited monarchy had not yet found acceptance anywhere, and the Provisions of Oxford would appear revolutionary in his eyes. Nor would he understand the complaints about "foreigners". These hated enemies of England were his own countrymen. The ties between the two countries had been close, and for generations their royal houses had been linked by marriage. If further persuasion were needed, perhaps Henry's plausible charm and show of piety played their small part.

In any case, the award was useless. Louis had laid down that the charters should be observed, but he did not suggest what measures should be taken to enforce them. Nor was there any possibility that the radical party would accept a verdict which undid all the painful and laborious work of several decades.

There has been much argument about whether the barons' attitude to the Mise could be justified. Having sworn to accept arbitration they now refused to accept the decision. On the other hand, it is clear that they expected a compromise, and not an outright annulment. The very word *mise*, or *compromissum*, must have led them to suppose that they would be asked to agree to nothing more than an amended version of the Provisions of Oxford. Simon himself, who knew the French King and his character so well, obviously took this view, confident that Louis understood the precise nature of his aims and presuming that he sympathized with at least some of them. What grounds he had for thinking that it is impossible to guess.

The royalists showed no sign of misgivings, and their mood

was one of confidence and self-congratulation. The Pope, of course, gladly and automatically pronounced in favour of the Mise. Queen Eleanor and Peter of Savoy sailed for England with the royal jewels and Henry, overjoyed by the verdict and with his incurable optimism believing that everything was set fair, serenely oblivious of the gathering storm, lingered on in France to celebrate.

Simon de Montfort kept in touch with events only by messenger, for soon after setting out for Amiens to be present at the arbitration, he fell from his horse and fractured a leg. Now he lay helpless at Kenilworth while the tempest raged about him. The situation must have looked hopeless. The King seemed to have everything on his side, including most of Simon's former supporters. Walter de Cantelupe and Peter de Montfort were among the few who had been faithful over the years, for death or desertion had taken most of the rest. Of the younger ones his sons Henry, Simon and Guy were eager to help but lacking in judgment and experience. Gilbert de Clare the young Earl of Gloucester was so far a dedicated supporter, and so was Nicholas de Segrave, but most of the others had drifted back into the safer waters of royalist favour.

One who changed sides was Henry of Almaine, a young man who had already suffered for the cause. After his arrest in Boulogne because he had courageously sided with de Montfort, he was released on the orders of King Louis. Shaken by doubts and abandoned by his friends, he now felt the lash of his uncle's scorn.

"And from that time arose a new error, worse than the first. For many nobles perjured themselves and withdrew from their fealty to the Earl of Leicester who was contending for justice. Henry, the son of the King of Almaine, having received the honour of Tickhill from Lord Edward, the King's son, came to the consul and said to him, 'Lord Earl, against my father the King of Almaine, and my uncle the King of England, and my kinsmen, I can no longer fight. With your favour, therefore, I would have licence to depart. Yet verily I will never bear arms against you.'

"To whom the consul mirthfully replied, 'Lord Henry, I

grieve not for your arms, but for the inconstancy which I discern in you. Go therefore, and return home with your arms, for I in no wise fear them.'

"At the same time Roger de Clifford, Roger de Leyburne, John de Vaux, Hamo L'Estrange, and many others, blinded by gifts, receded from fealty which they had sworn to the barons in common."[8]

The effect of the Mise was greatly to widen the gulf between the two parties. Père Daniel, the French historian, commented, "So celebrated and authentic a judgment had no other effect to make the least passionate of the rebels return to their duty, those who were dissatisfied with their party being glad of the opportunity to desert it."

In fact, as well as weeding out the faint-hearted it stiffened the purpose of the faithful. And the seething discontent of so many of the barons and clergy, the citizens of London and the Cinque Ports, some of the new urban middle class and a host of students and adventurous young men eruptied into rebellion. The Mise of Amiens had split the country wide open, and peace could only return as the exhausted aftermath of war.

VI

> "This so confused the Londoners that they armed themselves with staves, jerkins, etc. . . ."
>
> (*1066 And All That.*)

"AGAIN A PARLIAMENT was held at Oxford between the lord King and the said barons, but the Londoners and the barons of the Cinque Ports, and almost all the middling orders of the English nation, who indeed did not submit themselves to the arbitration of the King of France, entirely gainsaid his will.

"Wherefore the Londoners made for themselves their own constable and marshal, at whose summons when the great bell of Saint Paul's was heard all had to go out of the city, and not otherwise, with weapons and well armed, both by night and by day, following the standard of the said constable and marshal wherever they might wish to lead them. Afterwards Hugh le Despenser the justiciar, who was then Constable of the Tower, went out of the city with an innumerable crowd of Londoners to follow the standards of the said constable and marshal. Not knowing where they ought to go or what to do, they were led to Isleworth, and there destroyed and burned the manor of the King of Germany and carried off all the goods found there. They broke and ruined the mills and fish ponds, observing no truces, while he remained in the said parliament. And this was the beginning of calamities and the start of the fatal war through which so many manors were destroyed and so many men, both rich and poor, ruined, and so many thousands of men perished."[1]

The City of London, as well as joining in the national rebellion against the monarchy, was involved in its own private conflict. It had achieved a degree of self-government early in the thirteenth century, and with increasing overseas trade it was fast becoming an important mercantile centre. The pressure on south-east England had already started, and land values were rising. Political experience and growing prosperity led the Londoners to recognize their own importance and guard more jealously their civic rights and liberties. The King, with his greedy eye on this rich treasury so near his palace walls, took steps to grasp what wealth he could. And so London resented the King's interference on the one hand and distrusted its own aldermanic government on the other.

The mayor and aldermen tended to come from a small closed circle, and from time to time they were accused of corruption, irresponsibility, arrogance and discrimination in money matters. The royal sheriffs as the king's agents were, of course, unpopular with both sides. So bitter and so vital was the struggle between the monarchy and England's most powerful city that Henry hardly knew whether to try and render it impotent or curry its favour. He tried both expedients. Sometimes he deprived the city of all its rights and placed it under his own authority. Occasionally, on the other tack, he called a meeting of the Folkmoot and offered petty or meaningless privileges to win popular support against the aldermen. His hated clerk and factotum John Mansel acted as rabble-rouser. But the Folkmoot was a useful instrument in the hands of the aldermen too.

For years London swung uncertainly from one loyalty to the other, but after the publication of the Provisions of Oxford it became more and more de Montfort's ally against the King, and this was to be its traditional attitude in other anti-monarchist rebellions. In the thirteenth century it was not the most dependable of allies. At this stage in the city's development the Londoners were touchy, self important and unstable. Like dry tinder they were ready to burst into flames from a flying spark.

Rebellion spread rapidly and Prince Edward tried to restore order before it was too late. He attacked his de Montfort cousins at Gloucester, and again it was Walter de Cantelupe who arranged a truce between them. Edward moved north and the ravages of war spread through Derbyshire, Northamptonshire and to the walls of Simon's own home at Kenilworth, but his castle was impregnable.

King Henry assembled his supporters at Woodstock and dispersed the University of Oxford on the grounds that the high-spirited students might interfere with his solemn councils. In fact he was afraid of trouble.

The universities might have been expected to favour the King but they were strongly anti-royalist. In many ways Henry was a man after their own heart, for he was studiously pious and interested in all branches of learning. He had also intervened with the civic authorities in the interests of poorer students at Oxford and Cambridge. "But we have heard that when they hire your lodgings, you are so harsh and oppressive to the scholars resident among you, that unless you are more moderate and reasonable towards them in this respect, they will have to leave the town on account of your exactions, abandon their studies and depart from our land . . . So bear yourselves in this matter that no outcry comes to us because you have acted otherwise, and so that we do not have to take action in the matter."[2]

It is impossible to say how many students, influenced by their teachers and enflamed with the spirit of rebellion, marched out under their own banner to join the baronial army. When Walter de Merton founded his college in that same year he provided "for the perpetual sustenance of twenty scholars living in the schools of Oxford" but there must have been hundreds of young men who flocked to the town to attend the lectures by famous scholars and learn about the new discoveries of science as well as the older arts. On the other hand, it is impossible to believe that there were as many as fifteen thousand as some historians say. The little town had a Domesday population of about 1,700, and the university probably no more than doubled the population during the reign of Henry.

The King had now gathered most of the wayward back into the fold. His brother Richard, whose well-meaning efforts had often damped the fires of rebellion, was now strongly pro-royalist, and the savage destruction of his property at Isleworth no doubt quenched any remaining sympathy for the cause of reform.

He had been away in Germany for his coronation as King of Almaine when the barons drew up the Provisions of Oxford and imposed the oath. When he returned, piqued at their failure to consult him, he swore "by the throat of God, saying, 'I will not take the oath which you require, nor inform you of the period of my stay in England. I have no peer in England, seeing I am son of the late and brother of the present king, and Earl of Cornwall. If therefore the nobles of England wished to reform the state of the realm, they ought to have summoned me, and should not in impetuous daring have approached so difficult a matter without my knowledge or presence.' "[3]

The threats of the barons quickly changed his mind for him, and when the Earl of Gloucester, addressing him as Earl of Cornwall and not as King of Almaine which the barons refused to acknowledge, administered the oath, Richard "boldly and distinctly" made his vow. All who heard him believed he would keep faith with them except Richard Earl of Gloucester, who commented wisely "Inasmuch as we were often injured beyond measure in such cases, and as he who has once been scalded always dreads boiling water, I am by no means assured that we have not done too little, which Almighty God forefend".[3]

Both these men were quick to change sides and many others did so with little persuasion. Properties changed hands in quick succession. Roger Mortimer, a shifty member of the baronial party, was granted some of the de Montfort lands on the Welsh marches and became a devoted king's man. William Maudvit was hastily presented with the earldom of Warwick, and up and down the country rich estates were dangled to entice the waverers.

It is impossible to estimate the size of the army that rallied to the King's standard and encamped round his royal palace at Woodstock, but it was probably larger than the barons could possibly muster. Blaauw suggested that a line skirting the western boundaries of Hampshire, Berkshire, Oxfordshire, Warwickshire and Derbyshire roughly divided the main baronial support to the east of it and royalist support to the west. London and other commercial centres which had suffered from the King's shortsighted and avaricious policies threw their weight against him. The remoter parts of the country to the west and north were royalist by habit. They hardly felt the full weight of government interference, and continued the feudal custom of military service. The chieftains who came with their armies also welcomed an opportunity to plunder the rich merchants and traders.

In 1264 there were twelve great earls of England, and they were evenly divided in the struggle. On the King's side were his brother Richard of Cornwall; his son Edward of Chester; his half-brother William de Valence now Earl of Pembroke; his brother-in-law John de Warenne Earl of Surrey; Humphrey de Bohun Earl of Hereford and Essex, whose son fought on the other side; and William Maudvit the new Earl of Warwick.

With Simon de Montfort were Gilbert de Clare the young Earl of Gloucester; Roger Bigod Earl of Norfolk; Henry de Lacy Earl of Lincoln; Robert de Vere Earl of Oxford; and Robert de Ferrers Earl of Derby who was more trouble to his own side than to the enemy.

The King had lost one influential adviser, his factotum John Mansel the Treasurer of York, who had been an *éminence grise* in the royal household since 1242. This clever, crafty man had engineered many of his master's shady bargains, as well as arranging the marriage between Prince Edward and Eleanor of Castile and negotiating peace terms with Scotland in 1255. It was Mansel who went to Germany to bid for Richard's crown. He dispensed the rewards of royal favour and at the same time amassed a private fortune. Now that retribution seemed uncomfortably near he slipped out of the country and his property was confiscated.

Simon de Montfort had partially recovered from his fall and was on the move again. He called a meeting of his supporters at Northampton but before he reached there it had fallen to Prince Edward. The Prior of the Cluniac Priory of Saint Andrew, which lay just outside the town, breached the town wall and let the royalists pass in through his grounds. The garrison defended it stoutly, and Simon, the second of de Montfort's sons, stormed out so rashly that he landed headlong in the town ditch outside so that only the intervention of his cousin Edward saved his life. The whole garrison was taken prisoner including Peter de Montfort, his two sons, young Simon de Montfort and a strong force of students from Oxford under their own banner. The town was savagely sacked and from that time both armies indulged in all the viciousness and licence of total war.

Thus England suffered all the agonies of self-inflicted wounds and while Simon de Montfort was "raging like a lion robbed of his whelps" senseless and hideous atrocities were carried out all over the country. Properties belonging to both sides were looted and destroyed, and as so often before it was the Jews who were the undeserving victims of the worst acts of vengeance.

"Among other things I think that the slaughter of the Jews which was perpetrated at that time in London should not be passed over in silence. For when those who tarried in London became in want of necessary funds, especially when their own property could not suffice to sustain so large a party, they declared it a noble thing to redeem their own penury with the riches of others. Rushing therefore in unexpected tumult on the Jews, of whom a very great multitude dwelt with all confidence in London, little thinking that harm would happen to them, they, enticed not by the zeal of the law, but by the lust of temporal good, most cruelly slew as many as they could find in the city, forgetful at once of humanity and religion, sparing neither age nor sex; perpetrating unheard of murders, they slew without compassion the old men with the aged men, the suckling with the elderly, young boys at play, and babies not weaned, nearly four hundred Jews of both sexes and all ranks being slain. And although they were not signed with the mark of our faith, it seemed an inhuman and impious deed to kill them without cause, since we are bound, according to the canons, to cherish them if only for humanity, and also because they were made in the image of God . . ."[4]

There was nothing to be gained by pressing on to attack Northampton, and Simon de Montfort, with his greatly weakened and depleted force, turned southward. First he attacked Rochester which Roger de Leyburne had recently held for the barons but now defended in the name of the King. On Good Friday 1264, after fire-ships had been used to burn the wooden bridge, the town was taken and sacked. The cathedral was plundered, the cloisters were used for stabling and neither the authority of Simon de Montfort nor the influence of the bishops could prevent these acts of sacrilege. While the King's army was hurrying to the rescue rumours reached Rochester of a disturbance in London. A royalist rising in the city would be dangerous, for de Montfort could not afford to risk losing one of his main sources of strength. At once he abandoned the siege of Rochester Castle, which still held out, and hurried to London.

King Henry and his army made a forced march from Nottingham to Rochester, a distance of more than 150 miles in five days. This remarkable performance must have exhausted both the men and their horses. From there he moved to Tonbridge, which he took from the baronial garrison without difficulty. The castle belonged to young Gilbert de Clare who was married to Alais de Lusignan. The King allowed his niece to leave in safety.

His next aim was to secure the Cinque Ports, both to capture ships for an attack on London by water, and to ensure that the troops which the Queen was collecting in Flanders could enter England safely. But the wardens of the ports, backed by public opinion, put their fleets out to sea and Henry, finding supplies short in the densely wooded and hostile countryside, turned back. From Battle he went on through Herstmonceux, and there is a record of one of his knights, Roger de Tourney, being killed by an arrow when hunting in Herstmonceux Park during this journey. According to most authorities it was Sunday 11 May when the King and his tired army reached the small town of Lewes, nestling between the ridges of the South Downs, guarding the Ouse valley.

It had been a town of some size and importance since William the Conqueror gave the Rape of Lewes to his friend William de Warenne, but it was mentioned in records as early as Alfred's reign in the ninth century. Domesday Book showed a population of 1,484 with 426 burgesses in 1086, so in 1264 it may have numbered between 1,500 and 2,000 which was not inconsiderable for that time.

William de Warenne built castles on his lands at Reigate in Surrey and Castle Acre, near Swaffham, in Norfolk, but he lavished most care and expense on his castle at Lewes. It is remarkable for having two great artificial mounds, and he chose for it an ideal defensive position overlooking the valley. The castles at Chichester, Arundel, Lewes and Hastings formed a line of defence along this wide stretch of the south coast. The north-west boundary of Lewes Castle follows the line of the town wall, and on the other side the land falls steeply below the curtain wall. Two octagonal towers projecting from the keep were added during the thirteenth century, perhaps during the dangerous years of civil war, but the fine barbican was built a century later.

It is not difficult to imagine medieval Lewes. It is still a picturesque town with narrow streets winding up the steep hill-side, and some still bear names that tell their early history. L. S. Davey, in his scholarly and delightful account of the origin of street names in Lewes, provides many links between past and present. Once there were ten parish churches in the town and four outside its walls and although half of them are now destroyed their names are recorded in the lanes that ran beside them. And with a nice show of neutrality Lewes has honoured some of the leading figures in the battle, baronial and royalist, by naming roads after them: King Henry, Prince Edward, De Montfort, Leicester, Clare, Valence, FitzJohn, De Warenne and Ferrers are near neighbours in the area known as the Wallands where some of the fighting must have taken place. Robert de Ferrers, Earl of Derby, perhaps hardly deserves to be there. Rishanger believed that although he took advantage of the rebellion to plunder the royalists he never in fact paid more than lip-service to the barons, and failed to join them at Lewes.

The earliest town records date from 1542, but a map drawn by George Randoll in 1620[5] is probably some guide to medieval Lewes, where ruins of the ancient town wall still clearly mark its boundaries. L. S. Davey believes that the road from London ran over the hill from Offham and entered the town through the Westgate. On the other hand there is known to have been a Roman road from London that crossed the Ouse at Barcombe Mills and skirted the western bluff of Malling Down, where it turned west and became a causeway leading to the bridge over the river, to enter the town by the Eastgate. Later the Ouse was to become a busy waterway with shipyards and wharves that were still in use early in the last century, but in the thirteenth century drainage would be a problem and the low ground on the east and south of the town must have been a dangerous and tidal marshland. Cattle, sheep and goats were grazed and crops were grown to the west and north of the town where the land slopes up to meet the Downs.

The Lewes of today has spread outside its ancient walls. There are no longer a Westgate and an Eastgate to be locked and guarded at night and where tolls were levied on the carts that rumbled through with iron ore. The little hospitals originally built and maintained by the Cluniac monks, where poor wayfarers could find shelter, have gone, and so has the school that was founded by the Order as early as 1248. But it still has the charm of quaint streets and old buildings, and it is still dominated, as it was seven centuries ago, by the great flint fortress that stands, defiant and solid, high above the houses huddled under its protection.

Outside the town walls to the south, across the Winterbourne stream, lay the Priory of Saint Pancras at Southover, one of the wealthiest religious houses in England. This was the senior house of the Cluniac Order, founded by William de Warenne and his wife Gundrada in 1077, and the magnificent buildings included a church as large as Chichester Cathedral. The Priory later suffered under the Papal Schism, and eventually the buildings were destroyed when Henry VIII dissolved the monasteries. His nefarious minister Thomas Cromwell engaged an Italian engineer to demolish them, but even the ruined fragments that are left suggest the grandeur of the original design. There is now a plan to expose and preserve as much as possible of the ruins.

As the royal army approached Lewes the news must have spread like a forest fire, with neighbours bawling across the narrow alleyways and a clamorous mob gathering round the town gate. The town must have been in a ferment of excitement and panic. Faced with an added population many times its own size, the food problem loomed large in men's minds. Last year's stocks were running low by May, and the new corn crops were not yet ripe. Grazing was plentiful but hay must be stored against the winter months and there was little surplus to share with the horses of a visiting army. I doubt if they were welcomed with smiles and garlands.

Already this hungry army had impoverished many areas in the south-east, and when the rumours spread to Lewes the people no doubt tried to hide away some of their precious stores. But when the King himself appeared, escorted by his personal bodyguard and followed by his barons, bannerets and men at arms, riding over the narrow wooden bridge and along the causeway into the town, probably loyal emotion as well as expediency drew a great cheering throng to pay him homage. Both the men and their horses were famished and jaded. Wyke wrote that on the way there "from the deficiency of victuals in that barren province many persons wasted away from want of food, and the cattle were lowing and failing all around from scarcity of pasture".

King Henry usually chose on his travels to stay in religious houses, satisfying both his extreme piety and his taste for good living. On this occasion he made his headquarters in the Priory of Saint Pancras at Southover, where the Black Monks could offer suitably lavish hospitality. These were prosperous times for the Cluniac Order, and they were reputed to be intemperate and wild. A satirist, calling them "The Ordre de Bel Eyse" wrote:

"They must perforce get drunk each day
They know of life no other way;
But they only drink for company,
And not a jot for gluttony."[6]

Prince Edward was now a handsome man of almost twenty-five, fair haired, inheriting from his father a slightly drooping eyelid, and with a manner both proud and passionate. He was already regarded as a model of chivalry and a vigorous and efficient commander but he still had to learn discretion. Now, with William de Valence, Henry of Almaine and other leading royalists he rode through Lewes to stay at the castle with his friend John de Warenne, Earl of Surrey.

The earl was twenty-eight, and married to the King's half-sister Alice. Of all the intimate court circle only Prince Edward and the faithful John de Warenne were to survive the civil and foreign wars of the years that followed. When the earl died in 1305 after holding his earldom for more than fifty years his old friend, now King Edward I, had public prayers said for him, and the clergy promised remission of three thousand days from purgatory to those who should relieve his soul by prayer. He was buried before the high altar of the Priory at Southover.

The army was encamped outside the town walls, probably under canvas (for tents were in common use), and no doubt many men jostled in the town in search of beer and female company and a better meal than the camp provided.

It is impossible to say what plans the King had in mind, or whether he expected the barons to attack him there. Various chroniclers recorded that he placed a 'vedette', or mounted sentinel, up on the Downs. This was normal practice and would be the obvious precaution to take, for if he placed it on Offham Hill a man would have a fine view by day of the approaches from the north and it would take a matter of minutes for him to gallop down and raise the alarm. No signalling system was yet in use. Some writers have suggested that the 'vedette' was set on the higher Mount Harry further west, but it would not be as suitable for the purpose. There is no evidence of any further steps being taken to strengthen the royalist position. The King settled down to rest his troops and await events in his usual feckless fashion.

Prince Edward, less sanguine and more energetic than his father, probably took some pains to see that his army was under discipline and prepared for an attack. But even he must have believed, as he looked out from the castle battlements across the open country, that the wretched baronial army would hardly be so rash as to attack the royalists in their stronghold.

On Tuesday May 6 Simon de Montfort left London with his army. How large this army was it is impossible to say. Robert Brune wrote that there were "sixti thousand of London armed men full stoute" and the *Chronicle d'Angleterre* suggests this same figure, but as the total population was not much more than 40,000 it is manifestly absurd. Hardly more than 6,000 would be men of military age but with such ardent support there for the barons' cause a great proportion of them probably marched out of the gates with the rebel army. Most of them would be apprentices and journeymen, clerks and tradesmen, with little experience of fighting. No doubt they set out with wild enthusiasm while the city bells pealed out and cheering crowds lined the roads. But it is reasonable to guess that some soon found they had no stomach for the soldier's life, and that before many days were past they had found their way back to the more familiar city streets. From De Montfort's point of view they would be no great loss. An army has to be fed, and while well disciplined and accoutred cavalry made a valuable fighting force, a crowd of amateurs mainly on foot were little more than a liability.

The writer of the *Song of Lewes* wrote: "The Earl had few men tried in arms; the party of the King was swollen great, having the trusty warriors and greater men of England gathered together, and those who were called the flower of the knighthood of the realm. Those who were furnished with arms from London would be the three hundred preferred to the many thousands . . ."[7]

It is difficult to believe that the Londoners dwindled so much, but in any case they did not represent the main strength of Simon's army. The size of both armies is discussed in a later chapter and all that can be said here is that de Montfort, with a force running into several thousands, left London and headed for the Sussex Downs.

There is no evidence to suggest what route they followed.

A delightful map drawn by John Ogilby in 1695[5] shows pictorially the road "From the standard in Cornhill, London" through Croydon, East Grinstead and Lewes to Newhaven. It follows roughly the route of the present main road from London to Lewes by Wych Cross, and may well have existed in the thirteenth century. On the other hand, to the east of Ogilby's road lies the old Roman London-Lewes Way, running from the Watling Street in Peckham, along the Kent-Surrey border south of West Wickham, through Cowden, Hartfield, Camp Hill, Isfield and Barcombe Mills.

Simon de Montfort must have known the King's whereabouts and he was clearly bent on getting within striking distance at once. When the royalists reached Lewes, he was setting up his camp some nine miles north in the wooded country around Fletching, Piltdown and his own manor of Sheffield. There is no evidence that Simon had ever done more than draw his revenues from his manor of Sheffield, but he would now claim military service. Both armies must have gained new recruits when they marched through lands in friendly ownership.

While the King attended Mass in the Abbey Church at Southover, Simon de Montfort and his friends visited the lovely church at Fletching, a shining modern building finished only thirty years before. Apart from the weathering of the stone, and the spire which was to be added a century later, it looked then just as it does today, and as it was a large church for such a small village it possibly served some religious order. Later Fletching was to become of some importance for its production of iron arrowheads, but in 1264 it was just what it is now, a peaceful, secluded village.

As Monday, May 12, was the Feast of Saint Pancras and a day of celebration at the Priory, the following day may have been an unfortunate choice for opening peace negotiations. Although the barons appear to have made this, their final offer, in good faith, they were given no opportunity for discussion. The offer was rejected out of hand.

Again it was Walter de Cantelupe, Bishop of Worcester, who with Richard de Sandwich the Bishop of London rode through the woods, so bright in their spring greenery, down into the valley and skirted the town wall to reach the great gate of the Priory.

> "At Lewes the King began with his power to abide,
> The barons stayed without the town beside,
> And fair sent into the town to the King their sonde,
> That he should for God's love them better understand;
> And grant them good laws and have pity on his land,
> And they him would serve well with foot and with hand.
>
> The King sent them word again, without greeting, this,
> That he cared nothing of their serwice, iwis,
> And that out of love and truth he put them each one,
> And that he would them seek out, as his pure fon.
> The barons knew no other rede, when they heard this,
> But bid God's grace and battle abide, iwis."[8]

The terms Simon offered were now moderate and generous and could perhaps have resulted in a workable compromise had the King wanted one. If Henry would allow the Oxford Statutes to be amended by a committee of churchmen and accept their recommendations and abide by them, the barons would pay 50,000 marcs by way of compensation for damage and would loyally serve the Crown. The bishops also brought a letter declaring the allegiance of all the rebels to the King's person. This letter is recorded in *Liber de Antiquis Legibus* and several chronicles.

"May Your Excellency know that as we wish to preserve the health and safety of your person with all our might, and with the fidelity due to you, proposing only to resist by all means in our power, those persons who are not only our enemies, but yours, and those of the whole kingdom; may it please you not to believe their falsehoods. We shall always be found your liegemen, and we, the Earl of Leicester and Gilbert de Clare, at the request of others, have affixed our seals for ourselves. Given in the Weald, near Lewes, on the first Tuesday after the feast of Saint Pancras."

They were received with ridicule and fury. Prince Edward is said to have shouted, "They shall have no peace whatever, unless they put halters round their necks, and surrender themselves for us to hand them up or drag them down, as we please."

Some of the young men started bragging, the bishops were insulted and humiliated, and no doubt the latest to join the royalist side were loudest in protesting their good faith. The King was passionately angry and his reply was a challenge as well as a curt and unqualified refusal of the terms. This also is recorded in *Liber de Antiquis Legibus*.

"Since it manifestly appears by the war and general disturbance already raised by you in our kingdom, and also by conflagrations and other outrageous damages, that you do not observe your allegiance to us, nor have any regard to the security of our person . . . We, therefore, value not your faith or love, and defy you, as their enemies. Witness myself, at Lewes, on May the thirteenth, in the 48th year of our reign."

His brother Richard added his own portentous letter, which was also signed by Prince Edward and other leading royalists.

"Richard, by the grace of God, King of the Romans, always august, and Edward, the first-born of the illustrious King of England, and all the other barons and knights who firmly adhere to the said King of England, with sincere faith and force, to Simon de Montfort, Gilbert de Clare, and to all and each of the other accomplices in their treason. We have understood, by the letters you have sent to our Lord the illustrious King of England, that we are defied by you, although indeed this verbal defiance had been proved before by hostilities against us by the burning of our goods, and the ravage of our possessions.

"We therefore let you know that you are all defied as public enemies by each and all of us your enemies, and that henceforth, whenever occasion offers, we will, with all our might, labour to damage your persons and property . . ."

They had grounds for complacency. The King was surrounded by most of the powerful men of England. With his brother Richard and his son Edward were his half-brothers William de Valence and Guy de Lusignan, and Richard's son, Henry of Almaine. Humphrey de Bohun, a seasoned crusader, was willing to fight for the King against his own son. Henry de Percy was one of the great landowners of Sussex, the lord of Petworth. He had only recently turned to the royalist side.

Philip Basset the justiciar owned land at Berwick near Lewes, and was one of the most courageous of the King's friends. Roger de Mortimer was a fickle man but a ferocious fighter. Alexander III of Scotland, who was married to Henry's daughter Margaret, had sent strong forces under their chieftains to help his father-in-law, among them John de Balliol, John Comyn and Robert de Brus. The castles at Pevensey, Hastings and Arundel, as well as Lewes, were in friendly hands. Above all the royalists had the person of the king, the dispenser of all temporal power and rewards and the acknowledged head of the state.

To Henry and his friends the baronial army must have appeared little more than a band of stubborn fanatics roaring empty threats. Again because of the wide disparity in the figures given by chroniclers it is impossible to do more than guess at the numbers involved, but they all agree that the royalists had the larger army. The rebels, like all revolutionaries, had no doubt attracted a proportion of wastrels and trouble-makers. Simon had also suffered a very heavy loss at Northampton. His most experienced and reliable officer, Peter de Montfort, with his two sons, Simon's own son and at least fifteen 'bannerets' and their followers were still imprisoned there. A 'banneret' was a knight of high rank, sometimes achieved through valour on the battlefield. He commanded his own section and played a vital part in the hierarchy of the medieval army. It is not surprising that the royalists were complacent.

With the odds so heavily against him de Montfort must have hoped that the King, even at this eleventh hour, would agree to a peaceful settlement. Even so, while the bishops were away on their errand he was busy preparing to fight. When Richard de Sandwich and Walter de Cantelupe rode wearily back into camp and delivered the defiant and threatening royalist letters, careful and clever plans were already made for an immediate attack upon Lewes.

In the Priory the King and his friends waited indifferently for the next move, and according to an eye witness that night also was spent in revelry and dissipation.

VII

"This war was exceptionally inevitable and was caused by a number of causes." (*1066 And All That.*)

AMONG THE Cotton manuscripts in the British Museum is one, badly damaged and withered by fire, known as *Annals written by a certain Monk of Lewes from the Birth of Christ to the year 1312*. Blaauw once commented that "like many other monkish chronicles, it records much of which the writer could know nothing, and much which nobody wishes to know". But the entry for the year 1264 provides a concise account of the Battle of Lewes.

"This year on the 14th May, and on the day of the translation of Hugh Abbot, and of the Holy Martyrs Victor and Corona, there was a deadly battle between King Henry and Symon de Munfort and the barons, and so it was that the greatest part of the King's army was utterly over thrown between prime and noon. Firstly, the King was much beaten by swords and maces, and two horses killed under him, so that he escaped with difficulty, and his brother Richard, King of Germany, was soon captured. Edward, the King's son, delivered over in hostage to Symon de Munfort, and many of the greatest men of England who held with the King, wounded in their heads and bodies even to death, the number of which dead is reckoned at 2,700, more or less. All these things took place at Lewes, at the Mill of the Hide."

Other chroniclers have varied in detail but there is no reason to dispute this first-hand story, and in any case it is impossible at this distance in time to do more than speculate about the course of the battle.

Certain facts are clear, however. On the night of Tuesday, 13 May, the King was not alarmed by the thought of an enemy

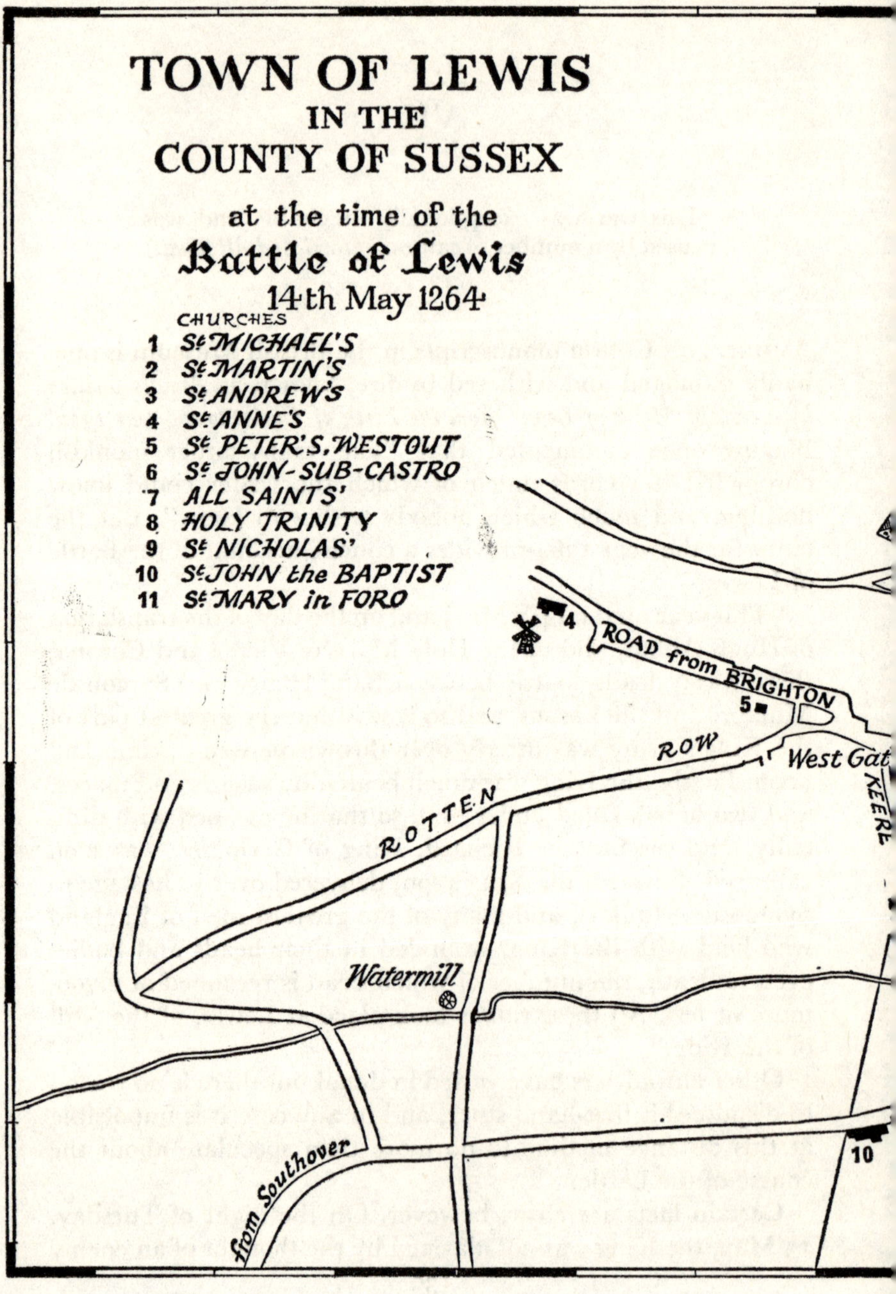
TOWN OF LEWIS
IN THE
COUNTY OF SUSSEX
at the time of the
Battle of Lewis
14th May 1264
CHURCHES
1 St. MICHAEL'S
2 St. MARTIN'S
3 St. ANDREW'S
4 St. ANNE'S
5 St. PETER'S, WESTOUT
6 St. JOHN-SUB-CASTRO
7 ALL SAINTS'
8 HOLY TRINITY
9 St. NICHOLAS'
10 St. JOHN the BAPTIST
11 St. MARY in FORO
4
ROAD from BRIGHTON
5
ROW
West Gat
KEERE
ROTTEN
Watermill
from Southover
10

Town Wall
River Ouse
6
ST. JOHN'S ST.
NORTH STREET
EAST ST.
Castle Wall
Castle
Castle Ditch
8
East Gate
SCHOOL HILL
9
Causeway
STREET
11
IGH
2
3
ST. MARTIN'S LA.
WATER GATE LA.
ST. ANDREW'S LA.
ST. MARY'S LA.
ST. NICHOLAS LA.
WALWER'S LA.
PINWELL ST.
PLANTAGENET ST.
FRIARS' WALK
7
ST. SWITHUN'S LANE
Pryorye of St. Mary
HEADQUARTERS OF SIMON de MONTFORT (After the Battle)
Winterbourne
ROAD FROM SOUTH-OVER
Watermill
COCKSHUT ROAD
Pryorye of St. Pancras
Scale of 10 Chains or One Furlong
0 1 2 3 4 5 6 7 8 9 10 Chains
M. A. Khan

army only nine miles away. A rollicking Victorian ballad suggests the mood of the royalist party at the Priory.

> "Long and loude were the cheeres theye rais'd
> And the wine cup circled free—
> No care had theye for the coming fraye,
> No thoughte of eternitye.
>
> Thus didde these gaye and waywarde menne,
> With wine inflame their heades—
> And Sir Symon in mighte, had ascended the height,
> Ere theye had left their beddes."[1]

While Henry and his friends revelled and slept, the baronial army in the woods around Fletching prepared for an early start. With so many disadvantages, Simon de Montfort had to depend on his one great asset: good generalship. It was essential that in the coming battle, unlike most medieval engagements, the enemy should be taken by surprise.

All through the day there was tremendous bustle and activity in the baronial camp, and when the bishops brought the news that there was no further hope of peace it kindled a flame of excitement that quickly spread through the army. The fight was on, and now the last preparations were rapidly completed. Armourers and farriers attended the knights and their horses. Cooks prepared a last hot meal. Messengers ran through the camp from one headquarters to another. The bannerets gave their orders and inspected their troops, and as the tents were taken down and loaded on the baggage horses each man was busy collecting and packing up his own possessions and checking his weapons.

During that crowded evening Simon de Montfort, with his sons and Gilbert de Clare, the 'bannerets' and the bishops probably went to pray again in Fletching Church where Thomas Esporoun the priest would have received them.

"Earl Simon passed that night without sleep, giving time, as was his habit, to divine offices and prayers and exhorting his men to make sincere confessions. Walter de Cantelupe, Bishop of Worcester, absolved them all, and commanded that for the remission of their sins they should manfully strive for

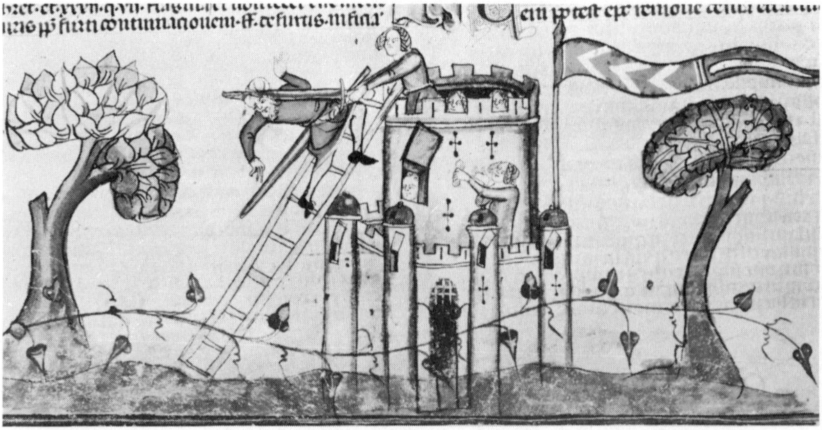

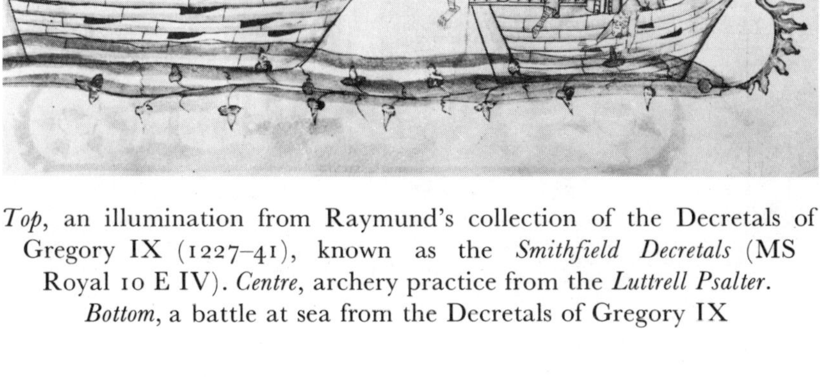

Top, an illumination from Raymund's collection of the Decretals of Gregory IX (1227–41), known as the *Smithfield Decretals* (MS Royal 10 E IV). *Centre*, archery practice from the *Luttrell Psalter*. *Bottom*, a battle at sea from the Decretals of Gregory IX

Knighting a young man. An illustration from the *Vitae Offarum* of Matthew Paris (MS Nero D I)

justice on that day, promising to all who should die thus the entry into the heavenly kingdom . . . Before the start Earl Simon de Montfort girt Gilbert de Clare with a knight's sword."[2]

Some chroniclers said that the ceremony of knighthood took place on the South Downs above Lewes just before the battle, but it seems more likely that Simon gave his young officers this honour before the army left Fletching. Robert of Gloucester believed that he did so in the woods:

> "Hii hovede under boskes and new Knights made,
> And armed and attired hom, and hor bedes gerne bade."

Among these new knights were Robert de Vere, John de Burgh, John FitzJohn, Geoffrey FitzPeter, a young man variously named John Befs, Bevis or de Bears who was soon to capture King Richard of Almaine, and Henry de Hastings, who with Nicholas de Segrave commanded the contingent of Londoners. There is a legend strongly held in the neighbourhood that the knights kept their vigil in the church at Fletching, and that a number who were slain in battle were taken back and hastily buried in full armour under the floor of the nave. But wherever it was spent their vigil must have been short. If they were to take the royalists by surprise the baronial army must have been on the march soon after midnight.

Rishanger says, "At daybreak before the rising of the sun they went out from the village of Fletching . . ." Burne, who made an expert appraisal of the battle, suggests that the head of the baronial army did not leave Fletching before four-thirty in the morning. There are good reasons for thinking, however, that the Monk of Lewes was right in saying that the battle took place between prime and noon. "Prime" is the first of the "Little Day Hours" laid down in the Roman Catholic breviary. It is at 6 a.m. On the day of the battle sunrise was at about four o'clock, and so I believe that just after midnight the main body of Simon's army was on the march, following their guides along the forest tracks. Low branches of beech and oak in young leaf brushed the cavalry on their sturdy horses. And as the last stragglers left the woods the dawn chorus began and the glades were loud with birdsong. Already, in more open country, the sky was luminous with the approaching dawn. In the tiny hamlets of Newick, Barcombe and Hamsey and the scattered cottages along the tracks to Offham, people stirred in their sleep.

The march from Fletching to Lewes was clearly a carefully planned exercise, probably using several routes, and each "banneret" would have been responsible for bringing his section, with the help of a local guide, to the appointed meeting place. Some perhaps crossed Fletching Common and rode through Chailey and Cooksbridge, turning off to the west just north of Offham and up the north face of the Downs. A second column may have ridden through Newick and Cooksbridge to climb the steep re-entrant south of Offham and reach the same area three or four hundred yards north and north-east of where the grandstand of Lewes racecourse is today. The Londoners, mainly on foot, possibly took the easterly route past Piltdown Pond, through Barcombe and Hamsey to Offham, to climb up the track that would lead them to a point on the plateau just below and to the west of Offham Hill. But this can only be guesswork.*

The meeting place was surely that flat stretch of ground some twelve hundred yards long and two or three hundred yards wide, that runs more or less due west from Offham Hill and then north-west for another five hundred yards beside and along the straight of the racecourse. There the whole army could be assembled, drawn up in "battles", out of sight of the guards on the castle tower and the Priory bell tower but within easy striking distance of the enemy. According to the chronicles the "vedette" had been deserted by all but one man, and he was asleep when the baronial army arrived. In any case he did not give the alarm, and so the rebel force reached the Downs safely and undetected.

As dawn broke the whole sky was diffuse with rosy light and the pale early sunshine glinted on the Priory bell tower. The great flint fortress must have looked quite impregnable, rising against the sky, and men felt on their faces the chill wind that brings the tang of the nearby sea. The guards who crouched

* *see endpaper maps.*

at the edge of the ridge and kept watch on the little town below could see the tents of the enemy, perhaps as Matthew Paris described the scene at the Battle of Taillebourg.

"When morning came our English saw the oriflamme of the King of the French and their banners and standards, and a great host of tents on the other side of the river like a large and populous town." And already, in the royalist camp, men were beginning to stir.

The baronial army must have had a sustaining meal before breaking camp, but now they were ready for another bite eaten on the march or while they formed up in their four "battles". On the left were the Londoners, rough and untrained, under Nicholas de Segrave and Henry de Hastings. De Segrave had fought in Gascony and was one of the very few to escape alive from Northampton. Henry de Hastings had been a ward of Guy de Lusignan and having experienced royal greed was ready to devote himself to the anti-royalist cause. His wife was a niece of Walter de Cantelupe.

The centre "battle" was under the command of Gilbert de Clare, who at the age of twenty-one was as keen as he was inexperienced. Fortunately he had two more capable commanders with him: John FitzJohn, a tough and vigorous man in his late twenties; and William de Monchensy, aged about thirty. These three men were connected by marriage with leading royalists, but only de Clare later deserted his friends.

The right battle was under the command of de Montfort's eldest son Henry and his fourth son Guy. The second son, Simon, was still imprisoned in Northampton. Almeric the third and Richard the fifth were destined for the priesthood and there is no mention of their fighting beside their father. Much has been written in condemnation of Simon's ill-fated sons, but in fact they appear to have done their best. Henry, rash and thoughtless as he was, remained his father's devoted and loyal lieutenant. As Grosseteste so curiously prophesied he died at his father's side. Young Simon's recklessness had already cost him his freedom. Only Guy inherited some part of his father's sagacity and military flair.

The fourth "battle" was kept in reserve under de Montfort's

own hand, and this most unusual but sensible step may well have decided the outcome.

Before launching his attack Simon de Montfort, in the traditional manner, addressed his troops.

"O my beloved comrades and followers, we are about to enter upon a war to-day for the sake of the government of the kingdom, to the honour of God, of the blessed Mary, of all the Saints, and of our mother Church, and at the same time for the observance of our faith. Let us pray to the King of all, that if what we now undertake pleases Him, He will grant us vigour and help, so that we may exhibit a grateful service by our knightly belt, overpowering the malice of all enemies. If we are His, to Him we commend our body and soul."[3]

The soldiers prostrated themselves upon the turf, each wearing a white cross upon his back and breast, and cried, "Grant us, O Lord, our desire, with mighty victory, to the Honour of your name." At that moment inspiration must have seized them all. Even the irreligious, the adventurers, the weak and faithless who would soon desert the cause and the hired mercenaries believed that they were indeed members of the army of God.

It is a pity we do not know what part Walter de Cantelupe played in the battle. It seems clear that he either rode back to Lewes with the army, or followed shortly afterward, as he was a most important member of the leadership and would be expected to be their spokesman after the fighting. The writer of a chronicle in the monastery of Melrose in Galloway wrote of him "setting aside the unarmed priest and becoming the militant soldier who bears a sword instead of a crosier and a helmet in place of his mitre". This was probably meant only figuratively, for Walter de Cantelupe was no longer a young man, and there was plenty for him to do in his role of priest, praying, absolving, pleading in time of defeat, treating terms of a truce and ensuring that the wounded and killed were properly cared for by the Church.

The commands were given and the Londoners were away down the gentle slope of the spur leading directly to the castle walls, their ranks already growing ragged as they disappeared out of sight over the slight ridge. De Montfort can hardly have hoped that they could storm the castle on foot. Centuries later a commander would have called them a "forlorn hope", a long-odds chance which occasionally succeeded. Perhaps he actually intended them to act as a decoy to draw off some of the defending forces. That, in any case, is what happened.

It is said that the first alarm was given by a squad of soldiers out foraging who met the Londoners coming down the hill. Supplying the royal army would be a complex operation extending to the villages for miles around. Tons of food were necessary to keep the men and horses of an army. In any case the Londoners must have been seen as soon as they appeared on the forward slope. Camp servants must have been astir early to feed and groom the horses and prepare breakfast for the troops, and even an over-confident army would keep a guard on the castle watchtower.

The confusion that followed, the clamour of shouting and trumpet commands must have been heard at the Priory barely five hundred yards away. There was no question of waiting for the whole royalist army to draw up in formation and engage the enemy in the accepted and traditional way. With the Londoners at his gates Prince Edward, with William de Valence, John de Warenne and the other leaders rode out of the Westgate to place themselves at the head of their cavalry "battle" and gallop to attack. The Londoners turned tail and fled up Offham hill and along the valley track towards Offham, trying in their terror to scramble out of reach of the pursuing horsemen. On the right of the track lay treacherous marshy ground, and on their left rose the steep, scrub-covered hillside. The royalist horsemen savagely hewed them down. Some believed that Prince Edward remembered the insults to his mother a year before, and took his revenge. Certainly his troops, lusting for blood, carried the chase to Offham and well beyond. It was even said in some chronicles that Prince Edward followed them as far as Croydon and returned to Lewes the same day, but as this would mean a ride of forty miles each way it is not credible. However, he certainly wasted his energies and wearied both men and horses while he slaughtered what in fact was the weakest part of the baronial army.

It does seem to be true that some Londoners who escaped eventually reached Croydon where they met a party of royalists. A number of skeletons were found under George Street there during excavations by the railway in the last century, and were attributed to men escaping from the battle. Up to ten skeletons have been found in small pits, by flint and chalk diggers working at various periods in the region of Offham chalkpits. It is reasonable to believe that at least some of them were skeletons of the Londoners who fled so desperately from their murderous enemies.

These men had served a useful purpose. While Prince Edward and his troops, a significant proportion of the whole royalist army, were away on this fruitless enterprise, de Montfort had already launched his centre and right "battles", and the King and his brother were frantically trying to hold the attack. The main gateway of the Priory gave onto the ancient highway that is now Southover High Street, and Henry and his troops would leave by this gate, cross the low water of the Winterbourne at the bridge of "Pankridge" (a corruption of "Pancras"), and line up on the Hides. His brother Richard, leading the left "battle", would follow Bell Lane and ford the Winterbourne to take up his position on Henry's left.

Historians have argued several theories about how and where the battle was fought, but none can be more than intelligent guesswork. Some, including Burne, believed that it was the normal set-piece event with the armies engaging each other by mutual consent and the almost comic ritual of a medieval battle. James Ramsay also held this view, and the ordnance survey maps mark the site of the battle on Racecourse Hill, based on his theory that the armies engaged there, high above the town. Burne wrote that the armies "engaged at the top in the opening clash and ended in strife at the bottom". The Monk of Lewes said quite simply that it took place "at the Mill of the Hide". The Hides were the grazing lands outside the town walls and would seem a logical area for the main clash to take place. W. H. Blaauw, after a lifetime of careful study and with an intimate knowledge of the subject, agreed with him, and said that "the greater portion of the Battle of

Lewes was fought in the vicinity of Lewes County Gaol, to the very walls of the town".

This seems to me the most likely answer. De Montfort, who already had the initiative and now depended for victory upon a quick strike and the advantage of his position at the top of the forward slope of the Downs, would surely press his attack before the enemy had time to form up clear of the town. He was far too ambitious and intelligent a commander to hesitate now or let the royalists dictate the site or timing of the engagement. When Wykes writes of *tubis terribiliter clangentibus* he conveys to me not the formal trumpet call to arms at the start of a set-piece battle, but the confused and rowdy tumult of trumpet commands when an army is taken by surprise.

It is impossible not to speculate. I also believe that when De Montfort loosed the Londoners he may have held back his centre and right "battles" on the plateau behind the rise where they were just out of sight of the town. Then as the leading royalist cavalry began the quite steep climb out of Landport Bottom preparatory to drawing up in their two "battles" for the usual set-piece engagement, Simon's cavalry could have charged down the hill into their disorganized and half-formed ranks sending them reeling back towards the Hides.

"When the King therefore was sure of the coming of the barons, he soon advanced with his men, with his standard unfurled and preceded by the royal banner, portending the judgment of death, which they call the 'Dragon'."[2] This famous banner was one of Henry's gifts to Westminster Abbey, and was made by Edward FitzOdo the royal goldsmith "of red samit, to be embroidered with gold, and his tongue to appear as though continually moving, and his eyes of sapphire, or other stones agreeable to him".

> "Then was ther a dragon grete and grimme,
> Full of fyre and also venymme,
> With a wide throte and tuskes grete."[4]

If the first clash took place where I suggest, the fighting must soon have swayed back to the Hides and the neighbourhood of the present Prison. The evidence of casualties given in the next chapter, as well as the shape of the ground, point to this as the main battlefield. Henry and his brother probably made desperate efforts to re-form their broken ranks before they were pressed back into the valley towards Southover and there was certainly fierce fighting around the town gates and the Priory as they made for the comparative safety of their headquarters.

This would have been the moment for Simon de Montfort to smash his cavalry reserve at the royalist left flank. If he held it for some time up on the Downs where they had first assembled, he could watch from the top of the ridge the course of the battle. He would see the terrified Londoners running towards Offham and Prince Edward's troops disappearing up the valley track after them. At any moment the avengers might return, either by the same route or over the Downs, to fall on the flank or rear of Simon's army, so he kept his position and watched. When his right and centre "battles" had engaged the royalists it was time to move. The champing horses felt the spur and the men, impatient to show their fighting skill, went winging down the hill to join the fray. De Montfort could have led them down the west side of the long spur that runs south-east towards the Prison from the grandstand, along the east side of Cuckoo Bottom and Houndean Bottom, cutting east just past the south end of the training gallop. In this way he would keep out of sight of the castle and the royalist army until the last moment. After a pause to draw up in close formation he hurled his crack troops at the left flank of the royalist army.

The main engagement must have been short and bloody. Hand to hand fighting with spiked maces and the savage battle-axes inflicted horrible wounds, and heads and limbs could be severed with the vicious swing of a heavy broad-bladed sword. Soon the green turf was littered with dead and dying. Many of the wounded tried to stumble to safety while loose horses added to the danger and confusion, as they reared and plunged in their panic, galloping over the Downs and thundering along the narrow streets of the town.

Rishanger described the scene. ". . . and then the courage of the barons flashed forth while they battled together for the sake of their country until they enjoyed at last a resounding victory

. . . Oh wretched sight when swords flash savagely on this side and that, son against father and father against son, kinsman against kinsman, citizen against fellow-citizen, drunk with the blood of slaughter, the fallen struggling to raise themselves, the mutilation, the trampling under horses' hooves, and those captured alive bound fast with tightest chains."

King Henry was now fifty-six, and he had never been renowned as a soldier, but he is said to have fought bravely and to have remounted when his charger was killed under him. His brother Richard, on the other hand, earned nothing but ridicule.

"In this battle Richard, Earl of Cornwall, Henry's brother (who a few days before had defied the barons to battle, calling them traitors to king and kingdom), being in fear of his life took shelter in a windmill, and there he barred the door on himself. When it was near evening on the day of the battle the barons came to it and called out loudly to him, 'Come down, come down you wretched miller; come out, unlucky master of the mill, come out!' They upbraided him with his timidity and cowardice, and added, 'It is a great pity for you that you must be made a miller—you who so lately defied us poor barons to battle; and when you defied us no less glorious title would serve you than King of the Romans and ever Augustus' . . . So Richard at last did come out of the mill, and the barons carried him off, after they had put him in chains; and then they placed him in close confinement."[5]

The satirists enjoyed the joke at the expense of this avaricious and pompous man.

> "The Kyng of Alemaigne wende do ful wel,
> He saisede the mulne for a castel,
> With hare sharpe swerdes he grounde the stel,
> He wende that the sayles were mangonel."[6]

T. W. Horsfield suggested that Richard's "castel" was a water-mill on the Winterbourne. Two are known to have stood on the stream, one at Pankridge and one at Eastport. Paul Dunvan who wrote *Lee's History of Lewes* in 1795, held the same view. "The King of the Romans was, about the same time, so closely pursued that he hid in a mill which stood on Winterbourne stream between Lewes and Southover, the exact site of which is still ascertainable from the well known denomination of the millpond which the place retains to this day." He goes on to remark that "chronologists say, no mills were erected in this island before the year 1299". But there is ample evidence to suggest that it was a windmill. The idea of harnessing the wind to grind corn was understood in the East in ancient times, and may have been brought to Europe by returning crusaders. They were certainly known here, even if they were not yet widely used, in the thirteenth century, and soon after they became a common device for providing power. The chroniclers seem clear on the point. The Monk of Lewes mentions "the Mill of the Hide". There is a damaged fragment of a curious document, mainly abridged from the work of Matthew of Westminster who was writing in 1375, which tells the same story. By the word *molendinum* someone wrote in about 1700 "call'd King Harry's mill to this day". This mill is clearly marked on Randoll's 1620 map, hard by St. Anne's Church. The Chronicle of Melrose, which was completed only in 1279, is quite clear: "*molendinum quod vi ventorum dicebatur molere.*" And Robert of Gloucester the contemporary poet who certainly drew on a knowledge of events even when he exercised poetic licence wrote:

> "The King of Almaine was in a windmill inome,
> For a young knight took him, a knight just made right,
> Named Sir John de Bears that was a very good knight,
> That much powess did that day."

In any case, Lewes was once ringed with windmills, and it was reasonable that Richard should barricade himself in one as the only place of safety when he found the battle going against him, and the way back to the Priory cut off by the enemy. After his capture Richard officially surrendered himself to the Earl of Gloucester, probably because he was the highest in rank on the baronial side. The battle went on, with skirmishing in the streets and the surrounding countryside, and the garrisons in the castle and the Priory tried to strengthen their defences and prepare for a state of siege. The royalist position was hopeless but the King would not yield easily, and soon the town was being sprayed from the castle ramparts with arrows bearing pellets of tow soaked in some inflammatory liquid. These incendiaries, known as "Greek Fire" or *tela ignita* were a technique learned from the crusades, and were probably composed of pounded resin, sulphur, naptha and nitre. The process was kept secret for centuries, but there is a strange receipt for making it in the Arundel MS.

"Most of the private buildings of the town were thatched with straw, and kindled into flames with the first wandering spark they caught. The town on fire, and its streets filled with objects of indiscriminate slaughter, together with the mingled cries and dismay of old age, female weakness and infancy, presented one of those scenes of complicated horror which mark the vestiges of civil war."[7]

While the town of Lewes bore the full brunt of the battle, Prince Edward, "with that impetuosity of valour, which ever after distinguished his martial career, strewed the lanes and woods with carnage for the distance of four miles, and halted not in the bloody chase, till the scattered fugitives ceased to afford gore enough to bathe his vindictive salchion."[8]

It was said that even when his lust for revenge was finally sated he dissipated his strength still further by attacking the baronial baggage wagon. There has been some controversy about this vehicle, some chroniclers describing it as a carriage or litter, designed to sling between two horses and used to carry de Montfort when he was helpless after his leg injury. Others have said that it was built especially to deceive the enemy and placed on high ground to lure them away from the battle.

"A few days before Simon set out against the King with the army of Londoners, whom he was about to lead into battle, he caused a cunningly-devised carriage to be built, the whole of the outside of which he covered with iron, and into it he thrust two old and honourable citizens of London because they were opposed to him and to the whole city.

"On the evening of the day previous to that on which the battle was fought between the King and the barons, when it grew towards nightfall, the entrance to the carriage, through which food used to be brought to these burgesses, was so firmly closed up by Simon's commands that from that time they had no longer any power of getting out. Round about the carriage Simon had caused to be hung those flags that are called pennons, that by this means the King and his force might be deluded into the belief that Simon was in the chariot; in which, however, the true Simon was not . . .

"So when the King went out to battle against the barons, those who were in the van of the army noticed those pennons I have mentioned as being hung about the carriage, and straightway hurried towards it . . . The Londoners had already told the royal army that within the carriage sat Simon . . . While they were engaged with all their energies in attacking this deceptive vehicle, and made no progress in their assault, they lost ground and their courage at the same time . . . The best of the King's troops seemed to have been seized with madness and they rent the air with the wildest shouts; crying out continually, 'Come out, Simon, you devil, come out of the carriage!' "[5]

There are so many references to this carriage in contemporary documents that it clearly played a part in the battle, though whether as a deliberate piece of deception or an accidental decoy it is impossible to say. Rishanger said: "Simon with his men ascended a hill and placed his chariot there in the middle of his baggage, and having purposely placed and firmly erected his standard upon it, he encircled it with many armed men . . ."

In the light of later military attitudes it would seem more likely that such a heavy vehicle was left under guard on the low ground near Offham, together with any siege machinery, the baggage horses and the rest of the tail of the army. As Burne pointed out, it would be more conveniently placed there in case of a sudden withdrawal, and there was no advantage in dragging such a weight up the steep, difficult track. But military sense did not necessarily prevail, and with plenty of available labour for just such jobs as this it is easy to believe that the crude, lumbering vehicle was dragged up onto the Downs to be a rallying point for the faithful in case of reverses and with its prisoners as an example to the faithless.

Whether he delayed to attack the carriage or not, when Edward and his tired troops limped back towards the battered and smoking town they expected to join in celebrating a victory. Instead they found the royalists crushed and beaten. The Prince tried to rally his men for a counter-attack but they had neither the strength nor the heart for further fighting. Many were already deserting him. When Simon de Montfort issued an ultimatum "in case of further hostilities, to put the King of the Romans to instant death, with his son Henry, and every other noble prisoner they had made"[9] the King had no choice but to surrender.

"And the King him yielded in doubt
To the earl of Gloucester as to the highest of the rout.
To the Friars Minor in the town sir Edward fled fast,
And there, as he needs must, yielded him at last.
Many a one stilly his arms away cast,
And changed them for cloaks, somewhat they were aghast.
And many fled into the water, and some toward the sea,
And some passed over and came never age.
About four thousand and five hundred, men said,
At the battle were slain. That was a piteous deed."[10]

During his travels through Kent and Sussex the King had collected a number of supporters, and no doubt they were glad to slip away and find their way safely home again in the confusion. Some royalists made a bolt for it, heading for Pevensey Castle and the safer shores of France. The Lanercost Chronicle gives a graphic account of the way men perished in the marshy ground as they were crowded off the narrow bridge over the Ouse, and were found half buried in the mud, sitting on their horses in full armour with drawn sword in hand, as they had died.

This dramatic story is hardly credible. Any horse and rider would struggle wildly to escape from the treacherous marsh rather than wait stoically for death. But the bridge was not more than eleven feet wide and armed horsemen would have little chance of crossing safely in a frenzied stampede. G. D. Johnston has suggested that many of them would in fact use the fords.[11] There were at least three Ouse crossings: one where the railway now crosses the river at Southerham; one by Old Malling Farm; and a third near the bridge itself, serving as a relief. Probably all these fords were used, and others too. Eighty skeletons were found on the north side of Malling Hill, near what is now Mill Road, during road improvements in 1820, and it has been widely believed that they were those of royalist fugitives. In fact they were Saxon.

There are many legends to suggest that men scattered through the countryside looking for friendly shelter, and were killed. It is said that some made a last stand by Terrible Down Farm near Halland, where the stream ran red with their blood, and that they were buried in a wood behind the present farmhouse. It is also believed that a number of Londoners were killed in the neighbourhood of Deadmantree Hill about a thousand yards north of the Rainbow Inn at Cooksbridge, where the east-west Roman road ran, and that they were strung to the trees as a public example. These and all the other stories point to one fact: that for Lewes and the villages around this battle was so important and so tragic that it became a part of the folklore, handed down from father to son through seven centuries. Every war leaves its wake of suffering and Lewes did not escape. Much of the town itself must have been badly damaged by fire. Parts of the town wall were breached and a murage grant was allowed two years after for their repair. A toll was levied on vehicles entering: "For every cart laden with iron for sale 1*d*; for every horse-load of iron for sale, through the week, a halfpenny . . . and for every tumbrel of squirrels for sale, a halfpenny."[12]

The townsfolk and villages for many miles round must have suffered too. Their men were among the casualties and their animals and crops had been taken to feed the hungry armies. Some families probably fell into the hands of the moneylenders. Some brought claims and counter-claims against each other for loss and injury, and the inevitable feuds divided relatives and friends and made for hatred between neighbours. And looting, that sorry postscript to so many battles, ancient and modern, robbed even the poorest of their paltry valuables.

Among the royalist fugitives who reached France were the King's half-brothers William de Valence and Guy de Lusignan; John, Earl de Warenne; Hugh Bigod; and according to both

Rishanger and Matthew of Westminster "about three hundred warriors". Other chronicles give a figure as high as seven hundred.

A contemporary satirist wrote about de Warenne:

> "By God, that is aboven ous, he dude much synne,
> That lette passen over see the Erl of Warynne;
> He hath robbed Engelond, the mores, ant the fenne,
> The gold, ant the selver, ant y-boren henne,
> For love of Wyndesore."[1]

How much in the way of gold and silver went with them in fact it is impossible to say. They were primarily concerned with saving their own skins, and although public opinion was quick to sneer, as they were able to form the nucleus of an army that would later return and trounce the King's enemies, their flight may have been expedient rather than cowardly. It is never suggested that they fled while any chance of victory remained, but they are said to have stirred up bitterness at the French court by telling a tale of Simon de Montfort surprising the King in his bed, which would be quite against the principles of honourable warfare.

In Lewes the flagging armies withdrew to lick their wounds, and the monks of Saint Pancras, the friars of Saint Mary's and all the brothers from the smaller religious houses were busy tending the casualties, ministering to the dying and burying the dead. Rishanger tells how the tragic day ended.

"In this state of uncertainty and civil rage, did the setting sun leave both parties; and the approaching darkness promised only an intermission of hostilities which were to begin again with tomorrow's dawn. But humanity, impatient to arrest the dire progress of bloodshed and devastation, trod the intervening gloom of night. Her venerable Heralds were the Friars Minor and Preachers, who constantly passed between the Camp and the Priory until they brought the King and barons to assent to an accommodation."

VIII

THE SONG OF LEWES

Calamus velociter scribe sic scribentis,
Lingua laudabiliter te benedicentis,
Dei patris destera, domine virtutum,
Qui das tuis prospera quando vis ad nutam;
In te jam confidere discant universi,
Quos volebant perdere qui nunc sunt dispersi.
Quorum caput capitur, membra captivantur;
Gens elata labitur, fideles laetantur.
Jam respirat Anglia, sperans libertatem;
Cui Dei gratia det prosperitatem!
Comparati canibus Angli viluerunt,
Sed nunc victis hostibus caput extulerunt.

THIS LONG, complex Latin poem is in effect a political manifesto, and was almost certainly written towards the end of 1264 when Simon de Montfort was the hero of the people and the ruler of England. Like most of the songs which have survived from that time it strongly favours the baronial cause, but in spite of its prejudice, the emotional arguments in favour of Simon de Montfort and the exaggerated malice toward Prince Edward, it contains a great deal that is wise and sensible. It shows every mark of scholarship and thought, as well as a knowledge of the law and legal terminology and, as one would expect, familiarity with the Bible.

The song appears in the Harley MS. 978, a volume of various works copied in several hands during the thirteenth century and probably originating in the Abbey of Reading. It is written in rhyming couplets of trochaic metre with a medial rhyme at the seventh syllable, and this complicated rhyme-scheme sometimes

A cavalry engagement from the *Vitae Offarum* of Matthew Paris (MS Nero D I)

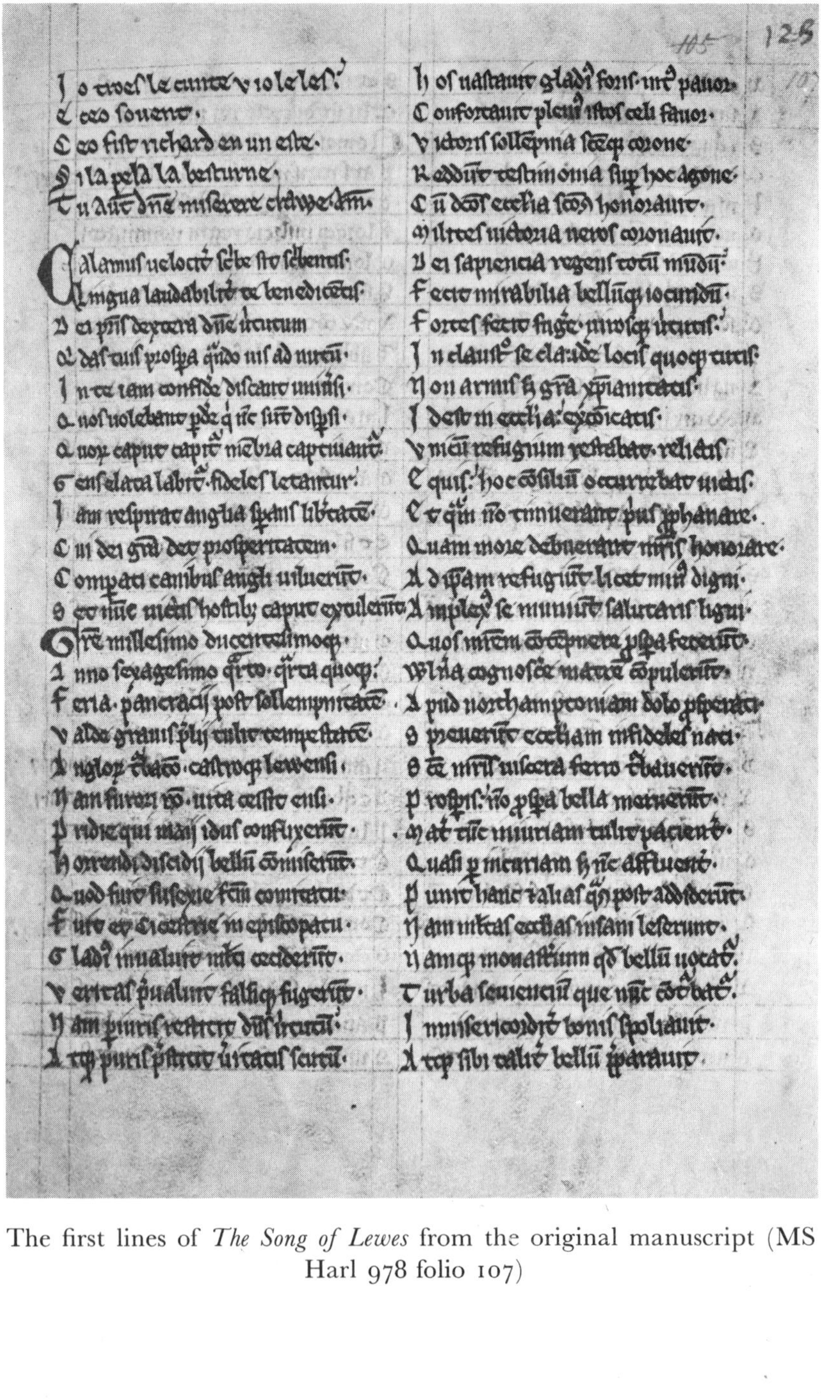

The first lines of *The Song of Lewes* from the original manuscript (MS Harl 978 folio 107)

means sacrificing elegance of style. But it is written with such vigour and freshness that in spite of occasional obscurity and repetition the message is never lost.

There are several clues to its authorship, but none lead as far as the man himself. Kingsford, who in 1890 published a carefully annotated edition of the work, brings evidence to suggest that he was a Franciscan friar of the Oxford school, and a former pupil of Adam Marsh and Robert Grosseteste. He believes that he was present at the Battle of Lewes and stayed with Simon de Montfort and the King during the days which followed. Kingsford concludes that it was one of the friars who accompanied Stephen de Berksted, Bishop of Chichester, and helped to negotiate the Mise of Lewes. He seems tempted to go one step further and suggest that it was Stephen de Berksted himself, but there is no evidence to support such a theory.

Whoever this unknown man may be, he left a work of immense value and interest. The first part is a hymn of triumph and thanksgiving, a eulogy of Simon de Montfort and a defence of his cause. The second part is a study of kingship and the supremacy of law. Even today the outlook seems so modern and the observation so astute that any government might profit from studying it.

The new translation which follows is by Jane Hodlin, a graduate of Saint Hugh's College, Oxford, who specializes in medieval French and Latin and has brought this little-known work to life again in the language of our times.

Speed on my pen, to write what is to come,
For I do sing in praise to bless, O God
And Father, Lord of Virtues, your right hand,
Who when you will, give to all faithful souls
Success and fortune at your single nod.
Let all men learn to place their trust in you,
All those attacked, and those now put to flight.
Their leader is in chains, with all his men,
Fallen the proud, the good are filled with joy,
For England can once more in freedom breathe;

Liberty hers, and fortune, by God's grace!
Like dogs the Englishmen were once despised,
But now their heads are high, their foe destroyed.

For in this year of grace, twelve sixty-four,
The feast of Good Saint Pancras four days past,
The English army rode the heavy storm
Of mighty war, at Lewes' Castle walls.
Then reason to blind fury did give way,
And life to the bright sword. They battle joined
The fourteenth day of May, and dreadful was
The strife in Sussex County, and the See
Of Chichester's Lord Bishop. Hundreds fell,
For mighty was the sword; virtue prevailed,
And evil men took to their heels and fled.
Against these wicked men, our great good Lord
Stood firm, and with the radiant shield of truth
Endued with righteous strength the pure of heart.
Routed their foes, by strength of arms without,
And craven fear within, on them did shine,
More to increase their valour, Heaven's smile.

The battle done, those rites to celebrate
The victor, and those crowns of sanctity
Bear witness to the justness of their fight;
As holy saints the Church did honour them,
And victory crowned these soldiers loyal and true.
For God, of all the world the only King,
In his great wisdom, miracles performed,
And joyful was the outcome of the war.
The strong He put to flight, and men of worth
He led to cloistered safety from their foes.

Sole refuge for the wicked could not be
In arms, but in the Christian's comforter,
God's holy church. This knowledge came to them
As they were leaving horse and battle both;
They fled to her, whom till this sorry day,

Most impious, without fear, they had blasphemed—
Though to her, as their mother true, they owed
All honour, love, and dutiful respect.
But they, unworthy, to protect themselves
Embraced salvation's cross, and recognized
In this adversity her whom in times
More prosperous they had cursed. For when by fraud
At Northampton they won, these faithless sons
Had spurned their Mother Church, and with their swords
Inflicted on her deep and grievous wounds.

So now, though prosperous once, they could not hope
To win again. As if she felt no pain,
And patiently, their Mother bore her wounds,
Which afterwards they added: in this hour
She punishes these madmen who spread fire
Through many churches, and the ruthless crowd
Now thrown into confusion, who ransacked
And cruelly despoiled a monastery.
For thus, at Battle, they had paved the way
For battle for themselves. At Robertsbridge
Cistercian monks were forced to buy their lives;
As ransom from the fury of the sword
Prince Edward ordered them, on pain of death,
To pay five hundred marks. For these great wrongs,
And others too, the punishment is just
That now before their foes they should give way,
And yield to righteous men. So now God bless
Sir Simon, with his army and his sons!
Courageously they ran the risk of death,
And fought with might and main, for they had felt
Such sorrow at the lamentable plight
Of those who lived in England at that time.

Plain words can hardly tell how they were crushed—
So little liberty remained for them
That scarcely could they call their lives their own.
Thus in great misery they lived oppressed

And, like the Israelites in Egypt, groaned
Beneath the yoke of tyranny and strife.
But God Almighty saw their suffering,
And now, at last, He sends to rescue them
A second Mathathias with his sons,
Who, eager to establish lawful rights
Would never yield to insults, or the wrath
Of England's King. Some men would have him named
A traitor, and corrupter of the people.
But his own deeds bear witness of a man
Faithful, loyal and true. In adverse times
The man who is a traitor will give in,
But he is on the side of truth and right,
Who in the face of death stands strong and firm.

But now the sly detractor, whose mean eyes
Still seek to cause more strife, will reason thus:
"If you can praise the constancy and faith
Of anyone who does not run from death
Or punishment, the same holds good for those
Who run to fight upon the other side,
For they expose themselves to equal risk—
They likewise could be killed or punished too."

But let us now see how our battle went.
The Earl had few men used to bearing arms,
But on the side of Henry mustered there,
The more to swell his ranks, the army of
Those older and more practised warriors,
Who throughout all the kingdom were then named
The flower of England's fighting men at arms.
Thus of the Londoners three hundred men
Stood armed to meet the thousands of the King,
Those veterans who held them in contempt,
And saw in them no danger to themselves.
For certainly the army of the Earl
Was for the most part of a tender age;
Novices in arms, they little knew of war.

With unaccustomed sword, the untried youth
Stood there in battle, with no time before
To grow acquainted with unwonted arms.
So newly a recruit, small wonder that
He trembled then, just as the new-born lamb,
Defenceless, cowers in fear before the wolf.
So those young men who fought on England's side
Were no match for their stronger foes, who jeered
And gloried in their prowess, with the thought
That safely without danger, they would soon
O'erwhelm and eat alive the tiny band
Who fought to help the Earl. For some of those
He brought to battle, and of whom he had
High hopes, were not long after terrified
And ran; as if awestruck they took to flight,
Thus leaving only two thirds to fight on.
But with his faithful few the Earl stood firm.

We may compare this battle with the one
Which Gideon fought; for in them both we see
A handful of the virtuous overcome
Their faithless foes, who just like Lucifer
Believed that in themselves lay victory.
But if God granted victory to the strong,
Then fools would tribute pay to fools, not God,
No praise for Him, but for those whom He helped.
These warriors had no fear of God therefore;
It was not steadfastness nor loyalty
They shared, but rather spiritual pride
And cruelty, for eager to destroy
The objects of their scorn, they rushed to fight
Unfearing, and as quickly were struck down.

The heart which swells with pride prepares the way
For ruin, but humility deserves
God's grace divine, for He will soon destroy
That overweening pride of faithless souls.
Look but at Aman and Mardocheus,

The former arrogant, the other one
True Israelite; their story tells that soon
Upon the gallows raised for Mardocheus
Aman himself was hanged. He blindly thought
That he was greatly favoured by the Queen
In sitting at her banquet, but vain hopes
Turned quickly to confusion and dismay
When after eating he was led to death.
The time of utmost joy was tinged with grief,
For with the ending of the feast there came
The ending of his life. A different tale
Is that of David, by God's holy will
Honoured by all, and favoured by his King,
For with the tiny pebble which he flung
Goliath was struck down. There is no help
For him whom God in anger has marked out;
And to all that, another fact is told,
That these disgraceful lechers had called in
No less than seven hundred evil whores.
They should have known these women to be false,
And followers of Satan, set by him
To lead astray men's souls, as sparks to fire
Their passions, and perfidious as those shears
Which cut the hair of Samson. Thus was set
On these contemptible and sinful men
The seal of wickedness, for they were weak,
Unfortified by God's great gift of grace,
Corrupted and unclean like animals
Who wallowed ever in their bodies' lust
Insatiate, and in their harlots' arms
Used up their strength; unworthy then were they
Of victory or the honour paid to knights.

For at that moment when the soldier true
Straps on the sword of knighthood at his thigh,
By this act he rejects all infamy
And evil deeds; it is the custom that
The body of a new-dubbed knight is bathed,

Which ceremony means that he must learn
To cleanse himself of all his sinful past.
Those who within the law had just been wed
Were totally unfitted on God's side
To fight, as Gideon's story shows, much less
Those who had once been scorched by burning flames
Of self-indulgence. Why should God therefore
Help these adulterers, and not give strength
To His true sons, those who were clean of heart?
Let those who wish to conquer in their fight
Be pure; for they are near to victory
Who over their own faults have mastery.
First let them fight and conquer their own sins
Who wish to triumph fairly in combat
Against the wicked. When it happens that
A virtuous soldier seems to lose his fight,
He should be looked upon as victor true,
For righteous men can never know defeat
And neither can the wicked long prevail
While they remain in sin outside God's law.

But now, hear of good Simon's probity.
His death alone would satisfy the King,
No ransom was allowed to save his head.
They hoped thereby completely to confound
The people, and disarm the greater part
Of the whole country, for they thought that thus
Disaster would then follow close at hand.
Long may it be before this comes about!

At that time when great danger threatened most,
(Here, truly I do not exaggerate),
For both sides were induced to talk of peace,
Good Stephen, who was Bishop by God's grace,
Of Chichester, and deeply was disturbed,
Received this message from the noble Earl:
"Choose some of your best men, in whom there burns

A lively faith, those who have read the laws,
Or who have rightly taught theology
And of God's sacred wisdom; those who know
How best to live as Christians. Let them meet,
And in their council base their findings on
Sound doctrine, and the holy rules of God,
For we are ready to believe as true
Whatever they with certainty decree,
No matter what they say, so that we may
Ignore the charge of falsehood, and keep faith
As true and honest sons of God on high."

So now may those who give their word with ease,
But have too little honour for their oath,
And though they swear to what is right and just
Soon break the very oaths which they have sworn,
And are not even wholly true to God,
Learn from this great example how they ought
With care to keep their vows. For here they see
A man who did not run away from death
Or torment, for his sacred word was given.
Not rashly so, but that he yet might change
The sorry state of all the English race,
Oppressed by vicious and malignant foes.

So Simon, ever faithful, had no care
For all the wealth he lost, but ran the risk
Of punishment, protector of the truth.
Thus openly, in deeds, not words, he showed
That truth with falsehood never can be joined.
So woe to those foresworn who fear not God!
In hopes of earthly gain, or to avoid
Imprisonment, or some slight punishment
They cast off God, but this new champion
Teaches that if for truth's sake we accept
The pain which this harsh world inflicts on us,
Then only can we gain full liberty.

The noble Earl before had sworn to uphold
Whatever was ordained by those wise men
At Oxford, that the honour of the land
Should be restored again; to call a halt
To foolish error. He would not, he swore,
Make any change in what their laws decreed,
For well he knew such sacred principles
And holy laws to guide the country back
To peaceful ways, which to uphold and guard
He had so greatly suffered in the past,
Should not be spurned or lightly cast aside.
Moreover, he had promised faithfully
To keep those promises which then he made,
With this proviso now, that if by chance
All the most learned doctors of the faith
Should say that those who pledged their word, could now
Withdraw, he'd pay no further heed to oaths
Which he had sworn before in Oxfordshire.
But when the bishop told the King of this,
Perhaps with some perfidious rogue close by,
The cries of courtiers swelled with pride rose high:
"See, now the soldier's ruled by clerks' dictates!
What degradation for his men in arms
To be subjected thus to simple clerks!"

So they condemned the wisdom of the Earl,
And it is said that Edward thus replied:
"From me they'll have no peace unless they come
To yield themselves, with halters round their necks
That I may hang or quarter them at will!"

What wonder that Sir Simon's heart leapt up,
Since only death could lie before him now?
He wanted to explain, as so he should,
But was unheard; the King knew no restraint,
Unmindful of the risk he ran himself.
But from the following day's events, he learned
Too late, what steps he should have taken then.
That evening there was nothing but contempt

For the good faith and honour of the Earl,
But his attack next day left them amazed
And quite persuaded of his victory.
This stone so long rejected by his foes
Was shortly to be fitted to both walls.
For England, so divided, fast drew near
To utter ruin, but good Simon's faith,
His shining and outstanding holiness
Was there, a corner-stone, to join the rift.

The honour and devotion of one man
Has given now the unity of peace
To all of England; he has brought down low
The rebels, and raised up those in despair.
The kingdom now is one, the proud downcast.
He had no praise for them, but in hard fight
Spilled their red blood, for truth demanded this,
Or that he should abandon truth and right.
So he chose wisely to devote his strength
To fight for them, and take the harder course
Of virtue, that rough road which is despised
By hearts which swell with pride, that road which leads
The active soul to ultimate reward.
For choosing otherwise he would have earned
God's vengeful anger at his cowardice,
And furthered the designs of evil men
By shrinking from his task. For some there were
Who sought with growing hatred to blot out
The name of Englishmen. But Heaven's King,
Unwilling that this country should be brought
To sudden ruin, sent the remedy.
So if the Englishman's desire is such
That he wants to be driven from his land,
Then let him call in foreigners. For those
Who further want to satisfy their pride,
And add to their prestige a glorious name
Which will live after them, call in support
From others of their race, who soon become

The greatest in the land. And then begins
The downfall of that troubled race of men
Whose rightful land it is, and hearts become
Embittered, as the chief men of the land
Feel more and more oppressed by foreigners
Who make themselves their equals, and acquire
By subtle means, all that by rights is theirs,
Usurping to increase their state, those powers
Which once they wielded in their native land.

A King should honour with escheats and wards
His loyal subjects who in many ways
Can serve him. Since it is in their own right
That they have power, they are in all affairs
More trustworthy. But those who nothing give,
Those who grow rich through his munificence,
Which brought them up from nothing to great power,
Continue to advance, until at last
They have replaced the native citizens.
And then they seek to influence the King,
And from his subjects turn away his love.
So, bit by bit, they undermine the rank
Of those whose downfall they desire to cause.
Who would put up with this without complaint?

So England should be cautious, and take care
That no such dire confusion should recur
Nor any such misfortune ever fall
Again upon the English race. The Earl
Did all he could to call a halt to this,
But that great sea of troubles was too strong,
So strong that one man singly could not hope
To stay its mighty flood; God's help alone
Could bring them safe across those stormy straits.
Let strangers come, but let them go back soon,
Like birds of passage, not long to remain.
Just as two hands are complementary
And neither of itself has all those gifts

Which must belong to both inseparably,
So one should help the other, but should not
Usurp the other's place, and in this way
Some profit can be drawn from everything,
The French could do some good for Englishmen,
Not with their guile, disguised by charming smiles,
Nor by relieving others of their goods,
But by accepting that they too must play
Their rightful part, and give as well as take.

Had self-advancement prompted the good Earl
Then after that alone would he have striven,
And he would not have fought with all his might
To right his country's wrongs, but power-mad
He would have sought preferment for himself
And for his family. In gaining wealth
For his own sons, he would have had no thoughts
Of safeguarding the welfare of us all,
But he would have disguised his perfidy
With the false mask of double-dealing, and
Cast off his Christian faith, and thus, exposed
To dreadful punishment, he could have found
No place to shelter from that heavy storm.
It is not possible that any man
Would thus court death to raise himself, and leave
His family and friends to risks exposed.
For if such huntsmen in their search for fame
And fortune, seek with cunning to disguise
The veritable object of their chase,
And always are preoccupied with thoughts
Of how they can escape the fear of death,
It is because they love more than most men
Their lives down here on earth; they never choose
To be where any mortal danger lurks.

Those men who thirst for honour hide their aim
And gently make the name for which they strive.
With good de Montfort it was never so,

A second Christ, who offered his own life
To save us all. But Isaac did not die,
Though he was ready for his father's knife,
For the death-blow was given to a ram,
While Isaac lived and tribute earned instead.
The good Earl's cause was furthered not by tricks,
Nor vile deceit, but by the grace of God
Who always knows to whom He will give help.

If you but now recall the time and place
Of that great battle, it will surely seem
That with such odds, it was more probable
That he would be defeated, rather than
The victor, but that would be to ignore
The fact that God had foreseen victory.
He did not come on them by night with stealth,
But fought in daylight when the sun returned.
The site was advantageous to his foes,
But, none the less, it once again was proved
That certain victory will slip from him
Who solely in his prowess puts his trust,
And military men, who recommend
For fighting—practice, tournaments, so that
The army should be highly skilled in war
May also learn a lesson from this fight,
On seeing how the strong and skilful men
Were battered by the weapons of the young.
So God, in order to confound the strong,
Gives to the weak both strength and victory,
But overthrows the strong and obstinate.

And now no more should any man presume
To think that he suffices to himself.
For he should learn that if he trusts in God,
He can take up his arms with confidence
And have no fear of anything, for God
Will always help the soldier on the side
Of justice; thus it was that He saw fit

To come to Simon's aid, for without Him
The Earl could not have overcome his foe.

But wait! Did I say then that he was just
The mortal enemy of the Earl? No, rather
Should I say "England's foe"—and more than that,
For he declared himself against the Church
And thus did he make war on God Himself.
If so, what grace can possibly be his?
He forfeited all grace because of pride,
And, fearing not in God, could not be helped.
So he who proudly boasts of his own strength
Must always come to grief. Praise be to God
Now and for evermore; for He saved those
Who of themselves were weak, and fools are crushed
By the great valour of a faithful few.

A vengeful God is He who sits enthroned
In Heaven above; all-powerful in Himself
He makes the proud and arrogant bow down
That lesser men may tread them underfoot.
He has brought down two kings, and heirs of kings,
And made them prisoners because they broke
The law; He has made infamous the pomp
Of knighthood and its following, because
The barons used those weapons which they seized,
Eager to fight for justice and their land,
Against the sons of pride, until at last
Undreamed-of victory was their reward
From God above; and glory was theirs too.
The mighty by their weapons are destroyed
And their frail army is endued with strength;
But this is Heaven's doing, as I've said,
So that no man can boast of it. And now
Let us pay all just tribute to our Lord
In whom we firmly place our faith and trust,
A general, a king, a conqueror,
All these is Christ, protector of His own,

To whom His word is pledged, and we pray God
That in their hearts, those who have won their fight
Shall kiss not their own hands, and look upon
The victory as their own, but that they should
Take note of what is written by Saint Paul:
"Let him who would rejoice, rejoice in God."

If any one of us should now be filled
With joy and hollow vanity, may God
Forgive him this, and keep His anger down!
So also, with His guidance, may our men
Keep careful watch, and so that idleness
Should not prevail, let them build up a wall!
And then may God with His almighty power
Complete the work which is now but begun,
And thus restore to honourable state
The English land and people, so that His
Will be all glory, and sweet peace shall fall
Upon those whom He loves, until such time
As they have safely come, with Him as guide,
To their true home. Now Englishmen, read on
About this battle fought at Lewes' walls.
Because of this you are alive and safe,
Though if the victory had gone to those
Now conquered, then for all posterity
The name of vanquished England would have been
Dishonoured and disgraced, to all our shame.

How best may we describe Edward the great?
It is perhaps most apt to say that he
Is like a leopard, for that word divides,
And we have then two animals in one,
A lion and a pard. He was most like
The lion when, unflinching, he went out
To fight against the mightiest of men;
Then no attack or onslaught frightened him,
But he would charge into the battle's midst
Most brave and unafraid, as if he thought

No living thing could ever bar his way.
He looked as Alexander must have looked
When he had set himself to win the world,
If only Fortune would hold still her wheel
Which turns, relentless and unceasing, on.
Therefore let him who now stands at the top
Beware, and understand that he must fall;
That he who reigns as master cannot long
Remain on high, but must come tumbling down
As Edward, noble Edward, fell just now
Before us all, from his precarious heights.

He, lion-like, in fierceness and pride,
Is also like the pard, so mutable
This man, and pliable; his fickleness
Leads him to break his word, and fail to keep
His promises, so that with blandishments
And soft words of appeasement he is forced
To make excuses to acquit himself.
In trouble, he will promise anything,
But just as soon as all goes well again
Such promises are banished from his mind.
And this is amply proved by what he did
At Gloucester, where when he was safe and free
From danger, he revoked all promises
And all those solemn oaths which he had sworn.
To him, however, this is not deceit
Nor treachery, but simply prudent means
Which he adopts to further his own ends.
The way by which he comes to what he wants,
However crooked, is called straight; when wrong
Can lead to the fulfilment of his aims
It is not wrong, but right, and everything
Is lawful when he wants it to be so.
He sees himself beyond the scope and reach
Of laws, and greater even than a king,
For every king is governed by those laws
Which he himself enacts. In olden days

King Saul was thrust down from his lofty throne
Because he broke the law, and we see too
That David was chastized for doing so.

So as you read, mark well, and learn this truth,
That anyone who does not keep the law
Is no fit man to rule, and such a man
Should never be elected as their king
By those whose heavy task it is to choose.
And Edward, now you wish to be made king—
But king outside the law! What misery
For those who have to live in such a reign!
Whatever can there be more just than law
Which governs everything? And what more right
Than justice by which everything is ruled?

So if it is a king you wish to be,
First you must learn to have respect for laws.
For if you go against them, you set forth
On steep and treacherous paths, which have no end
And cannot lead you home, but if you serve
And act as guardian of these holy laws,
Then they will shine to guide you on your way
As brightly burning lamps to light the road.
Then will you flee from hated treachery,
Strive after truth, and shun all perfidy.
Though fraud may seem to thrive and grow apace,
It never will know fruitful harvest-time,
For God has told His faithful on this earth,
As you may learn from reading Holy Psalms,
That He Himself decrees that they shall live
With Him for ever to the end of time.

So now, what did you gain by treachery
At Northampton? So false a victory
Is but a fiery spark, it gives no warmth
As true flames do; and since we now compare
Such treachery with fire, it is with straw

That you now strive to keep this spark alight.
But straw is fast burnt up, and leaves no glow,
It is consumed as soon as touched by flame.
And so to nothing came all rootless things,
But truth, well-planted, can admit no change,
So may it please you now to do alone
That which is right according to our laws,
And not to be misled by wicked men.
A virtuous Prince will have a mind and will
As noble as his rank. Protect the law
And you will then deserve your royal name
And fittingly rule over many men.
You will be worthy of their loyal help,
And of these great and splendid courts you hold.

But why have you no feeling in your heart
For those whose king you wish to be? It seems
That you want rather to be served by them
As mighty ruler, than that you yourself
Should do them service as a kindly friend.
But he who looks for glory for himself
And no one else, will cause by his own pride
The downfall of his kingdom. You have seen
The ruin of your subjects and your land,
And that great glory which was all you sought,
Has now shrunk back into the distant past.

But here we touch upon the very root
Of all the troubles which beset our land
And of the quarrels of the sides who fought
This battle, for their aims were not the same.

On one hand was the King, with all his men,
Who wanted to be free, as, so they said,
He ought to be, for without liberty
He was no king, and must give up that claim,
Or else he must, as king, enjoy the right
To act just as he wished. So other men,

The great ones of the land, presume too much,
In telling him on whom he must bestow
Some earldom, or to whom he should entrust
His castles, or those whom he should appoint
As fit to mete out justice in the land,
Or be his Chancellor and Treasurer.
He trusted to his own judgment alone,
And from whatever race he chose, he took
His counsellors and all his ministers.

And all this time the Barons of the land
Were powerless to act; the Prince's word
Is law, so that whatever he decrees
Is binding on all men. For every Earl
Is likewise his own lord, and therefore gives
Of his own property, to whom he wills,
As many castles, lands and revenues
As he is pleased to give; and though he is
A subject, all this freedom is allowed
And granted by the King. If wisely done,
He will reap profit from it, but if not,
That's his affair, the King will not prevent
That he should harm himself. Since this is so,
Why should the status of the Prince be such
That Barons, soldiers and free men enjoy
A greater liberty in their affairs?

Those then who seek to lessen the King's power
Want nothing but to make of him a slave,
And take away his princely dignity.
With treason in their hearts, they want to seize
And make a captive of his power as king,
To force it to submission and restraint,
To take away all he inherited,
So that he can no longer rule the land,
As strongly as those kings of days gone by.
For they would not submit to any man
But were in full control of all affairs.

According to their pleasure they bestowed
All that was theirs to give, and rightly so.
So reasoning thus, the King supports his claim,
And outwardly, it would seem fair and just
This statement made to save his royal rights.

But now my pen shall state the other case,
The one in opposition, and describe
As well what all the Barons had in mind,
So that when both sides have been justly heard
Their arguments may be compared, and then
With all the evidence, we may decide,
And clearly see which side is in the right.

The people are more likely to obey
The truer side, so let the Barons speak
And argue for themselves, and in their turn
Describe what drives them on. They first protest
Quite openly that they have no designs
Upon his royal honour and prestige;
That, on the contrary, they rather want
Both to reform and to exalt still more
The status of the King. For just suppose
The kingdom were laid waste by enemies—
Without the Barons' aid it could not be
Put back again to rights, and they would be
The ablest and most fitted for this task.
But if someone refused to help in this
The law would seize on him, and he would stand
Accused of being traitor to his King
And false to all the oaths which he had sworn.
For by these he is bound to give such help
And service as he can, that he may save
The honour of his lord in jeopardy,
And save his country from the dreadful threat
Of utter desolation.

There are foes
Who openly make war against the King.
Enemies too those counsellors who praise
And flatter him, and with their idle talk
Seduce their lord, and lead him straight into
The byways of false judgment. These it is
Who are worse enemies by far than those
Who openly refuse to go with him,
For they pretend to be good, honest men,
While really all they seek is to corrupt,
And win thereby more honour for themselves.
So frequently they manage to deceive
Those who, without due caution, trust in them
Because of all the pleasing words or deeds
That they have said or done, and so it is
That, free from all suspicion, they go on
And what they say is heard with great respect.

Such men as these can do more to deceive
Than those whose deeds are seen, for they build up
Around themselves the false impression that
In them there is no malice nor no wrong.
So if such liars and such wicked men
Should cluster still around the Prince, with all
Their aptitude for malice, treachery,
And empty words, and, urged still further on
By envy's pricking spur, should then commit
That crime of high depravity, that is,
To seize upon the country's sacred laws,
And by adapting them to suit themselves,
Add both to their own standing and their power,
And if they should contrive and scheme to find
Some argument, however harsh, whereby
Eventually they may confound and throw
Into confusion all the common men,
And crush them underfoot, until at last
They are reduced to direst poverty,
If thus they lead the country further on

The road to utter ruin and despair,
And warp and twist the judgment of all men
Until no justice can be found except
By him who will consent to feed their pride,
And nourish it with no small sums of gold,
If all this should be so, can any man
Bear such abuse or such outrageous shame?

And if these men for their own ends, should change
For worse, the face of this fair land, and thus
Throw justice from its sacred seat on high,
And in its place put vile abuse and wrong,
And if they crush true Englishmen, and call
Usurpers from abroad to make of them
The masters and the rulers of the land,
If then without respect for all the great
And those of noble birth in England now,
They should place over them in highest rank
Unworthy and dishonourable men;
If by such means they should humiliate
And bring down low all those of high estate,
If all the social order is by them
Reversed, and totally upset, so that
All good is then abandoned and replaced
By evil and wrongdoing, surely this
Is to disrupt, and what is more, destroy
Our native land? For though they wage no war
With foreign weapons, yet those arms they use
To violate the state so wrongfully
Are none the less pernicious, and although
The harm they do is not the same as that
Caused by invading armies, it is just
As great, and equal in destructive power.

So whether it is that the King, misled
By flattering talk to giving his consent,
And truly ignorant of their designs
Unknowingly approves such wrongs as these
Whose only end can be destruction, and

The ruin of his land; or whether he,
With malice in his heart, and ill-intent,
Commits these shameful crimes by raising up
His royal state and power far beyond
The reach of all his country's laws, so that
His whim is satisfied by the abuse
Of royal privilege and strength; if thus
Or otherwise this land of ours is brought
To total rack and ruin, and at last
The kingdom is left destitute, it is
The duty of the great and noble men
To rescue it, to purge the land of all
Corruption and all false authority.

So if it falls to them to rid the land
Of such wrongdoing, and if they it is
Who must establish and put right the code
Of common usage, then how can it be
That it is not their duty too to watch
And guard against all evil which could harm?
But should such wrong have come about, they must
Remove it, stamp it out, so that no hurt,
No sudden happening should be a source
Of grief to those caught unawares. So now,
In order to prevent such shameful crimes
Which could disrupt all harmony and peace,
And overthrow all customary rights,
And if the wisest and most learned men
Should work to find the greatest good for all,
Why should reform as they suggest not be
Accepted, since in it would be no taint
Of false corruption? Kingly clemency
And royal majesty should rightfully
Approve such zeal, which mitigates and makes
More bearable unwelcome laws which, since
They thereby are less burdensome, become
More pleasing in the sight of God on high.

For great oppression of the people finds
No favour in His eyes; what pleases Him
Is rather that great mercy which allows
The people to devote some time to Him.
The Pharaoh, who so grievously oppressed
God's chosen people, that they scarcely could
Find time to hear the counsel which He gave
Through Moses as His prophet, in the end
Was punished thus; he had to let them go,
The Israelites, albeit unwillingly,
And when he planned to bring them back again
And thought that he could too with safety cross
As they had done, the water's great divide,
Then it engulfed and drowned him as he passed.
Great Solomon himself had no desire
To crush the Israelites, or make of them
His slaves, for he knew that this holy race
He ruled, was God's own people, and he feared
To hurt those on whom God had set His seal.
And thus was he to mercy more inclined
Than to harsh judgment, and preferred the peace
Of fatherly affection, to the sin
Of torture and oppressive punishment.

So since it is the Barons' proven right
To bring about all this, it now remains
To answer to the claims made by the King.
For he wants to be free, with all restraint
Removed, so he refuses to submit
To men by birth inferior to him,
For they it is whom he wants to command.
The King demands to rule, not to be ruled,
And he will never show humility
Within himself, or to those officers
Whom he appoints, not over him, but more
As nobles to uphold and keep the law.
For otherwise, though there would be in name
One king, he would not rule alone, for if

He once gave way to them, then they would rule
With him as equals. This is difficult,
A problem which seems insurmountable,
But with God's help, an answer can be found.
For we have faith and still believe that God
Wills only what is right and just, and so
With Him as guide, this problem will be solved.

For He who governs all the world, and rules
With highest and most glorious majesty,
Is said to be, and truly is, sole King.
For He can rule alone; He needs no help,
No counsellors, for He can never err.
His wisdom and His power are infinite
As is His majesty; how greatly then
Does He surpass all those to whom He gives
The power to reign, and as it were, to rule
His people, still subservient to Him!
For these, His deputies, can fail and err,
They have not in themselves alone the means
To win success, and independently
To conquer all their foes; no more have they
As single men, that wisdom which they need
To govern kingdoms, for they go astray
And wander in the paths of shameful wrong.
They must have aid to come to their support,
And good advice to set them on their way.

But then the King will say "This I accept,
But still maintain that all such counsellors
Must be of my own choosing, picked by me.
I will associate with whom I wish,
And with their help, will govern over all.
For if in this, some prove inadequate,
If they are poor in wisdom or in strength,
Or should they prove so full of ill-intent
And so entirely lacking in good faith
That they could be accused of treachery,

Why then, I ask of you, why then should I
Be so restricted to a certain few
When by myself I could find better help?"

To this an answer quickly may be found
If we but now consider what this means
And what is the true nature of restraint
Upon the King. For all restraint does not
Mean loss of liberty, nor is it true
That power is lost if it is limited.
All princes want to have unbounded power,
No ruler will submit to servitude.

All this we know, but let us now ask this:
What limits will a free law set on kings?
This only: that they will reign undefiled
By laws which are corrupt, and such restraint
Is far from being that of slavery,
But rather by it is the power of kings
Enhanced, and brought to its full majesty.
For royal offspring are protected thus,
Yet they are not reduced to slavery.
For their own good they are restricted so,
As are the very angels, even though
Such spirits are made stronger to resist
Temptation to be false or lose their faith.
The Author of all things can never err,
Nor can He sin from whom all things began,
But this is not a lessening of power,
But power at its greatest, that of God
In all His glory and His majesty.

So that if man, who easily may fall,
Is so protected that he can live free
From fear of this, then from such guardianship
He can reap only profit for himself,
And to depend on such support is not
To be reduced to vilest servitude,

But rather to ensure the maintenance
Of what is right and just in terms of power.

It is a holy gift of God that kings
Should freely be allowed to do all things
Provided they are good, but should not dare
To tread the paths of wickedness and wrong.
So those who stand on guard for him, and watch
That he, though tempted, does not stoop to sin,
They serve the king, and to them he owes thanks.
For they ensure that he will never be
A slave, and that themselves who guide him so
Will never take his power away from him.
But he who truly would be king is free
If he can rule with righteousness and truth
His kingdom and himself; then will he know
What liberty he has to do those things
From which his country will reap benefit,
But not those things by which it is destroyed.
Resistance to the law brings in its wake
Destruction, which is very different from
Such rule as is befitting to a king.
The law derives its name from words which mean
To bind, but is the perfect attribute
To liberty, which to the law owes much
For all the great protection that it gives.

Let every king accept that he, to God,
Is but a servant; let him therefore love
That only which is pleasing unto God.
So let him reign that he will glorify
His master, and not seek to satisfy
His pride by the rejection of his peers.
And if a king should want obedience
From those who are his subjects, let him then
Acquit himself of all he owes to God.
For he should know that he can make no claim

To be obeyed, if he does not fulfil
That contract by which he is bound to God.

Moreover, he must understand this fact,
That all the people are not his, but God's,
And are there but to help and serve him well.
But he who for so short a span of time
Is set as sovereign power over them,
Must soon in marble casket be enclosed,
And lowered deep into his country's earth.
So let him then toward his people turn,
And humbly thus become as one of them.
He has good precedent if he recalls
That David danced with humble handmaidens.
If only our next king could be like him!
Like David, with those virtuous gifts he had
Of prudence and humility, a man
Who would not dream of harming those he loved,
Much less his subjects, but cast over them
A smile of loving kindness, who would seek
Both safety and prosperity for them.
The people certainly would not allow
That such a man, their king, should suffer wrong.
But it is difficult, unloved, to love,
And it is hard, despised, not to despise,
Nor to resist when ruin threatens us.
But it is human nature to approve
And lend support when things go well for us.

The duty of a prince is not to crush
Nor to oppress his people, but to stand
As their protector: so he will deserve
Their loving favour and affection true
For all the benefits bestowed on them,
As Jesus Christ has won the love of all
For those great blessings which He gave the world.
For if a prince shows love, then in return
He should be loved; and if his rule is just,

He should be honoured for his righteousness.
But should he err, then he should be set right
By those on whom the burden fell of some
Injustice done by him; for though at first
Perhaps he would not listen to advice,
If, later, he should wish to make amends,
Then those same persons should both offer help
And lend support to raise him up again.
A prince must strictly keep to such a way
Of governing, that he will never say
That he can rule and never feel the need
To call upon his people for support.
Those unwise princes who beat down and crush
Their subjects will discover to their cost
That men who are outraged and angered thus
Cannot with ease be tamed or quieted.
But if a prince should claim that he alone
Is in possession of all truth, that he
Has greater knowledge, more intelligence,
More grace with God, more of His holy gifts
Than any other man, if he can claim
All this without presumption, but with truth,
Then with his teaching he will so inflame
And so infuse with light the loyal hearts
Of those who are his subjects, then from him
They will learn moderation and restraint.

We have already seen that Moses and
King David, and the holy Samuel
Were true and virtuous leaders among men,
Who suffered greatly at the hands of those
Who were their subjects, but these saintly men
Did not abandon them or cast them off
As richly they deserved, and furthermore,
Did not set strangers over them, but ruled
With loyal help from men of their own race.
God turned to Moses once, and spoke these words:
"I will destroy these people, and instead

Will make you ruler of a greater race."
To which the gentle Moses thus replied:
"O Father, I would rather die myself
Than see my people perish for my sake."
So he was proved a worthy man to rule,
And thus a wise prince never will reject
Or cast aside his fellow-countrymen,
Although a foolish one will throw the land
Into confusion. So that if a king
Is shown to lack that wisdom which he needs,
How can his country profit from his reign?
Should such a king be left to choose himself
Those counsellors on whom he must depend
To supplement his own deficiency?
If such a choice is left to him alone
He could be very easily misled,
Because he is incompetent to judge
How useful to him certain men could be.

Therefore the kingdom as a whole should choose,
And popular opinion be made known,
Because it is the people who best know
The laws which govern them. It is not true
That all the country's men are ignorant,
And so untaught that they are less aware
Of all those rights and customs handed down
From generations past, than foreigners
Who come as strangers to their country's shores.
For men whose lives are governed by such laws
Must know them best, and those who practise law
Become more skilled and learned in its use.
And if the cause concerns their own affairs,
In their own interest they will take more care,
And will contrive a way of finding peace.
But knowledge must come from experience,
And those who serve the country best, are those
Who have the surest knowledge of its laws.

And so we see from all these arguments
That it concerns the nation as a whole
To see that just selection must be made
Of such men as will serve the country best.
For it is those who have the will to serve,
As well as great ability and skill,
Who should become advisers to the King,
Such men as have become from day to day
Familiar with the customs of the land,
Who suffer when their country suffers harm,
And make themselves its guardians, for if
The kingdom should be harmed in any way,
Each several part of it will suffer too.

And at this point most aptly we recall
The noble justice of King Solomon:
The woman who did not recoil or shrink
In horror at such ruthless cruelty,
When he suggested that the child she claimed
As hers, should be divided into two,
Proved, as the King foresaw, that since she felt
No stirring pity, no maternal love,
She could not be the mother of the child.

A prince, therefore, should seek as counsellors
Those men who will feel sympathy for all,
Who will be fearful, as a mother is,
Lest any suffering oppress the land.
If any man can bear to watch, unmoved,
The ruin of most of his fellow men,
While he alone obtains what he demands,
Then he is no fit man to set above
The suffering majority of men,
Since he devotes his every thought and deed
Entirely to himself. A man who feels
Compassion for his fellows, will do good,
And is acceptable to all of them,

But he who has a heart of stone, so hard
That he is dead to feeling, has no care
If troubles and misfortune rain on them,
And such a wall as this is no defence
Against the massive onslaught of such woe.
So if the King cannot judge for himself,
Or wisely choose those who are best equipped
To be his counsellors, we have shown here
How best this problem then should be resolved.

For it concerns the nation as a whole
To see that worthless men do not become
The guiding lights of royal dignity,
But rather that such powers behind the throne
Should be the most exceptional of men,
The best that can be found, those who have proved
That they are the most worthy of this task.
For since whatever government we have
Can save or be the ruin of us all,
The choice of those who are to rule the land
Is of great consequence, as in a ship,
For chaos reigns if those men in command
Know nothing of the working of a ship,
Or if a passenger should wrongly seize
Its rudder, and should steer it, all untrained,
Since he as steersman has the most control.
Then higher officers may give commands
Both good and bad; they will have no effect.

So those who rule the kingdom must take care
And watch for anyone who misbehaves,
Who treads along forbidden paths which he
By chance, perhaps, has chosen for himself.
For national affairs are dealt with best
If all the kingdom is embarked upon
The way of truth and right. And furthermore,
If any subjects should then be inclined
To waste and to misuse their property,

Those in authority can call a halt
To such temerity and foolishness,
So that the arrogance and idiocy
Of stupid men should never undermine
The power of the kingdom, or inspire
A greater boldness in her enemies.

No matter in what part a wound is felt,
The body's total strength must be thereby
Diminished, so that if some are allowed
To misuse and destroy their property,
Although this may be detrimental to
The kingdom as a whole, soon other men,
Enjoying this same harmful liberty,
Will so extend the folly of this wrong
That in the end the whole land will be lost.
For licence which allows such foolish men
To govern so unwisely, should not be
Called liberty, for this is limited
And held in check by laws, but if these bonds
Are spurned and cast aside, then such a deed
Should be regarded as grave infamy.
For otherwise a raving lunatic
Will be called free, although he is at odds
With all that is devised to work for good.

All those objections which the King has raised
About his subjects' being ruled by men
Whom they have freely chosen to elect,
Are, therefore, answered here, and overthrown,
Since everyone who is a subject has
A greater man in power over him.
For we have said that no man has the right
To act just as he wants, but that he has
A lord, a master, who will act as guide,
To give correction should he ever err,
To lend support, and give encouragement
When he is doing well, to raise him up

If he should ever fall. And so it is
That to the nation as a whole, we give
The place of prime importance; we say too
That laws must regulate the scope and power
Of royal majesty, for we believe
The law to be a light, without whose rays
A ruler will, unguided, go astray.

The law which rules the world, and holds its sway
In all the many kingdoms of the world,
Is likened to a fire, within whose depths
Lie sacred and mysterious properties,
Of deep and far-reaching significance;
So all at once it shines, it burns, gives warmth,
And with its flames it bars the way to him
Who is about to stray away from truth.
It drives away the cold, and purifies,
Or burns some things to ashes; it makes soft
Things which were hard, and cooks with fiery heat
Things which were raw; it brings to life again
Limbs which were numb and dead; all these and more
Are benefits bestowed on us by fire.

And so there are within our sacred laws
Such properties as can serve well the King.
For Solomon sought wisdom in the law
And strove with all his might to make of it
His ally and his friend. But if the King
Should rule without the guidance of the law
He soon will go astray, and if he then
Refuses to uphold and keep the law
He will be guilty of the foulest wrong.
With law as his right hand, a king will have
The grace to rule both virtuously and well,
But if he casts it off, then all the land
Will suffer total ruin and be lost.
And if the law could speak, it would be thus:
"It is through me that mighty kings can rule,

Through me that justice is inspired in those
Who formulate and found your country's laws."

So right a law is fixed, immutable,
No king can alter it, though he will find
Within it that stability he lacks.
If he obeys the law, he will stand firm,
But he will found his reign on shifting ground
If he should contradict its sacred truth.
There is a common saying which goes thus:
"The law is but the servant of the King."
But truth says otherwise, for kings may fall,
While law still stands unshaken and rock-firm.
For truth and charity, together with
A zealous striving to protect and save,
These are the sacred properties of law,
All that can be prescribed for virtuous rule.
For truth, and light, and charity and warmth,
And such a burning eagerness for good,
Are all the flames of that fire which is law,
And so, with this diversity of gifts
The law is armed to combat any crime.

So let the King's decrees conform with this,
If not, the people will be full of grief,
And all the land confounded, should the King
Be blind to truth, or cold to charity,
Without the inspiration of the law
To act with moderation as he rules,
To temper that severity he needs
In order to fulfil his role as King.
For if he is possessed of these three gifts,
This love of truth, of men, of clemency,
Then he may do whatever pleases him,
But if his thoughts are opposite to these,
Then he defies the law in all he does.
For Heaven taught Saint Paul, and we have learned
Through him, this sacred truth from God on high:

However we resist it, we can do
No harm to any stimulus for good.

And so the King is not deprived of rights
Which must be his by reason of his birth,
If some conditions are imposed on him
According to a just and upright law.
For wickedness will never change the law,
So steadfast is its teaching, it will stand
Immutable until the end of time.

And so if something which has power for good
Has long been left unused, it must not be
Condemned when, late, it comes into its own.
A king must never set his private needs
Above those of his people, for he thus
Subjects the common welfare to his own.
For he is not appointed over them,
To live entirely for himself alone,
But rather that he shall devote his life
To seeing that his subjects are kept safe.
A kingly title is but relative,
And thus implies protection for all men,
So kingship can allow no selfishness,
But by its very nature it demands
That those of royal birth should live their lives
As guardians and protectors of us all.
But he who lives entirely for himself
Should never be allowed to wear a crown,
But rather should be left to live alone
And separately from all his fellow-men.

The glory of a Prince consists in this:
That for so many he can do such good,
That by self-sacrifice he can raise up
So many of those over whom he rules.
So let him not choose first to serve himself,
But rather let him have regard for those

Who are entrusted to his royal power.
He who has lived as guardian of his land
Has done the proper duty of a king,
But if he has done anything to harm,
To persecute his kingdom, he has failed.

And so we see from all these arguments
What is the rightful duty of a king,
That he who dedicates himself to that
Which furthers his own good, will never know
Wherein the dignity of kingship lies.
For such a loving kindness is opposed
To selfishness; it forms a lasting bond
With all the people, like a fire which melts
Whatever can be melted in its flames,
Which grows as it is fed with logs of wood,
Which dies if it is not thus kept alight.
So if a prince's heart is warm with love,
A love which is as great as it can be
Towards his people, if he strives to rule
With righteousness and justice as his guides,
And mourns to see his kingdom overwhelmed
Or laid waste by disaster; if he loves
The great men of the land, for though a king
Will, prophet-like, know best within himself
What government the kingdom really needs,
What duties are incumbent on himself,
What it is necessary to achieve,
Yet he will never hide from these great men
Whatever he decrees, for without them
His orders would have no authority.

If this be so, then he will yet consult
His people, and discuss with them those things
Which by himself he would not undertake.
Why will the King not make his plans more known
To those from whom he will in time beg help?
For if he has in mind some enterprise

Which done, shall fill his people with good will,
Inspire true friendship, foster unity,
Then in his royal wisdom it is fit
That he should first reveal it to those men
Who can increase the glory of his reign.

Our Lord disclosed all things to those great saints
Who once were His apostles, chose His friends
From humble serving men with whom He talked,
And often, seeming not to know, He asked
For their opinions, though in truth He had
A great and perfect knowledge of all things.
If only royal princes would seek first
To pay due honour to the Lord their God!
Then rightly would they govern, and avoid
All defects, all mistakes in thought or deed.

If princes had true knowledge of their God,
Their justice would be freely shown to all.
But, ignorant of God, and blindly, they
Want only to be praised, and take delight
In all the hollow vanities of life.
And you may all find written in the Psalms
That badly will he govern other men,
Who has not first learned how to rule himself
As Joseph did, so that his King saw fit
To give him power over other men;
And this should be a lesson to all kings.
So David, pure of heart, with wisdom ruled,
And lovingly he cherished Israel.

From all that has been said, we clearly see
That in the drawing up of policies
To further the well-being of the land,
And to ensure the maintenance of peace,
The King should first consult with his great men,
And as companions should choose Englishmen,
Not foreigners, nor favourites, to be

His counsellors and leaders in the land.
For they are but usurpers, and reject
The customs and traditions proved so good.
And discord thus provoked does not love peace,
Gives rise to battles, and breeds treachery.
For just as death was brought into the world
Because the envious devil tempted man,
So hatred will destroy all unity.

The King will find great joy in governing
If he upholds the orders of his land,
But if this social order is upset
And he deprives his subjects of their rank,
How can he wonder vainly why it is
That those whom he has put down in this way
Refuse to show obedience to him?
In such a situation, it would be
The very height of folly if they did.

IX

> "Simon de Montfort saved the situation by announcing that he had a memorable Idea."
>
> (*1066 And All That.*)

The Monk of Lewes was probably among those who looked after the sick or helped to bury the dead and he gives the figure as "2,700, more or less", who were killed on the royalist side. Estimates have varied so widely, and so little can be accepted as fact, that even speculation seems dangerous. Two questions arise: what was the size of each army; how many were killed in the battle.

It can safely be said that there is always a tendency to exaggerate both the size of armies and the number of casualties. It was certainly possible in the thirteenth century to put a large army in the field, even if only for a limited time, but it could not be greater than the population from which it was drawn, and it is clear that the chroniclers liked to tell a good story. When Robert Brune wrote of "sixti thousand of London armed men full stoute", he ignored the fact that the total population of London was no higher than forty thousand, and probably a great deal less. The Worcester Chronicle recorded that the King's army before the battle consisted of sixty thousand men, and the barons', including the Londoners, of forty thousand.

In more modern times W. H. Blaauw, writing in the nineteenth century, weighed all the information with great care and formed the view that some fifty thousand men were engaged altogether with a higher proportion on the royalist side. The historian J. R. Green born some thirty years later stated in his *History of the English People* that Simon's army was "reinforced by fifteen thousand Londoners". Twentieth century historians are more reluctant to commit themselves, although A. H.

Burne, the military historian, made the conservative estimate of under ten thousand in the King's army and little more than five thousand with the barons. As he also accepted the monk's figure of about two thousand seven hundred killed on the royalist side he was suggesting the high death-roll of more than one in four.

Perhaps a likely figure for both armies together is somewhere between the higher and lower estimates, say thirty to thirty-five thousand, with the weight of numbers on the King's side. But Peter Langtoft had the best answer when he wrote:

> "The numbre non wrote, for tell tham mot no man,
> Bot He that alle wote, and alle thing ses and can."[1]

Apart from the natural inclination of a story-teller to embroider a tale, some confusion may have arisen from the temporary nature of armies. A good many of the brave Londoners for instance may never have got as far as Lewes. Support for both sides fluctuated, and many a feudal baron on his way to help one cause or the other digressed to plunder enemy lands or church property. A summons did not ensure that a baron would turn up, for he might be a rascal like Robert de Ferrers, Earl of Derby, or he might set out with good intentions and fail to find his way. It would be no easy matter, even for a historian of the time, to judge the size of the actual armies engaged in a battle.

Even population figures are not dependable. The total population of England and Wales in 1279 calculated on Domesday Book figures was approximately 3,000,000. At that time the population of Surrey and Sussex together was shown by a poll tax to be 35,326 not including children under fourteen, and priests, who would add another third. So if a total of up to 50,000 men were involved in the Battle of Lewes this would represent the total population of those two counties.

Another sidelight on this subject is the interesting study made by Denholm-Young into the actual number of knights in England during the Middle Ages, and the size of the social class from which they were drawn.[2] He concludes that in Henry III's reign there were no more than four hundred knights available for fighting in any campaign, and although Blaauw said that

"England probably contained some 12,000 who had taken out their knighthood or might be compelled to do so; and it is reasonable to assume that half of these took part in the (Barons') War", he is unable to account for more than three or four hundred of them.

There is some evidence on which to base an estimate of the numbers killed in the battle. Here again the chronicles vary widely. The remark in the Fabian Chronicle, "some say twenty thousand", can reasonably be ignored. The Monk of Lewes offers the low figure of "about 2,700" on the royalist side. Matthew of Westminster and Rishanger, among several others, mention five thousand. Polidore says 6,500, and the Melrose Chronicle reports "in this battle many thousand men were slain, as well as horse as foot".

Fortunately large numbers of skeletons have been found in the neighbourhood of Lewes which help to indicate the probable site of the main fighting and the numbers killed. The skeletons of some dozens of the Londoners are already accounted for near the chalkpits at Offham. There have been other, more dramatic discoveries. In the second edition of his book *The Barons' War*, published in 1871 after his death, W. H. Blaauw reported his discovery that in 1810 Mr. Barrett, the road surveyor, was lowering the Brighton turnpike road and found three pits filled with skeletons near the eastern entrance to the County Gaol. Each pit was estimated to hold quite five hundred bodies, and carts took several days to move them to the grounds of Saint Anne's poor houses where they were re-buried. Blaauw reported this information in a letter to the Sussex *Express* in 1863, and it confirmed his view that the heaviest fighting had been "in the vicinity of Lewes County Gaol to the very walls of the town".

L. S. Davey has brought further information to light. In 1795 Dunvan wrote in his *History of Lewes*, "As they were making the new turnpike road . . . the workmen dug into one of those pits and threw up a great quantity of bones . . . Most of the slain were interred in pits in the field or croft adjoining the hospital." The original turnpike road from Brighton to Lewes was made in 1769, but unfortunately the Brighton Road papers are missing. The question of course arises whether there were two discoveries of skeletons in the same area, or only one. Probably there were two. Blaauw is so precise in his account that he must have had some source of information that is now lost. But Blaauw apparently knew nothing of another discovery which was reported, also in the *Sussex Express*, on 17 January 1846:

DISCOVERY OF THE REMAINS OF THE KILLED IN THE BATTLE OF LEWES

"On Friday night the excavators employed in the cutting at the Priory" (this would refer to the railway which was cut across the Priory grounds) "came across a mass of human bones, nearly 6 feet thick and 10 feet in diameter, which were deposited 18 feet below the surface, in a well of that extent.

"There is no doubt that these are the remains of the bodies which, after the battle of Lewes, were collected in the town by the monks, whom history records as having busily occupied themselves on the occasion burying the dead.

"That this was an original burial is established by the fact that when the bones were first exposed the effluvium was so obnoxious as to cause the men to desist from their work until next day—several, in fact, were taken ill.

"The bones were conveyed away in about 10 railway wagons and were thrown into the mass of rubbish which forms the embankment through the brooks, midway between the river and Southerham corner.

"It is a source of deep regret that human bones should have been employed for such a purpose—there is something so revolting in this appropriation that we cannot bring ourselves to speak on the subject, lest our feelings should be excited to censure with severity the despoilers of the dead. Surely it would have been more consonant to public taste to have reburied the remains of the warriors within the walls of the Priory. The expense would have been trifling, and this outrage have been prevented."

There is another account of this, with only slight variations, in *A Day's Ramble in Lewes* (1846) by Gideon Mantell, a surgeon and geologist who lived at Lewes. "A very remarkable discovery was made near the eastern termination of the foundations by the railway excavators," (this suggests a site near the entrance of the Brighton railway into Lewes Station). "At a distance of eighteen feet below the surface, they cut through a wall or pit, 18 feet thick and 10 feet in diameter, which was completely full of human bones; the skeletons of bodies that had evidently been interred in a promiscuous heap. This mass of human remains, when first exposed, emitted so nauseous an exhalation, that several of the men were ill from its effects. It has been suggested, with much probability, that these bones are the relics of the persons who fell in the Battle of Lewes in 1264, in the streets and immediate vicinity of the town, and which were gathered up and afforded Christian burial within the precincts of the Priory, by the monks of Saint Pancras."

He adds an outraged footnote. "In perfect accordance with the spirit of this railway age, this heap of skeletons of the patriots and royalists of the thirteenth century, which filled thirteen wagons, was taken away to form part of the embankment of the line in the adjacent brook."

Mantell reported another find in his Journal: ". . . Some workmen employed in digging flints near the Walloons discovered the remains of eight or nine skeletons; one of them had the mouth wide open; they are evidently the remains of the bodies interred after the battle between Henry III and his Barons . . ."

This was certainly one possibility. By "Walloons" he must have meant the Wallands, which adjoined the Hides and were also open grazing lands. It is there that the battle is commemorated in the names of the roads.

Several questions arise from the two main discoveries. Once again it may be supposed that there was a tendency to exaggerate the number of skeletons. There could be no question either of such an ancient burial pit giving "so nauseous an exhalation" but it clearly provided a fair excuse for a holiday. It is also important to consider whether they were more likely to be battle casualties than plague victims. The two are commonly confused.

I am indebted to Richard F. Dell, the East Sussex County Archivist, who has very kindly looked into the question for me. He writes: "The parish registers of the five Lewes parishes, which are deposited here, make it perfectly certain that no devastating visitation of the plague since 1558 could account for the size of the mass graves you mention. For the waves of bubonic which swept England in the 14th and 15th centuries we have no reliable evidence from Lewes. A rural community under one lordship, for which court rolls exist, can give a good idea of the decimation from the vacancies of tenancies, but such evidence is not available for a town in which numerous freeholds were intermixed with the copyholds. Nor is it likely, I should have thought, that plague victims would be massed together; the visitation would spread over weeks and to leave the graves open to receive the succession of victims would appear dangerous. A heavy concentration would surely suggest a burial at one time hence a battle, and in this case the graves are where we know the heavy fighting took place—on the hill approach to the town in the morning and around the monastery on Prince Edward's return later in the day."

There may well be other burial pits not yet discovered, but it is significant that so many bodies were buried just where one might look for them after studying the battle. Men who fell at some distance from the town would probably be buried on the spot, as the chalkpit graves suggest, but there is no evidence of large numbers of casualties on the Downs. As Blaauw said it is unlikely that there are large pits up there "for nearly every portion of the Downs has, within the past century, been sufficiently turned up to mark such a spot if any existed". Bodies around the town itself would be taken by the survivors for burial in hallowed ground nearby, and so it is reasonable that a large grave should be found within the Priory boundaries and another near the church of Saint Anne. This church, originally dedicated to Saint Mary, stands beside the Hides, and the greater part of it dates from the twelfth and thirteenth centuries.

It is sometimes suggested that if in fact these pits held battle casualties they would also yield remains of armour and weapons, if only in the form of metal particles. Unfortunately the workmen appear to have been so overcome by their experience that they neither called an expert nor studied the remains with any care. It would be helpful, for instance, to know if they were mainly the bones of adult males. But generally speaking armour and weapons have always been too costly and useful to bury. The victorious army stripped the corpses and kept or sold anything of value.

In view of the evidence of the skeletons already found, and the weight of opinion among the chroniclers, it is a fair assumption that about 5,000 were killed in the battle or died so soon afterward that they were counted among the dead. There must have been many who did not recover from their wounds, which would so easily become gangrenous or infected, and no doubt many of them remained at Lewes in the care of the monks. There was certainly a heavy loss of life. The writer of the Oxenede Chronicle said: "It was there seen that the days of man were as the grass of the field; a huge multitude was slain, whose number I know not." Yet it is curious that out of all this number very few were important enough to be mentioned by name. One was William le Blund, who had been left in charge of the baggage cart or "chariot" that delayed Prince Edward's return. Another on de Montfort's side was Ralph Heringaud, whose family held lands in Kent, Surrey and Sussex. The most famous of those killed on the royalist side was Fulk FitzWarren, who was drowned in the Ouse. William de Wilton is the only other royalist who died to be mentioned by name.

Most of the more important who did not escape were taken prisoner, for the attitude to killing an enemy was not the same in medieval warfare as it is today. It was not mercy, but good sense that made kings, queens, princes, bishops and knights almost inviolate. They were more useful alive than dead, and like their castles they served a purpose as bargaining counters. This is particularly the case in a rebellion against the monarchy, for there was every advantage in having the person of the king as a figurehead of the new regime. The royal seal was the ultimate in sanction, and a royal puppet was needed to add recognizable authority to new regulations. Those who were killed were the ordinary citizens, the apprentices from London and the cottagers and villeins who obeyed the call to arms.

A great cross was cut in the chalk on the north slope of the Downs at Plumpton, thirty yards across in each direction, and it is said that the monks of Saint Pancras chose this way to honour the men slain in the battle. The chalk-white cross on the short green turf of the hill would be visible for a considerable distance to the north, and its outline can still be seen in certain lights. It has also been suggested that they chose this spot because Simon's baggage train waited there (for which there is no evidence) and that some of the Londoners took refuge with the garrison left in charge and were killed when Prince Edward's men stormed it in the belief that Simon himself was there. But the Cluniac monks were not among those who regarded Simon as a saint, nor did they support the baronial cause.

In 1924 at the 660th anniversary celebrations a memorial stone placed in the centre of this chalk cross by the Brighton and Hove Archaeological Club was unveiled, and although partly buried it is still in good order. Instead of choosing a site to mark the battle itself the members chose to strengthen the tradition linking the chalk cross with the Battle of Lewes. The monks from the Priory of Saint Pancras reminded future generations to pray for the souls of the men who fell in battle. Centuries later men remember that out of this destruction sprang an advance in England's constitution.

While the soldiers were collecting their dead and attending to their wounded comrades, the leaders on both sides were urgently trying to reach a settlement. According to some chronicles negotiations began on the evening of the battle. The interruption of government exposes a country to grave dangers, just as the human brain is quickly damaged when the heart fails. With enemies watching and waiting across the Channel, and powerful mischief makers at home only too ready to fish in troubled waters, even hours were precious. So perhaps through the night, while the wounded were carried to the Priory and other religious houses, messengers were busy carrying their leaders' arguments from one headquarter to the other.

Simon de Montfort probably set up his headquarters in the newly-founded Priory of Saint Mary just outside the town wall, where the railway goods station now stands. There the Franciscan monks, known as Greyfriars, would remind him of his old friends Robert Grosseteste and Adam Marsh. It would explain why chroniclers say that two Greyfriars acted as emissaries on the baronial side, and two Black Monks of Saint Pancras on the royalist side. Blaauw argues that it was more likely once more to be Walter de Cantelupe and Richard de Sandwich who went back and forth amending the terms of peace. But the barons had now won a decisive victory and this time their terms were arbitrary. While Simon de Montfort, Gilbert de Clare and the bishops discussed the practical steps to be taken, the emissaries were probably empowered to do nothing more than serve as letter-bearers.

"On the next day, with the friars, preachers and minor, acting as intermediaries, it was decided that Edward and Henry should surrender themselves to Earl Simon in the place of their fathers, the Kings of England and Germany, under the hope of peace and quiet, so that there might be deliberate discussions as to which of the realm be kept and which overthrown, and that the captives might thereupon be given back without ransom."[3]

The Mise of Lewes, setting out the provisional peace terms, has not survived, and although it has been commonly believed that its contents were clearly set out in Rishanger's *Chronicon de Duobus Bellis* and elsewhere, Denholm-Young has shown that this is not so.[2] This and similar documents related only to the amendment of a peace already made, and the immediate truce can have provided only the urgent safeguards needed by the victorious party and for the King's unconditional surrender. One of these would be an amnesty for Simon de Montfort and his followers and arrangements for the release of prisoners from former engagements. Another immediate condition of surrender may have been that Prince Edward and his cousin Henry of Almaine were to be hostages for their fathers' safety. In this way the King himself could retain the dignity of apparent freedom in public. Finally, there may have been some restatement in general terms of the main Provisions of Oxford.

The seven articles of the fuller peace terms appear, with little variation, in a number of chronicles, and they were no doubt intended to be a working basis for the new government but subject to amendment.

The first two confirmed the Provisions and named a body of arbitrators to enforce them. H. W. C. Davis wrote in *England under the Normans and Angevins*, "The beaten party negotiated better than they fought." Certainly the choice of arbitrators and the system of voting seemed destined to help the royalists and make the Mise unworkable. The committee consisted of the Archbishop of Rouen, the Bishop of London, Hugh le Despenser who was again appointed justiciar and Peter le Chamberleyn the chief minister of Louis IX. In the event of their being divided a casting vote was given to Guy Foulquois Bishop of Sabino, the papal legate. In fact, this meant that the Pope through his legate was able to bring his powerful influence to bear against the new government, and when Guy Foulquois was found to be mischief-making and refused entry to England the committee itself could no longer operate.

The third article directed that these arbitrators should swear to choose only English counsellors. The fourth said that the King was bound to act on the advice of his counsellors in administering justice and choosing ministers "and shall not exercise his vast liberties until the old debt shall have been paid and he can live of his own without oppressing the merchants and the poor . . ."[3]

Under the fifth article Prince Edward and Prince Henry of Almaine were to be taken as hostages. The sixth provided for the indemnity of the Earls of Gloucester and Leicester and their associates. The last article stated that the terms of peace should be amended as necessary and confirmed by the following Easter. Peace was declared on 25 May and published in London on the 11 June.

Stephen de Berksted, Bishop of Chichester, took a leading part in these peace negotiations, and some writers have believed that it was he and not Walter de Cantelupe who was with the baronial army at Lewes. The Bishop of Worcester was such an active supporter of the barons that he was probably with them through these important days, but Stephen de Berksted, in whose See the battle took place, is mentioned in the Song of Lewes and as he was suspended from office and excommunicated in the following year he clearly played a part in forming the new system of government.

As soon as the armistice had been agreed, Simon was anxious to be on the move. Provisions were running short, and manpower was needed on the land again. All over England estates had suffered from the ravages and neglect resulting from civil war. Also, there were immediate problems of government to be tackled and there could be no security until the Cinque Ports and the royal castles were in baronial hands.

Unrest and violence had spread through the country like some contagious disease, and lawless elements everywhere took advantage of the state of rebellion. For more than ten years order had been kept in towns and villages by a form of police system laid down by law. In every city and town a number of men guarded the gates each night, and in every village, according to size, from four to six "stout and good men, armed with bows and arrows and other light weapons" were responsible for keeping the peace. Now it needed stronger guards and harsh measures to restore order. Armed robbers lay in wait for travellers, and plundered many of the northern chieftains on their way home after the battle.

The royal hostages, Prince Edward and Henry of Almaine, were first sent to Dover in the custody of Henry de Montfort. Only a few years before Edward had publicly knighted his cousins, Henry and Simon de Montfort. They had grown up together as friends. Now his confinement appears to have been neither strict nor painful. His youngest de Montfort cousin, Eleanor, was allowed to write to him in prison.

Henry of Almaine was one of the tragic figures in this story. He was a gentle boy, perhaps overshadowed by his ebullient and self-opinionated father and his mother Isabel, daughter of the great regent William of Pembroke. He was by nature both loyal and peaceable, but he found himself fighting against a man he admired and many of his own friends, involved in a struggle for power which he never coveted for himself.

On Saturday 17 May the King dismissed his court and was moved to Battle. Care was taken to give the illusion that he was a willing negotiator and that orders carried the weight of his authority, but in fact he was as helpless as a performing bear. He was taken where the new rulers decided and paraded before his subjects with all the outward respect due to his rank, but he was powerless. On 21 May he was moved on again to Canterbury, and each day orders were sent out under his seal to strengthen the hand of the new government. The prisoners at Northampton were to be released, and the University of Oxford had its position restored. There was a prohibition on the bearing of arms without a licence, and the penalty was death or amputation. Special wardens were appointed to keep the peace in each county, and Simon de Montfort's sons were among them. Royalists were removed from the office of sheriff, and royal castles were handed over to baronial hands. Even the Jews were allowed to enjoy the new peace, for they were removed from the talons of Richard of Cornwall and commended to the protection of the Mayor of London.

Richard of Cornwall had escaped with his life but he had to part with much of his money. When the royal party eventually reached London he and many other important prisoners were lodged in the Tower and had to pay heavily for their freedom. The King was kept at Saint Paul's.

Remembering with bitterness the Mise of Amiens it seems surprising that the victorious barons turned again to France for arbitration. But there were powerful reasons for this. It was still from France that the worst threat could come. With hostile elements just across such a narrow strip of water, as well as divided loyalties at home, the new regime desperately needed to bolster its position. Recognition by France would be a major diplomatic success. Also, feudal habits of thought died hard. Henry III personally owed allegiance in respect of certain lands to Louis IX of France, and in other ways too England was subservient to her more powerful neighbour. It would be a bold step for such a small and vulnerable kingdom to defy public opinion in France as well as in Rome. Most revolutionaries presently seek to become respectable and to have their governments recognized by greater powers. And since every action was taken and every proclamation issued in the name of the King, who still served as the mouthpiece of the government, it must be technically his wish that the new state of affairs should be accepted by France.

On 22 June a Parliament met in London, where is not known, but not at the Palace of Westminster which to Henry's great grief had been damaged by fire two years before and was not fully restored. It was attended by the magnates and bishops and each county was ordered to send four "discreet and loyal knights chosen by them" to represent "the whole community of the realm of England". This was not a new step. In 1258 the King had issued a similar summons, probably at the insistence of the barons.

There is no record of the discussions that took place at this Parliament or how long it sat, but it was attended by barons and bishops of both parties. With the advantage of numbers on the royalist side, de Montfort no doubt hoped to adjust the balance by stronger representation of "the community of the realm", and to give added force to the statement that was to be drawn up known as the *Forma Regiminis*, "A Form for the Government of the King and Kingdom".

"This is the form of peace approved in common and in concord by the Lord the King, the Lord Edward his son, by all the prelates and lords, and by the whole community of the realm of England, to continue firm, stable and unshaken both during the reign of the King and of Prince Edward after his death, until the treaty previously settled between the said King and the barons at Lewes by the form of a certain *Mise* be fulfilled."[4]

The new government was formed. At its head was a triumvirate of Stephen de Berksted, Bishop of Chichester, "my beloved and faithful" Earl of Leicester and Gilbert, Earl of Gloucester. They appointed an executive of nine to govern in the name of the King.

The two "estates of the realm" were the aristocracy and the

Church, the one dominated by the King and the other by the Pope. No new government could hope to enforce its will unless it embodied these two estates, and ultimately it was fighting a losing battle if it was opposed by the leading monarchists and the powerful Curia. The new form of government was an attempt to rule moderately and wisely, with safeguards against corruption. "And the counsellors and all officials, greater and less, shall swear on their appointment that they will faithfully execute their offices according to their power, to the honour of God and the Church and to the profit of the King and kingdom, without reward except the food and drink which are customarily presented at their table. But if the said counsellors, or any, or one, of them, shall be guilty of malversation in the administration committed to them or him, or shall be changed for any other cause, the King, by the counsel of the three first elected or nominated, shall remove those whom he sees fit to remove, and appoint or supply in the place of them, through the same persons, other fit and faithful men . . ."[4]

But already, in spite of stringent efforts to establish order, danger threatened. The royalist defenders of Tonbridge had remained under arms and made their way to Bristol where they formed a rallying point for others. There were signs of disaffection in the victorious baronial party, and loud complaints about the way in which the spoils had been distributed. The Church of Rome kept a watching brief, and encouraged any signs of mutiny and disunity. In France the English Queen and her friends, now joined by the fugitives from Lewes, were preparing for an immediate invasion. On 10 July the King, no doubt under orders, wrote to King Louis, "Do not allow hostile preparations to be made in France under cover of liberating the hostages given at Lewes."

There was an immediate call to arms, and this national danger briefly united the barons and stirred a fleeting sense of patriotism in the people. A large army, royalist and baronial, encamped on Barham Downs near Canterbury, conveniently placed to hurry to any vulnerable point on the Kent coast, and prepared to drive away the invaders. But as on so many later occasions England was saved from invasion by adverse winds, and the force that had collected across the Channel never put to sea.

It is possible to take the view that the barons' rebellion was only the reflection of a deeper and more important struggle between the Church of Rome and the Church in England. At the same time, in the thirteenth century it was hardly possible to separate the clerical from the secular. The Pope was one of the political powers of the world, and held a politician's weapon in the monopoly of propaganda. The parish priest not only advised his flock, but he commanded them. He told them what to believe as well as how to behave, and every order sent out from Rome reached the village pulpit unless there was a priest brave enough to resist and so risk his living or even his life. The Church held a large proportion of the country's wealth and all learning was rooted in it, and when all other influences had struggled for supremacy in men's minds, the Church still had the threat of Hell and eternal damnation to tip the balance. As Matthew Paris once wrote, the Pope "had no bowels of affection for England".

There was no way in which the new government could evade the Pope's stranglehold. His power was felt in every section of the community and in every aspect of national life, not only in England but on the continent. He could interfere with trade, order boycotts, impose extortionate taxes, and dictate the policy of most of Europe's rulers. The small, brave band that defied the King of England were challenging a more far reaching and powerful enemy than they knew. From the moment the Pope pronounced the Provisions of Oxford to be null and void the baronial party was doomed, for ranged against it were most of the resources of Christendom. Out of their brave struggle were to come valuable reforms and a new stirring spirit of self respect, both in the English Church and in the middle class of society, but it was mainly the dictatorship of the Church of Rome that made it almost impossible for de Montfort to establish any durable reforms during his brief term of office. Rome only understood the concept of absolute monarchy, and it was Edward I therefore who was able to give those same reforms a permanent place in England's constitution.

The new government decided to try and win over the enemy diplomatically, and the bishops of London, Winchester and Worcester, with Hugh le Despenser the justiciar, Peter de Montfort who was now freed from Northampton, and the Archdeacon of Oxford were sent over to treat with the French arbiters named in the Mise of Lewes. The visit failed utterly. Guy Foulquois, formerly Bishop of Sabino, was now Archbishop of Narbonne, and one of the most powerful men in the Church. Later he was to be Pope Clement IV, and a strong advocate of the theories of Roger Bacon. Now he refused to acknowledge the Mise of Lewes, excommunicated the whole baronial party and threatened that their lands would be confiscated unless he was allowed to land in England. He also laid a boycott on any trade with England in wine, wheat and other commodities. There were riots in Boulogne where some of the envoys and their attendants were killed, and it is said that when the bishops reached Dover, the enraged customs guards snatched their documents and flung them into the sea.

The boycott was pointless, for trade was already almost at a standstill. The Cinque Ports, perhaps over-zealous in defending England's coastline, had closed their harbours to cargo, and the new government's views on commerce were far from liberal. Wyke commented, ". . . the Earl of Leicester, in order to tickle plebeian ears, had given out that the English might be well supplied without the intercourse of foreigners, which, however, was impossible, for the interchange of goods from diverse realms furnishes all sorts of advantages."

Prices rose sharply. Wine cost three times the normal figure and so did wax. Fine coloured cloth was soon out of reach of all but the rich, and as in Cromwell's dictatorship an unwilling people had to suffer puritanical restrictions. A few traders exploited their advantage, but the majority of them knew hard times and the country generally resented the changed way of life.

There were personal griefs too. Young Eleanor of Castile, the wife of Prince Edward, had never been separated from her husband for long before. She waited unhappily at Windsor for his return, and received a peremptory letter ordering her to Westminster ". . . because we will undertake to excuse you toward the said Edward your lord, and will preserve you harmless". The months apart must have brought sorrow to them both. She was a gifted and courageous woman, and Edward showed his devotion to her on her death in 1280 when he erected crosses at the thirteen places where her coffin rested on its journey from Harby to London. Her heart was given to the church of the Friars Preachers of London, and her body was buried at Westminster Abbey.

In September Henry of Almaine was taken from Dover and sent as envoy to the King of France "in order more fully to treat of and confirm the peace". Nine bishops went bail for his return, and three French envoys swore that he should not be held in France. Even so, this action suggests a degree of faith in the young man's personal honour. Some slight progress was made. Emissaries were exchanged between England and France to discuss amendments, and King Henry commended to King Louis the new terms of peace which he declared "well suited to God, to ourselves and to our kingdom". But those Provisions of Oxford relating to the rights of aliens were not amended.

There are indications of growing intrigue, both abroad and at home. Although the King's letters to his wife in France, and to King Louis, are models of propriety and follow the Government line, it is quite possible that a more private correspondence was also carried on between them. It would not be difficult for members of the royal household, or men already growing jealous of de Montfort's powers, to arrange a postal service for the humiliated king.

On 18 November 1264 Henry wrote to his wife in France, "The King to the Queen of England, health and sincerely affectionate love . . . blessed be God, that we have a well-grounded hope of having a firm and good peace in our kingdom, on which account be cheerful and merry. Moreover, we have heard that certain persons at this time propose to make a sale or alienation of our lands, and of the prerogative of ourself and our son in those parts, to the disinheritance of us and our heirs, against our will, which you ought by no means either to wish or permit, wherefore we send to command you that you suffer nothing to be done or attempted in such matters . . ."[5]

He wrote in similar terms to Louis IX, and there was clearly some move afoot to pledge his remaining property in France to raise men and money. The letter does not sound at all like his own spontaneous work, nor can it have deceived the French King.

Jealousies and feuds were now splitting the reforming party. The bright vision of a new world was tarnished as self-interest took its place. There was a revival of allegiance to the King, instinctive to them all, and perhaps a growing sympathy and affection for the humiliated men whom they had often scorned but rarely feared. If hardships were to be borne they preferred to suffer under a rightful monarch than an upstart dictator.

While many of his supporters fell away Simon was left with his family, a few close and faithful friends, a strong following in the church and among the poorer classes who, with little to lose or gain, still regarded him as their saviour. He was also hampered by the need to take the King with him wherever he went, both to cloak all his actions with royal authority and to prevent royal conspiracy.

The hostage princes were evidently moved from place to place, for at one time they were recorded as being at Berkhamsted, and at another at Wallingford, the castle which Richard of Cornwall had once lavishly furnished for his own use. The care of them seems to have been little more than "house arrest", although some chronicles describe them as prisoners, and others as being "on parole". Their freedom would be a great asset to the royalist party and the partisans from Tonbridge who were still encamped at Bristol, reinforced by men who escaped from Lewes, made an attempt at a rescue. The guards threatened to hurl Prince Edward off the castle ramparts fastened to a *mangonel*, a siege weapon designed as a powerful catapult to hurl rocks over the battlements. The Prince himself had to appeal for his own safety.

> "That hii wolde Sir Edward vawe out to hom sende,
> Tithered with a mangonel home with hom to lede."[6]

Edward was transferred to Simon's own fortress at Kenilworth where his aunt, the Countess of Leicester, received him with every courtesy and kindness "and wat she might dude hom of solas".[6] And there restraint was so easy and faith so great that Mortimer, Clifford and Leyburne, who were now three of the mainsprings of the royalist cause, were allowed to meet the King at Pershore one December day, and then travel under safe conduct to Kenilworth to talk to their friend Prince Edward for "the promotion of peace". It was probably during that meeting that plans were outlined to rescue the Prince and restore the King and the old guard to power.

X

"Simon de Montfort's Idea was to make the Parliament more Representative . . . thus causing the only Good Parliament in History."
(*1066 And All That.*)

WESTMINSTER HAS been the home of the Kings of England and the seat of government since the time of Edward the Confessor, and perhaps even earlier. There is a tradition that Cnut lived there, early in the eleventh century, and that it was the waters of the Thames that he commanded to turn back. It is quite possible. Westminster was built by the broad Thames estuary where fording was safe and easy in fine weather, and small tidal streams, like the Tyburn, formed a delta. Water lapped against the palace walls, St. James's Park was a lake, and the little medieval town may have looked something like a corner of Venice. The two arms of the Watling Street from Dover and Chester met at the river crossing, and a highway ran from Westminster to the City of London.

The Palace of Westminster could better be described as a village consisting of royal apartments, banqueting chambers, assembly halls, courts of law and other rooms where the King personally or through his agents could administer justice and collect taxes. There he "lived over the shop". Some of the buildings were already old when Henry III lavished money and artistic skill on their improvement. Others, like Whitehall Palace which Hubert de Burgh built for his own use, were modern. Fire caused such frequent damage or destruction that rebuilding went on throughout the Middle Ages.

The Great Council was not always summoned to Westminster, but met in other places at the King's convenience. Eight times it assembled at Gloucester. Occasionally it was called to the Augustinian Priory at Merton, ten miles south-west of London. In 1258 it met at Oxford, and several times it used the Temple, the headquarters of the wealthy and influential Knights Templar. During the thirteenth century, however, as Parliament came to meet more regularly and to act as a representative consultative body, it became the established custom to meet at Westminster.

It was there, probably in the Great Hall, that Parliament was to meet on 20 January 1265, and the summons that was issued a month before marked an important constitutional advance.

"Henry, by the grace of God King of England, Lord of Ireland, and Duke of Aquitaine, to the venerable father in Christ, Robert, by the same grace Bishop of Durham, greeting.

"Since after the grave occurrences of disturbance which have long prevailed in our kingdom, our dearest first-born son Edward, has been given as a hostage for securing and confirming peace in our realm, and as the said disturbance, blessed be God, is abated, for providing deliverance in a salutary manner for the same and confirming and thoroughly completing full security of tranquillity and peace to the honour of God and the profit of our whole kingdom, as well as concerning divers other matters which we are unwilling to decide without your counsel and that of the other prelates and magnates of our realm, it is needful that we have speech with them. We command you, desiring you by the faith and love by which you are bound to us, that putting aside all excuse and other business, you will be with us in London on the octave of Saint Hilary next, to treat and to give your advice on the said matters, with the prelates and barons whom we shall summon thither. And this, as you love us and our honour, and your own, and the common tranquillity of the kingdom, in no wise omit.

"Witness the King, at Worcester, the fourteenth day of December.

"Also it is commanded all the sheriffs of England that they cause two knights from the loyal, honest and discreet knights of each shire to come to the King at London as above.

"Also in the same form it is written to the citizens of York, the citizens of Lincoln, and to other towns of England, that they should send in the said form two of the discreet, loyal, and honest citizens and burgesses.

"Also in the same form it is commanded to the barons and good men of the Cinque Ports."[1]

Individual writs were sent to the Archbishop and the Dean of York, the Bishop of Carlisle, to ten abbots and nine priors of the northern province and to ten bishops and four deans of the southern province. Ten days later a similar writ was sent to 55 abbots, 26 priors, the Master of the Temple and the Prior of the Hospitallers; and to five earls and eighteen barons.

After the summons had gone out Simon de Montfort, taking the King with him, went to celebrate Christmas at Kenilworth. Even the faithful Rishanger censures him for his extravagant ostentation, and it is difficult to guess whether this man, normally so austere and frugal, was now enjoying the rewards of an ambitious policy, or merely providing what seemed necessary for the comfort and dignity of the king. Simon de Montfort can hardly have felt much confidence about the future. Although he still appeared to be the paramount ruler and was strongly supported by the Church, most of the great barons were either openly hostile or becoming evasive and silent.

The January Parliament has rightly become famous for what it was, not for what it did. For the first time not only the knights of the shires, who were accustomed to visiting Westminster on legal business or representing the lesser barons in Parliament, but members of the new urban middle class which had until then played no part in national affairs, were to take their places beside the powerful churchmen and leading magnates who decided matters of state. As a concept of democracy it was more illusory than real. No one can have imagined for a moment that these burgesses, sent from the nearly two hundred cities and boroughs throughout England, were to be allowed to offer opinions or play any active part in the government. They were to be there as witnesses; to see justice done and spread the news throughout the country that England was now wisely and fairly governed. They were also there to pledge their constituencies to pay a share of the aid that this government, like the old one, would demand. Above all, they were needed to add weight of numbers to the pitifully thin ranks of de Montfort's supporters. All he dared to muster from the governing class as we have seen were five earls, eighteen barons and a hundred and twenty churchmen.

The introduction of this new class of citizen into Parliament was not even a popular step. The knights of the shires were too poor to pay their own expenses at Westminster and had to claim them from the barons. Now the burgesses became an expense to their boroughs, and brought back no obvious benefit. In fact this broader conception of Parliament, which became an integral part of England's unique political system, sprang out of weakness rather than strength. When de Montfort summoned what Disraeli described as "that fatal drollery called a representative government" what later looked like the progressive act of a statesman was in part a hopeful expedient.

Again there is little information about the proceedings of this Parliament. "On this parliament, on St. Valentine's day (14 February), it was published in the chapter house at Westminster that the lord king had bound himself by his oath and charter that neither he nor the lord Edward would in the future trouble nor cause trouble to the earls of Leicester and Gloucester, the citizens of London or any of their adherents, by reason of anything done in the time of the late disturbances in the kingdom, and he expressly commanded that the charters of liberties and of the forest which were made in the ninth year of his reign should be inviolably kept with the other articles which were made into statutes in the month of June in the forty-eighth year of his reign."[2]

In March the royal princes "who had given themselves as hostages at the battle of Lewes until peace should be restored to England, were set at liberty by the lord king freely and quietly, in the presence of all the people in the great hall of Westminster, and then were read certain letters binding upon the lord king and the lord Edward in which was contained how and under what penalty they promised on their oath to preserve the tranquillity and peace of the realm. Then nine bishops in their pontificals with lighted candles excommunicated all those who should dare anything against the charters of liberties and of the forest, or against the statutes made in the preceding year".[2]

This act of showmanship was clearly intended to impose long term restraint on the monarchy and discourage their supporters. Edward had to swear that he would not leave the country for three years and would keep a bodyguard of trustworthy Englishmen; he would not appeal to the Pope for absolution; he would surrender as guarantees five royal castles for a period of five years; and he would "not bring nor allow foreigners to be brought into the realm of England, and if any came and he had been forewarned by the king's council, he would thwart them with all his might".[2] Finally, as well as pledging all his lands, tenements, honours and dignities as forfeit if he broke his word, his cousin Henry was to remain a hostage on his behalf, in the custody of Henry de Montfort, until "Saint Peter's Chains" (1 August).

It is confusing to learn that after this ceremony the prisoners were taken back into captivity. No doubt Simon de Montfort had good reason to fear and distrust his nephew. Not only was Edward an energetic young man and a clever military commander, but he was a determined and ambitious monarchist, and more and more the royalists and the waverers were attracted to him, rather than to the King, as their future leader.

Parliament was dismissed. All these proceedings were embodied in an Act of 31 March 1265 and the burgesses and the knights of the shires were free to return home and tell their constituents that peace was established and the new regime strongly in command. They possibly also reported that Prince Edward was free again and that the King was a willing partner, if not the predominating power, in all these matters. It was a false picture. Not only was the King helpless and Prince Edward back in strict captivity but Simon de Montfort was neither in control of events nor of his own party. Under a veneer of stability the cracks were appearing, and the most damaging of them was jealousy.

There is no doubt that in the first flush of victory Simon de Montfort and his friends, especially the churchmen, intended to show mercy and moderation, to establish peace through a stable government, and to refrain from those vindictive and greedy actions that so often follow victory and the seizure of political power. Prisoners on both sides were to be released without ransom, and as far as possible it was determined to heal the wounds and not to exact a price. In practice things worked out rather differently. For military reasons it was necessary to clip the wings of the royalists, and for financial reasons some ransom money was needed to repair the ravages of war. Men who have risked everything for a speculative revolutionary cause often expect to be paid. The crusading spirit rapidly grew weaker, and the years of bloodshed seemed to have reduced the country to a state of exhaustion and apathy. The enthusiastic band of idealists, and the students from Oxford and the citizens of London, had returned to normal life. Apart from a small nucleus of loyal friends, de Montfort was constantly jostled by the inevitable hangers-on looking for jobs and personal gain.

Justly or unjustly, Simon de Montfort himself was bitterly resented by many, including former admirers. Wyke says that when the royalist estates were confiscated he took eighteen baronies for himself. T. W. Horsfield wrote in his *History and Antiquities of Lewes and its Vicinity* (1824) ". . . his tyrannous exercise of the power which the chance of war had thrown into his hands, is corroborated by so many circumstances, that we must be indeed wilfully blind, not to recognize in the popular chieftain, an unprincipled, overbearing, and ambitious spirit". On the other hand the writer of the *Song of Lewes*, who was just as biased the other way, wrote: "His habitual prayer to God was that divine grace would preserve him unstained by avarice and the covetousness of worldly goods, which had ensnared so many in his day."

When properties and titles changed hands so frequently it is difficult to learn the truth. Wardenship and ownership were not the same thing, and Simon had good military reasons for taking the strongholds in strategic places under his direct or indirect control. He had few friends he could trust. Among them were his own foolish but well-meaning sons, and the responsibilities he gave to them incensed some of his more competent but less reliable supporters. When Simon died he held,

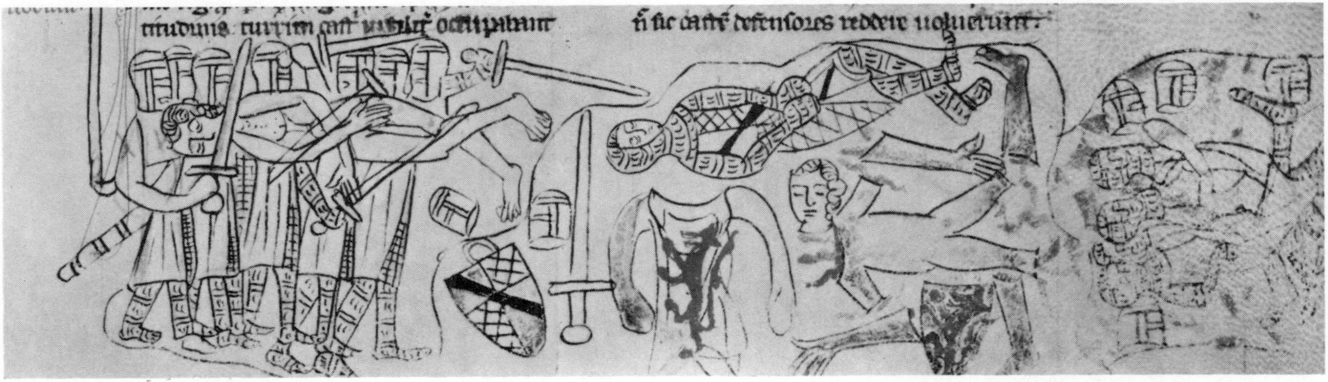

Top left, Simon de Montfort arrests the King at Lewes. *Top right*, Henry III slays Simon de Montfort at Evesham—two imaginative sketches from the *Chronicle Laudunense a Bruto usque ad* 1338 (MS Cotton Nero A IV). *Below*, the mutilation of Simon de Montfort's body at Evesham, from the Chronicle of John of Oxonede

Top, an early illustration of a windmill from the Decretals of Gregory IX and, *below*, another illumination from the same work according to the records, no more than his hereditary property and office of High Steward, and a property in Cheshire gained by legal exchange. On the other hand Gilbert de Clare, who complained most loudly of Simon's greed, had amassed the estates of Philip de Savoy and William de Valence as well as some of de Warenne's properties, although Simon considered "that he ought to think it quite enough to have saved all his own property by the battle".

Winston Churchill once wrote: "Dictators ride to and fro upon tigers which they dare not dismount." It is difficult not to believe that if Simon de Montfort had been less rigid and more tactful, a more experienced politician and a more generous and imaginative thinker, if his courage had been tempered by a little humour and he had exercised magnanimity and charm, he might have ridden the tiger more successfully.

Of all the personal quarrels that crippled the government the most serious was between Simon de Montfort and Gilbert de Clare. It seemed almost traditional for Gloucester and Leicester to fall out. Like his father, de Clare could be truculent, jealous and opinionated, and he probably regarded himself with some justification as senior in rank. He had inherited great wealth at an early age and his earldom could be traced back in his family to a natural son of Henry I. His father had made his mark on his times, and towards the end of his life had been a sworn enemy of de Montfort. At the age of twenty-two, his youthful hero worship changed to a soured and resentful hatred. He now saw the older man as a foreign upstart and was afraid of finding himself on the losing side.

"In this year, while Edward, the King's son, was still held in ward in the Castle of Hereford, dissension arose between Simon Earl of Leicester, and Gilbert de Clare on the following occasion.

"The Earl of Leicester was not content with keeping the King of England a captive, but took the royal castles in his own power, disposing of the whole realm according to his will. And his chief offence was that he claimed the entire possession of the revenues of the realm, the ransom of the captives, and other profits, which according to the convention ought to have been equally divided between them. He seemed to be held in contempt also by his sons, who at that time caused a tournament to be proclaimed at Dunstable against the Earl of Gloucester, to which came the Londoners and a vast multitude of knights and armed men.

"When their father Simon heard this he rebuked their presumption, straitly enjoining them to cease from their undertaking and threatening that if they did not obey his orders he would put them in such place that they should no more enjoy the light of sun or moon. When the Earl of Gloucester heard this he was incensed beyond measure, and many who were ready for the aforesaid tournament bore it ill to be frustrated in their desire, especially on account of the expense which they had incurred in the matter, uttering reproaches and saying of the earl that it was ridiculous that this foreigner should presume to put the whole realm under his yoke. And it increased Gilbert's indignation that the said Simon, when asked by him to return to him the King of Almaine and certain other captives taken in the battle by Gilbert and his men, replied with brevity or levity. For which cause the old friendship was turned into hate, so much so that neither the consideration of his oath nor former devotion could thenceforth pacify the said Gilbert.

"And Gilbert went over to the party of the nobler knights of the March," (Roger Mortimer, James Audley, Roger de Clifford and others), "whom Earl Simon had ordered by public edict to leave the realm, and joined them in alliance. They were joined also by John de Warenne, Earl of Surrey and Sussex, and William de Valence, Earl of Pembroke, who landed at Pembroke on their way by sea to the west parts of Wales. Therefore Earl Simon, taking the King with him, set out for Hereford and collected a strong force that he might crush the said knights. Meanwhile an endeavour was made by certain prelates to restore the Earls of Leicester and Gloucester to their former union; but they could in no wise succeed."[3]

By May 1265 the situation was growing desperate. Simon de Montfort could not be in several places at once, and wherever he went he was hampered by the captive king who had to be "honourably and royally received, the earl showing him all reverence". There were outbreaks of fighting in the north. The

Earl of Gloucester had gathered an army together and made an agreement with Roger de Mortimer in Wales. The exiles from France were mustering their force in Pembrokeshire and the friends of Prince Edward who had failed to rescue him from Wallingford were again a source of trouble in Worcestershire and Herefordshire.

The military position was dangerous, and Simon once again tried to gain a diplomatic advantage. He sent a letter dated from Hereford on 18 May to King Louis of France. It was signed by the King, Simon de Montfort, Peter de Montfort, Roger de St. John and Giles d'Argentein. Again it was Henry of Almaine who was sent to "ask and require, with all possible urgency, by our prayers and by our love, that your serenity will be pleased to deliver to speedy effect those matters which concern us; for we, who cordially desire the expedition of the said business, will always be prompt and ready for all things, relating to these matters, on our own behalf and on that of our dependents, as our nephew, who is more fully acquainted with our willingness on this point, may also report to you by word of mouth."[4]

It was too late. War again became inevitable when ten days later Prince Edward escaped from custody at Hereford by a ruse. He asked permission to arrange a little innocent fun racing his own horse against those of his guards outside the town.

> "Leave was to him granted, God wot to what end,
> So that Sir Edward without town began to wend.
> A steed he began to spur well for the mastery,
> And with him he had of knights a fair company.
> And then he took another, and weary them made anon,
> And then he took the third, the best of each one.
> As it was before bespoke the which he should trust,
> He spurred it first softly as him little lust.
> When he was a little from the folk, with spur he
> smote to ground,
> The sides ran a-blood in a little stound.
> Then of steeds a good and quick they found.
> Away went this good knight. When he was out of hand,
> 'Lordings,' he said, 'have now good day,

And greet well my father the King; and I shall, if I may,
Both see him well betime and out of ward him do.'
What need of a long tale? He escaped so,
And to the castle of Wigmore his way soon he nome.
There was joy and bliss enow, when he was thither come."[5]

The links in the royalist chain were now almost complete again. Only the King himself was missing, and he may have served a more useful purpose in enemy hands as an inspiration to his supporters. In the King's name Simon ordered the Bishop of London to excommunicate Prince Edward, and publicly denounced the Earl of Gloucester, John de Warenne and their friends as rebels and traitors. The garrison at Bristol Castle was ordered to surrender to the baronial army, but refused. Civil war had broken out again with all the attendant cruelty and misery.

Prince Edward and his army wisely strengthened their hold on the border country by taking Chester, Shrewsbury and Bridgnorth and then moved to the royalist stronghold of Worcester. There was severe and prolonged fighting at Gloucester where de Montfort ravaged de Clare's lands before marching into Wales where he spent nearly a month trying to raise troops. He promised his daughter Eleanor in marriage to Llewelyn ap Griffith, the last native Prince of Wales, and gave him royal recognition of his status in return for help, but the expedition was not a success. The English soldiers were uneasy in the mountainous and unfriendly country and suitable food was scarce.

Simon de Montfort was now in considerable danger. His army was small and exhausted, and the Bristol Channel cut him off from reinforcements. While he waited at Newport in Monmouthshire a rescue fleet prepared to sail across from Bristol, but the armed ships of the royalists attacked and scattered it. With great difficulty Simon and his hungry army crossed the Usk at Abergavenny and made their way to Hereford.

Young Simon de Montfort, who had been appointed Warden of the Peace for Surrey and Sussex, escorted his mother from her castle at Odiham to stay in greater safety at Dover. At the end of June he was ordered by his father to attack the royalists wherever he could, but while he was accordingly besieging

Pevensey Castle another urgent message arrived asking him to go to help his father with all possible speed. Whether the messenger failed to convey the imperative need for haste, or whether through lack of judgment Simon waited to enlist more troops, it is impossible to say. He appears to have spent three days in London, where he undoubtedly appealed for help. He paused to make a senseless attack on Winchester and slaughter a number of Jews. The Waverley Annals record that he rested for three days at Oxford, but there too he may have increased his army. The journey of 135 miles from Winchester to Kenilworth took fifteen days, and it was 31 July when he reached the comparative safety of his home.

Prince Edward and his army now stood between de Montfort and the relief force at Kenilworth, and on the following morning after a forced night march he surprised his cousin Simon and his flagging troops "who, as we have said, had on the previous day, unfortunately for themselves, abandoned the castle with the idea of sleeping in the various houses adjoining it. This was why they left the castle: they chose to go out for baths so that, after rising from their beds at daybreak comfortably bathed, they might because of the baths bear themselves more sprucely for battle on the following day, and in the town they could have a great abundance of vessels for bathing than they could well have in a castle . . .

"When, in the middle of the night, Edward's men burst in upon Simon's sleeping forces, they raised a very loud noise throughout the town, and when these heard it, they were exceedingly terrified by the awful clamour, and especially were they seized with fear and trembling, terror and dismay when they heard the noise of horses, and armed men shouting horribly at them and saying, 'Get up, get up, rise, rise from your beds, and come out, you traitors and servants of that worst and most obstinate traitor, Simon, for by God's death you are all dead men!'

"Then those who had been thus shamefully betrayed got up and escaped by the back of the houses, leaving behind them their horses, arms and clothes, and all the baggage which they possessed. Some of them might be seen running off entirely naked, others wearing nothing but a pair of breeches, and others in shirts and breeches only, for of all of them there were very few, probably not one, able to dress completely. Many of them carried off their clothes under their arms, and just as they had hurried out of the houses in this plight in the hottest haste—God in His infinite mercy giving them their lives—Edward's men rushed in and carried off the horses and armour and everything else which the fugitives had left behind them."[6]

This time young Simon was lucky enough to escape with a few friends and reach the little town of Alcester, about twenty miles south-west. His relief force was now impotent. Twenty bannerets, including several who had fought at Lewes, were now prisoners at Kenilworth and the best of their horses and arms were lost.

While Edward's back was turned Simon de Montfort made one last despairing effort and pushed his tired and hungry army across the Severn by boat, four miles downstream from Worcester at the village of Kempsey. There, with his sons Henry and Guy and, of course, the King and his entourage, he spent the night of 2 August.

The Manor of Kempsey belonged to Walter de Cantelupe the Bishop of Worcester. No doubt the two old friends talked together far into the night, remembering Robert Grosseteste and Adam Marsh and other former colleagues, retracing the story of their efforts and their triumphs right to this point of imminent failure. They probably tried to comfort and encourage each other with false hopes, and the bishop prayed again for God's blessing on the cause he believed in so passionately.

On the following day, Monday 3 August, de Montfort pressed on toward Kenilworth still hoping to meet his son with a strong army to reinforce his own. That night was spent at Evesham which lies in a loop of the River Avon and so is hemmed in on three sides. To the north, the open side, the ground rises fairly steeply. From a military standpoint the position was most dangerous. For such an experienced soldier to allow himself to be trapped there suggests either that he failed to foresee the risk of attack or that he was too exhausted and despairing to exercise his usual keen judgment. He was a man of nearly sixty and the hardships of the past months had possibly dulled his alert and vigilant mind. It is said that King Henry persuaded him to rest there, where the lovely Benedictine Abbey would provide suitable royal lodging. With only a few dedicated friends left, and his remaining troops in a state of near-mutinous despair, Simon no longer exercised his judgment, or enforced his strict standards of discipline. One of his men, Ralph de Ardern, was treacherously keeping Prince Edward informed of his enemy's movements.

This time it was the Prince who showed the cunning of an experienced commander. On that same Monday evening he set off from Worcester towards the north-west as if making for Shrewsbury, and no doubt made sure that this news reached the baronial camp. Suddenly he turned about and marched rapidly through the night south-east towards Evesham. At the same time Roger de Mortimer and Gilbert de Clare were also converging on the town with their armies to cut off any possible retreat by the river crossings.

The main street of Evesham crossed the river at the bottom of the loop and climbed the hill to meet a road running east and west which was probably the main route from London to Worcester. Early on Tuesday morning, 4 August, after attending mass with the King and for the last time receiving absolution from Walter de Cantelupe, Simon led his army north out of the town. It was a thin column of cavalry, probably no more than a few hundred, that jogged along the cobbled street with harness jingling and brought the people out of their cottages to see them pass. As the first ranks climbed the slope they saw an army approaching from the north.

The news brought fresh heart to them all, for when Simon climbed the Abbey tower he saw in the distance the emblazoned banners of the de Montforts. For a moment he was deceived, but then, above the ranks that followed, he made out the lions of Prince Edward and the chevrons of de Clare. He watched the orderly formations with a fleeting sense of pride. " 'By the arm of Saint James they come on well. They learned that order from me.' " And then, his last hopeless prayer. " 'May God have mercy on our souls, for our bodies are the foe's.' "[3]

The engagement was brief and inglorious. It lasted barely an hour or two and amounted to a massacre rather than a battle. A mob of ill-armed Welshmen who had followed de Montfort across the border turned and fled, to be cut down in the cornfields as they tried to hide from the relentless royalists. Robert of Gloucester, who was thirty miles away at the time, describes a thunderstorm that raged over the battlefield.

"Such was the murder of Evesham, for battle none it was,
And therewith Jesus Christ well ill pleased was,
As he showed by tokens both grisly and good.
As befell with Himself when He died on the rood,
That through all the earth darkness there was enow,
So also the while the good men at Evesham men slew,
In the north-west a dark storm there arose
Suddenly swart enough, that many a man agros.
And it overcast all the land that men might scarce see,
A grislier weather than it was might not on earth be.
A few drops of rain there fell great enow.
This token fell in this land when men these men slew,
For thirty miles from thence this saw Robert
Who first this book made and was well sore afraid."

It is said that as the enemy bore down upon the band of men surrounding their leader each implored the others to escape. All refused. There was no thought of surrender on their side nor of mercy on the other. Only the King, whose situation was both dangerous and bizarre, escaped severe hurt.

The story is told in the Melrose Chronicle. "As for King Henry, who had fostered injustice in England by means of foreigners, he went out in arms to wage this battle with Simon in order to restore justice to England, wearing, however, the armour of some other person. I might have said that the King had gone out to fight for the justice of England unless his escape from the battle and his restoration to royal power had again enabled him to have gathered together aliens against native Englishmen, and so the last error had become worse than the first.

"It seems then that the barons wished that the King should die with them, if it were necessary that they should die in the battle in which the King was engaged; their plan was that he should be unknown to his own adherents and should fall under the heavy weight of their blows.

"Being unable to fight like the others he kept calling out at the top of his voice, 'I am Henry, the old King of England'; swearing sometimes, 'By the love of God,' at other times, 'By God's head', and constantly affirming that he was the King; and he cried to the men who were hitting at him, 'Do not hit me, I am too old to fight.' It was his use and wont to swear such oaths as these.

"As he was thus exclaiming, they took his helmet off his head; and, discovering by his countenance that he really was the King, he was taken out of the battle."

Nothing could save the baronial army now. When Simon's horse was killed under him he continued to fight on foot, "stoutly like a giant for the liberties of England", but the end was near. "The gallant old man lay, with the few who remained faithful to him and to his cause, dead upon the field, and with him the curtain seemed to fall upon all that was free and noble in the land. The tempests which raged throughout the country that day were remarked as shadowing forth the grief of heaven. The accompanying darkness, which was so thick that in some places the monks could no longer see to chant their prayers, was nothing to that which must have fallen on many when they heard of the death of their protector."[7]

Simon's son Henry died beside him as well as Peter de Montfort, Hugh le Despenser, Ralph Basset, William de Perons and many more; in all, it was said, one hundred and sixty knights and gentlemen. The Earl of Leicester, pierced by blows from behind, died commending his soul to God, but his body was not left in peace.

"And among all others most ruth it was ido,
That sir Simon the old man dismembered was so,
For Sir William Mautravers (thanks have he none)
Carved off his feet and hands, and his limbs many one.
And his head they smote off and to Wigmore it sent
To dame Maud the Mortimer who right foully it shent;
But though that men limbed him, he bled not, men said,
And the hair-cloth was to his body nearest weed."[5]

Even some of the prisoners were butchered to death. Among those who narrowly survived were Guy de Montfort, who nearly died of his wounds; Henry de Hastings and Nicholas de Segrave who together so gallantly led the Londoners at Lewes; Humphrey de Bohun the son of the Earl of Hereford; and two sons of Peter de Montfort.

After Simon's body had been mutilated with almost ritualistic savagery the Benedictine monks came to the deserted battlefield to rescue what remained of his body and give it loving burial in the Abbey church, in the north transept under the High Altar. The Abbey, like the Priory of Saint Pancras at Lewes, was demolished by Henry VIII and is a total ruin, but for many years after the battle simple people came to worship at the tomb of the man they called a saint, and more than two hundred miracles were attributed to his power. The first, recorded in the Melrose Chronicle, concerned the hands, which were sewn up in a cloth and taken with Simon's head to Maud the wife of Roger de Mortimer. She was at prayer when the messenger arrived, and he took these grisly gifts and the news of the royalist victory into the chapel to her. Although the cloth remained intact, the hands of the martyr were seen by the whole congregation to stretch up, clasped in prayer, and Maud sent them back to Evesham.

A monk at Evesham left an account of the men and women who came seeking cures for themselves and their families and for their horses and cattle.[8] The first page of the manuscript is so badly defaced, evidently with hostile intention, that it cannot be deciphered but it appears to have described the Battle of Evesham. The rest deals with the miracles, and shows that men came from all parts of the country, from Canterbury, Salisbury, London, Northamptonshire, Leicestershire, Essex, and as far north as Newcastle. They came with congenital deformities, blindness, paralysis, fevers, and to intercede for people who had died from drowning or fire. All of them recovered, and often their testimony is witnessed by abbots, priors or women of high rank. The whole village of Cordebregge in Berkshire testified that a boy recovered his hearing after three years' deafness. "Guido de Phynele juxta Warrewyk" recovered after being paralysed for ten years. Most of the stories refer to "*mensuratus ad Comitem*" which means that a string used for measuring the relics of the earl was passed round the forehead of the diseased person and effected the cure.

In spite of every effort to prohibit them, pilgrims continued to visit de Montfort's shrine for more than twelve years and still in modern times he is remembered at Evesham. In 1918 a memorial cross was erected on the site of his burial by the Reverend James Manders Walker, D.D., then rector of Evesham, and every year on the Sunday nearest the anniversary of his death a service of thanksgiving is held to honour him.

"After the precious death of this Simon, the Friars Minor, whom he had always loved as became a religious man, and who also were acquainted with the inmost thoughts of his heart in many things, taking matter of a speech from his life, published a history out of his good deeds, consisting of lessons, responses, verses, hymns, and other matter appertaining to the honour and respect due to a martyr; but as long as Edward survives this compilation does not attain that acceptance by being chanted within the church of God, which was hoped for."[9]

"*Salve, Symon Montis-Fortis,*
Totius flos militiae,
Duras poenas passus mortis,
Protector gentis Angliae.
Sunt de sanctis inaudita,
Cunctis passis in hac vita,
Quemquam passum talia;
Manus, pedes amputari,
Caput, corpus vulnerari,
Abscidi virilia.
Sis pro nobis intercessor
Apud Deum, qui devensor
In terris exterritas.

Ora pro nobis, beate Symon! ut digni efficiamur promissionibus Christi.[10]

XI

"These Revolts were thus clearly romantic episodes, and a Good Thing . . ." (*1066 And All That.*)

ON 7 AUGUST, three days after the Battle of Evesham, Henry moved to Worcester, revelling once again in the full exercise of kingly power. He was not an especially vindictive man, but the opportunity to flaunt his restored dignity and at the same time replenish his coffers was too good to miss. Having declared that every order issued during his time of captivity was given under duress, which they obviously were, and so null and void, he began systematically to exploit the situation.

The defeated rebels released their prisoners and handed over their castles, ready at once to swear allegiance to the King and enjoy the peace which a conciliatory policy would soon have brought to the wounded country. Instead, Henry enforced penal forfeits, confiscated lands and distributed the spoils of victory among his royal favourites with his usual lavish hand. The earldom of Leicester was given to Prince Edward's younger brother, Edmund Crouchback who so nearly became King of Sicily; the Londoners were forced to yield the keys of their city and surrender themselves, their lives and property to the King's pleasure. Even Richard of Cornwall could not curb his brother's foolishness.

These shortsighted measures revived the dying spirit of rebellion, and a group known as "The Disinherited" doggedly continued the fight, establishing themselves in the marshes on the Island of Ely. Winston Churchill wrote: "In isolated centres at Kenilworth, Axholme, and Ely the followers of de Montfort held out, and pillaged the countryside in sullen despair. The Government was too weak to reduce them. The whole country suffered from confusion and unrest."[1] The Earl of Gloucester had another change of heart and began to collect support in London. At Kenilworth Simon de Montfort's fortress was defended against strong royalist attack all through the summer of 1266. The Norman keep, with its walls sixteen feet thick, was virtually unassailable and the siege was apparently so lax that the garrison was sometimes able to send out parties to replenish their stocks of food. All the roofing and other timbers were burnt, and when *mangonels* and *ginnes* failed Prince Edward and his brother Edmund devised structures with platforms from which rocks could be hurled with even greater force. Barges were brought from Chester to launch an attack from the lake, but the garrison of about a thousand men with a number of women and children, held out for sixteen months. On one occasion they amputated the hand of a royal messenger and sent it to the King. When Archbishop Boniface and the papal legate tried to reduce the garrison by spiritual means, and declared them excommunicate, they produced a wit to climb on the ramparts and excommunicate the Archbishop.

"The legate and the archbishop with them also nome
Two other bishops, and to Kenilworth come,
To make accord between the King and the disinherited also
And them of the castle, if it might be ido.
But the disinherited would not do all after the King,
Nor they of the castle any the more, nor stand to their liking.
The legate with his red cope amansed (excommunicated) tho
Them that in the castle were, and full many mo,
All that helped them or were of their rede
Or to them consented, in will or in deed.
They of the castle held it in great despite.
Copes and other clothes they let make of white.
And master Philip Porpoise, that was a quaint man,
Clerk, and hardy in his deeds, and their chirurgian,
They made a mock legate in this cope of white
Against the others' rede to do the legate a despite,
And he stood as a legate upon the castle wall,
And amansed King and legate and their men all."[2]

At last hunger and disease forced the garrison to surrender, and even the King was exhausted by his own stubbornness. The Pope himself advised a more moderate policy, Prince Edward was taking more power into his own hands, and neither side had the heart for further fighting. In October 1266 after fourteen months of restiveness and misery, in an edict known as the Ban of Kenilworth, the rebels were offered terms by which they might repurchase their rights and inheritance. The articles were drawn up by the bishops of Exeter, Bath and Wells, Saint David's, and the new Bishop of Worcester, and eight laymen including the Earl of Gloucester who had worked hard to achieve an acceptable compromise, Philip Basset the former justiciar, and John de Balliol. If the Provisions of Oxford established that a King should accept the counsel of wise men and govern for the good of his people, the *Dictum de Kenilworth* was a reminder that the King's prerogative is absolute.

In this ordinance it was laid down that the King should "have, fully obtain, and freely exercise his dominion, authority, and royal power, without let or gainsaying of any man . . ."[3] but the council went on to ask the King to appoint honest and impartial men to dispense justice to his subjects. The King would keep and observe "the ecclesiastical liberties, the charters of liberties and of the forest". Article 5 asked for an amnesty for all who had committed "any wrong or offence against him and the crown royal" during the disturbances, but with certain exceptions including all the family of de Montfort. All properties and rights were to be restored to the crown, and all "writings, obligations, and instruments" issued under the terms of the Provisions of Oxford were made null and void.

One article referred to Simon de Montfort. "We humbly ask both the lord legate and the lord king that the lord legate himself forthwith forbid, under ecclesiastical distraint, that Simon, Earl of Leicester, be held by any one as a saint or righteous person, since he died under excommunication, as holy Church holdeth that the vain and foolish miracles told by some of him be uttered by no lip hereafter, and that the lord king strictly forbid the same under pain of corporal punishment."[3]

The ordinance provided for the reform of the state of the city of London "as far as lands, rents, domains, and liberties, and that provisions for this be quickly made". All who had fought against the King at Northampton, Lewes, Evesham or elsewhere, or committed acts of plunder, murder, arson "and other mischiefs" were to pay as ransom "as much as their land is worth for five years" before their property would be restored to them. Under article 23 "the lords, the legate, the king, and Henry of Germany, shall see chosen twelve men, who shall diligently and faithfully execute these things, and the King and his heirs shall cause them to be firmly observed and maintained".

The King at last seemed ready to let state matters drift into the capable and energetic hands of his son Edward, and his last years were mainly devoted to his beloved Abbey and his art treasures. In 1269 the new Westminster Abbey was consecrated and the remains of Edward the Confessor, the ancestor he worshipped, were moved to the new and ornate shrine which they still occupy today. The triumphant occasion was spoilt by the bishops who jealously wrangled about their order of precedence, but the day marked the culmination of Henry's work. With projects like this absorbing his interest, rather than government affairs, "a sort of twilight happiness"[4] filled the end of his long and troubled reign.

It would be difficult to bring a chosen period of history to an arbitrary end without backward and forward glances at some of the main characters who walked the thirteenth-century stage. King Henry, who had strutted across the boards in no very heroic role, died in November 1272 at the age of sixty-five and was buried in the old tomb of Edward the Confessor. After the funeral rites his Great Seal was broken according to custom and his son Edward, who was away on crusade, was declared King. Rishanger says that he brought back precious stones of jasper to adorn his father's tomb, and certainly in spite of the very different temperaments of these two men there was a strong bond of affection between them. Matthew Paris described a touching scene when Henry sailed for Gascony in 1253, and Edward was fourteen years old.

"On the 6th of August, after appointing Earl Richard and the Queen guardians of the kingdom, and intrusting his eldest son Edward to their care, the King bade farewell to England and put to sea with a favourable wind; he embarked at

Portsmouth and was accompanied by three hundred large ships and a numerous fleet of other vessels. The young Edward, after his father had many times embraced and kissed him, stood crying and sobbing on the shore, and would not leave so long as he could see the swelling sails of the ships."

There is little to praise in this bossy, vain and inept king, with his extravagance and humbug, his comical pretensions and posturings; yet there is something endearing about such an essentially ordinary, affectionate spendthrift.

Edward inherited some of his father's warmth and passion, but they were tempered by great qualities. By nature he was just, liberal and diplomatic, and although when the crown was actually endangered he flung himself into the royalist cause, he always had a certain sympathy with the aims of the reformers. It was said that he never forgave the Londoners for their insults to his mother, but in general he was not a man to nurse a grievance, and he was big enough to learn from his father's follies and to profit from the example of his uncle, Simon de Montfort. The wholesale murder at Evesham was not by his wish. When he learned that Simon de Montfort had been killed he followed the mutilated body to its tomb and wept over the corpse of his cousin, Henry de Montfort. During his reign he consolidated the painful and costly advances of the previous years, and emerged from the bitter experiences of civil war to become "the first English king since the Conquest who loved his people with a personal love, and craved for their love back again. To his trust in them we owe our Parliament, to his care for them the great statutes which stand in the forefront of our laws".[5]

Richard Earl of Cornwall, King of Almaine, "King of the Romans, always august" died in the same year as his brother the King. He too was an affectionate father, and he was heart-broken when in 1271 his son Henry of Almaine was assassinated. Father and son were buried side by side in the Cistercian church at Hayles. He shared his brother's love of finery and pomp, and he was fickle, histrionic and corrupt, but whereas Henry loved money only to have the spending of it Richard loved money for money's sake, and at one time he was probably among the

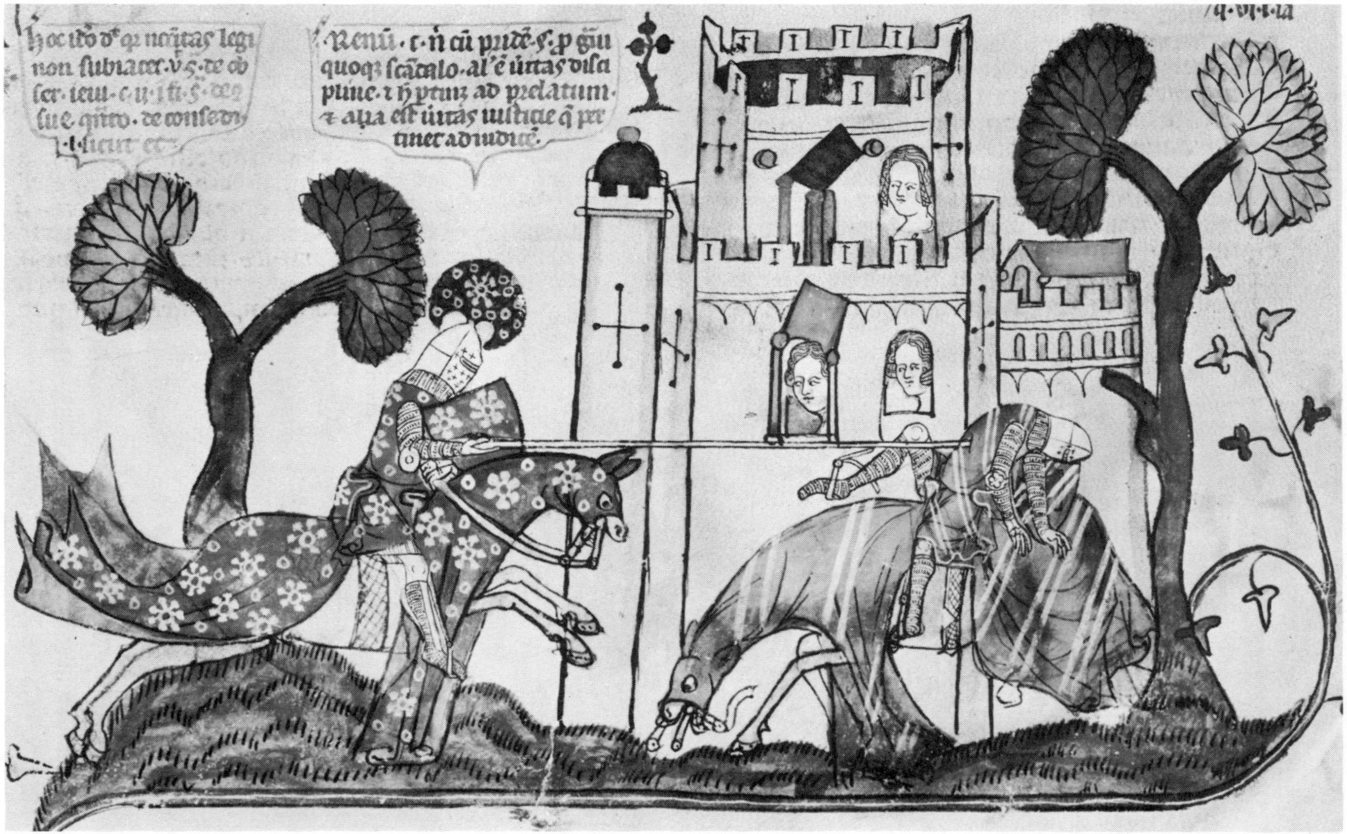

Jousting. An illumination from the Decretals of Gregory IX

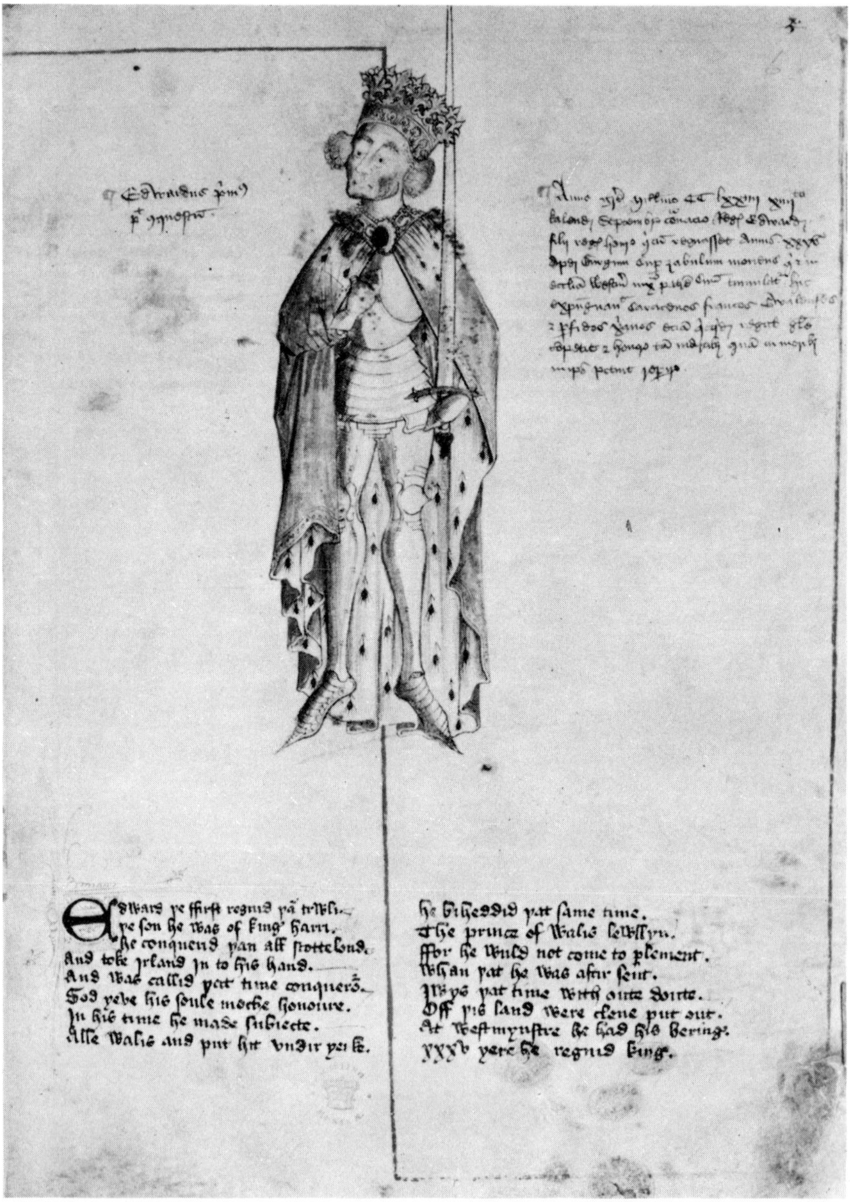

A posthumous portrait of Edward I (MS Cotton Julius E IV)

The verses tell of Edward's conquest of Scotland and Wales, the taking of Ireland "into his hand", and his execution of Llewelyn, Prince of Wales richest men in Europe. In spite of his faults he was a stronger character than his brother and he could have served a useful and important purpose as peacemaker if he had cared less about his own pocket.

When Simon de Montfort married the King's sister Eleanor, Archbishop Edmund Rich placed a curse upon them both and prophesied that their family would pass into oblivion. It was evidently fulfilled, for not one of their six children appears to have survived the turn of the century or to have left an heir, and the line that had been so illustrious on both sides of the Channel passed into obscurity.

If any of their sons seemed to bear something of his father's stamp it was Henry, who died on the battlefield of Evesham. His brother Simon, now the head of the family, made a powerful friend at court by releasing Richard of Cornwall and his youngest son from imprisonment at Kenilworth, unharmed. When the garrison there refused to yield to the King and "The Disinherited" continued their resistance Simon refused an offer of peace terms and took to piracy. When Guy, the fourth son, had recovered from the severe wounds he sustained at Evesham, the two brothers became soldiers of fortune in Italy. It was they who avenged their father's death by murdering their cousin Henry of Almaine.

It was a senseless act inspired only by revenge, for Henry had not been present at Evesham and had shown no malice toward the baronial cause. He was a young man of gentle temperament with the qualities of a statesman rather than a soldier. While he was visiting Italy on behalf of his uncle the King he attended Mass at the parish church at Viterbo. The de Montfort brothers dragged him from the altar and murdered him, together with a priest who tried to intervene. Henry's heart was taken to Westminster Abbey in a golden phial and placed in the tomb of Edward the Confessor. Guy paid heavily for the crime. After taking temporary shelter with his father-in-law in Tuscany he suffered poverty and imprisonment and after long intrigue and changes of fortune died in irons in 1292. His brother Simon was spared this misery by dying shortly after committing the atrocity.

Little is known about Richard, the fifth de Montfort son. He was mentioned in a charter of 1266 but left no further trace of his life or death. Almeric, the third, had been given a stall in the cathedral of York with the title of Canon and Treasurer of the Chapter. After the Battle of Evesham he fled to Italy and became a papal chaplain, studying medicine at Padua. He escorted his sister Eleanor for her promised marriage to Llewellyn but was captured and imprisoned in Corfe Castle. He died in 1295. Eleanor, the only daughter, married Llewelyn in 1278 but died in childbirth in 1282 and her only surviving child, a daughter, entered a nunnery.

Eleanor, Countess de Montfort, must have been a woman of real courage and stamina. In spite of her royal birth and upbringing, her piety, and her worldly and volatile nature, she never tried to evade the difficulties in which her marriage to this fanatical man frequently placed her. All through her married life she identified her own ideals with his, sharing his dangers and hardships, bearing the enmity of nearly all her relatives and former friends, and defying the greatest powers in the world familiar to her: the Pope, the King of France and her brother the King of England. However it may have started, their marriage surely grew into a love match which nothing but death could destroy.

After her husband's death this lonely, mourning woman received neither compassion nor protection from her brother Henry. In his mood of uncontrolled revenge he robbed her of most of her possessions and drove her to take refuge, almost penniless, in France. Sir James Mackintosh in his *History of England* (1834) described his behaviour as "the unmanly insolence of a feeble mind intoxicated by undeserved success". Fortunately, her brother Richard of Cornwall befriended her, and she entered an Augustinian convent at Montargis where she died in 1275.

A word must be said of Walter de Cantelupe, Bishop of Worcester, who played a key role for thirty years. The date of his birth is not recorded, but he was the son of William, Baron Cantelupe, and was consecrated bishop in 1237. He has been called the greatest of the bishops of his time after Grosseteste, who was his intimate friend. A great diocesan administrator, a militant Christian and an ardent worker for peace and political reform, he was suspended from his See after the Battle of Evesham and called to Rome to answer for his sins. He never made the journey, dying less than a year after his friend, on 12 February 1266. Because of his part in the rebellion he was never canonized, but the trumpets surely sounded for him as for the greatest of the saints.

AFTER THE long years of quarrelling and bloodshed, when men had fought against their own friends and families and defied their king, it must have been difficult to see what had been gained. Simple people continued to make pilgrimages to de Montfort's shrine although they hardly understood what he had been fighting for. Civil war always leaves scars that do not heal easily or quickly, and constitutional changes are slow to affect the lives of poorer citizens. Yet it was not only the monks in their prayers and writings who kept Simon's memory alive. When Prince Edward became king he paid the finest possible tribute to his defeated enemy by enshrining in the constitution the habit of regular consultation with a more representative Parliament.

Pollard says: "The House of Commons was not, in fact, created either by Simon de Montfort or by Edward I." But he goes on, "It was not until Simon de Montfort and Edward I popularized parliaments that England became really conscious of itself and acquired the means of national action. Even then the action must not be exaggerated; there was no will on the part of the English people to determine or direct a national policy, and it was little more than a formal expression of national acquiescence that Edward I sought in parliament. Consent, and not direction, was the object of its summons . . ."[6]

We have a bird's eye view of these distant centuries. Henry II was a modern-minded king, the architect of a professional civil service and a system of government that answered the needs of the people. During the reigns of King John and King Henry III these needs were changing. The system was found wanting and feudalism, having served the country well, was nearing its end. It had never been as firmly entrenched in England as it was in France, and it did not need a major holocaust like the French Revolution to destroy it, but over the years it was replaced by a government built on four corner-stones: the monarchy, the aristocracy, the Church and, now, "the community of the realm".

There was no possibility that the attempt to place restraints upon the King, the main object of the reformers in 1258, would be really effective for several centuries to come, but other important advances remained. Arthur Bryant points out just how important these were in his book *The Age of Chivalry*. "The attempt of de Montfort to make such authority independent of the Crown had failed, as, in an intensely monarchical age and country, it was bound to fail. But in the Statute of Marlborough of 1267 Edward, in his father's name, had legalized the baronial reforms of the past decade by a solemn public act of the Crown, issued in parliament under the great seal and enrolled in writing as a permanent national record. By this means he had given to the royal decisions that resolved the controversies of the civil war an enduring validity which, despite his unchallenged right to declare law by ordinance, they could have had in no other way. Henceforward such statutes, as they became called, were cited in pleadings in the royal courts. Like *Magna Carta* they became part of the continuing life of the nation."[7]

The young statesman-king incorporated in the Marlborough Statutes all that seemed to him to be practical in the Provisions of Westminster, and so preserved the best of the Oxford Statutes which his father, urged on by the Pope and the French King, had rejected with such awful consequences. The reforms remained, even if the restraints on the monarchy were lost. Edward carried the full weight of kingship so readily that he willingly accepted the limitation of wise counsel.

Equally important if less obvious gains were made by the Church. Most of the country's wealth was in her hands, and she was constantly engaged in her bitter struggle to free herself from the clutches of Rome on the one hand and an avaricious monarchy on the other. Ill-fitted to fight her own battles, her leaders saw in the reform movement a hope of achieving greater liberty, and in Simon de Montfort a man strong enough to lead it. The bishops and church scholars, the political theorists of their time, were also the negotiators, and frequently called upon to suggest the terms and safeguards for political compromise. With each attempt at agreement between the warring parties a prime demand all through the centuries was for liberty within the Church to control its own affairs. Although Edward I took steps to limit the independence of the Church within the state he also helped to sever its ties with Rome.

"It is to your ancestors, my Lords, it is to the English Barons, that we are indebted for the laws and constitution we possess; their virtues were rude and uncultivated, but they were great and sincere; their understandings were as little polished as their manners, but they had hearts to distinguish right from wrong, they had heads to distinguish truth from falsehood; they understood the rights of humanity, and they had spirit to maintain them."[8]

This interpretation by Lord Chatham is more idealistic than we readily accept today, but it would be a mistake to believe that there was no spirit of reforming zeal to motivate Simon de Montfort and his followers. Professor Treharne has said that the barons "changed parliament from an occasion into an institution", and it is possible that Grosseteste, Adam Marsh and their friends, the thinkers behind the reform movement, recognized to some small extent the principle of rule by consent. They certainly understood the concept of freedom, and the true function of law. "That is not true liberty which is totally unlimited. On the contrary, true liberty is not lost by wholesome restraint . . . Law is like fire, for it lights as truth, warms as charity, burns as zeal; with these virtues as his guides the King will rule well. He will then remember that he holds office not for his own but for others' good."[9]

How far Simon de Montfort understood their theories and shared their bright vision it is impossible to say. This man, who fused all the elements of rebellion into one coherent group, remains something of an enigma. He was without question an outstanding military commander for his day. In the light of modern techniques his success at Lewes and his record of successes in Gascony and Palestine may seem of little moment, but the idea of adding science and imagination to brute force was new. He did not accept that the smaller army must always concede victory to the larger and he proved that a battle may be decided by forethought and planning. He also had the gift to inspire, as well as discipline his followers even if he lacked the generosity and tact that might have kept their allegiance.

In the field his "appreciation of the situation", as soldiers call it today, must have been one of his great abilities. He must often have accurately sized up the strength, the character and the likely moves of his opponents before he fought his battles. He was in sole command and he saw to it that his orders were carried out. But as a politician he constantly miscalculated the strength, the character and the future moves of his opponents. There could be no absolute victory, and he often came too late to the idea of compromise. As a political leader he all too frequently left events to drift or be controlled by others. He was only in sole command for brief moments, and as often as not his orders could not be enforced. As a soldier, until his inexplicable blunder at Evesham, he was nearly always master of events. As a politician events in the end mastered him. So the very qualities that helped in the field, his military approach to problems, his fanaticism and his dislike of compromise may have hampered his efforts to govern a divided country. Winston Churchill, who greatly admires him, has this to say: "Though a prince among administrators, he suffered as a politician from over-confidence and impatience. He trampled upon vested interests, broke with all traditions, did violence to all forms, and needlessly created suspicion and distrust. Yet de Montfort had lighted a fire never to be quenched in English history. Already in 1267 the Statute of Marlborough had re-enacted the chief of the Provisions of Westminster. Not less important was his influence upon his nephew, Edward, the new king, who was to draw deeply upon the ideas of the man he had slain. In this way de Montfort's purposes survived both the field of Evesham and the reaction which succeeded it, and in Edward I the great earl found his true heir."[1]

History is subject to fashion, and Simon de Montfort has at one time or another been worshipped as a martyr, reviled as an anarchist, respected as a democrat, sentimentalized as the first Whig, and denounced as an ambitious revolutionary. Neither the high-sounding phrases of his supporters nor the vituperation of his enemies gives us any picture of the man himself, and the churchmen who knew him intimately and worked closely with him through many stormy years left no spontaneous and revealing comment.

The writer of the Melrose Chronicle left an account of his almost excessive devoutness. "A wax taper was his horologe, which it was his wont to light each night as he went to bed; and God so adjusted this taper, with reference to the length and shortness of the night, as the case might be, that when it reached the point which indicated midnight, immediately he arose from his bed, as if awoke by God, and yet so noiselessly, that none of those who were sleeping near at hand either heard him or were aware that he had so risen . . . While Simon was thus in watching and prayer, he knew by heart the primer, the psalter, and other prayers, which he repeated during the night with alacrity and devotion; for he was not forgetful of the love and commands of his Creator."

This is not a picture that accords with the late Sir Maurice Powicke's description of him as "a dark force", an arrogant and self-righteous fanatic, nor with the commonly held view that he was an unprincipled rabble-rouser inspired only by personal ambition. "He that goeth about to persuade a multitude that they are not so well governed as they ought to be, shall never want attentive and favourable hearers."[10] It would certainly not be difficult to encourage the complaints against King Henry III, to spread a subversive doctrine and deliberately foster the discontent never far below the surface among a serf population. But when the lunatic fringe had melted away and the majority of his party had been ravaged by jealousy there remained two faithful groups: the Church who had made him their champion, and the poor who loved him.

Arthur Bryant has pinpointed the weakness in Simon's character that was a major factor in his downfall. "The jealousy and alarm which the proud, unbending Frenchman awoke in his associates, and in moderate and conservative men generally, created a party for the King which had not before existed. For Simon's violence and intransigence sooner or later alienated everyone who tried to work with him as an equal. He was incapable of sharing power: he could only give orders and be obeyed. Compromise—the breath of self-government—was alien to him. He wished to establish the rule of righteousness on earth and viewed everyone who opposed him as the agent of unrighteousness."[11]

It is impossible not to admire him for his strength and single-mindedness. His qualities may have been greater than his achievements, but there is no doubt that he belongs in the ranks of England's great leaders, and we have much to thank him for. To like him is more difficult. If he was an affectionate husband; if he ever laughed at his own absurdities or was torn like other men by self-doubts and fears; if he was capable of gentleness, humility and good humour, we do not know, for we only see the stylized figure of a hero and a rebel. Perhaps it was well said "too great for a subject, which had hee not beene, he might have beene numbred amongst the worthiest of his time".[12]

NOTES

CHAPTER I

1 Thomas of Eccleston, *De Adventu Fratrum Minorum*, translated by Margaret A. Hennings, *England Under Henry III*. Longmans, Green and Company, 1924.
2 *Song of Lewes*, translated and edited by C. L. Kingsford. Clarendon Press, 1890.
3 *Opus Tertium of Roger Bacon*, published by A. G. Little, 1912, translated by Margaret A. Hennings, *England Under Henry III*.
4 *Medieval England*, Volume I, edited by Austin Lane Poole. Oxford University Press, 1958.
5 *Burton Annals*. Rolls Series.
6 Ernest Walker, *History of Music in England*. Oxford University Press, 1907.

CHAPTER II

1 Matthew Paris, translated by Margaret A. Hennings, *England Under Henry III*. Longmans, Green and Company, 1924.
2 *The Political Songs of England*, Volume 6, edited and translated by Thomas Wright and printed for the Camden Society, 1839.
3 *Westminster Abbey and the King's Craftsmen*, by W. R. Lethaby. Duckworth, 1906.
4 *Liberate Roll*, translated by Margaret A. Hennings, *England Under Henry III*.

CHAPTER III

1 *Chronicle of Aubrey de Trois-Fontaines*.

2 Roger of Wendover, *Flores Historiarum*, translated by Margaret A. Hennings, *England Under Henry III.*

3 *Close Rolls*, 1234–7, translated by Margaret A. Hennings, *England Under Henry III.*

4 *Chronicle of Melrose*, edited by the Rev. J. Stevenson for the Bannatyne Club, 1835.

5 *Simon de Montfort*, by Charles Bémont, translated by E. F. Jacob, Clarendon Press, 1930.

CHAPTER IV

1 *Chronicle of Matthew Paris.*

2 *The Political Songs of England*, Volume 6, edited and translated by Thomas Wright and printed for the Camden Society, 1839.

3 Letters from Adam Marsh to Grosseteste, *Monumenta Franciscana*, translated by Margaret A. Hennings, *England Under Henry III.* Longmans, Green and Company, 1924.

4 Letter from Pope Alexander IV to Henry III, *Annals of Burton*, 1255. Translated by Margaret A. Hennings, *England Under Henry III.*

5 *Chronicle of William de Nangis.*

CHAPTER V

1 This and subsequent extracts are taken from the *Burton Annals.* Rolls Series.

2 *Annals of Dunstable.*

3 "Witness ourself at London on the eighteenth day of the month of October in the forty-second year of our reign; and this was done in the presence of our sworn councillors:

Boniface, Archbishop of Canterbury,
Walter of Cantelupe, Bishop of Worcester,
Simon of Montfort, Earl of Leicester,
Richard of Clare, Earl of Gloucester and Hertford,
Roger Bigod, Earl of Norfolk, Marshal of England,
Peter of Savoy,

William of Fortibus, Earl of Albemarle,
John of Plesseiz, Earl of Warwick,
John Geoffreyson,
Peter of Montfort,
Richard of Grey,
Roger of Mortimer,
James of Aldithel, and before many others.

And these same words are sent into every other shire over all the kingdom of England, and into Ireland."

4 Matthew Paris.

5 *The Political Songs of England*, Volume 6, edited and translated by Thomas Wright and printed for the Camden Society, 1839. Wright attributed this work to later than 1264, but others think that it was written at this time, and I agree.

6 *Song of the Peace with England*, from a thirteenth-century manuscript in the Bibliothèque du Roi in Paris. Thomas Wright attributed it to the time of the Mise of Amiens, but it seems more appropriate to connect it with the peace negotiations of 1258–9. It is translated by Jane Hodlin.

7 Rymer's *Foedera*.

8 *Chronicle of William Rishanger*.

9 *Annals of Dunstable*, translated by Margaret A. Hennings, *England Under Henry III*. Longmans, Green and Company, 1924.

10 *Notes and Documents: The Barons' Argument at Amiens. English Historical Review, July 1958*. By Peter Walne. Translation by Jane Hodlin. "The burdens by which the land of England was oppressed, and which demanded some reform of the state."

11 *Liber de Antiquis Legibus*.

CHAPTER VI

1 *Liber de Antiquis Legibus*, translated by Margaret A. Hennings, *England Under Henry III*. Longmans, Green and Company, 1924.

2 *Close Rolls 1231*. Henry III to Mayor and Bailiffs of Oxford

and Cambridge. Translated by Margaret A. Hennings, *England Under Henry III.*

3 Matthew Paris.

4 *Chronicle of Thomas Wyke.*

5 This and other ancient maps are in the Barbican House Library at Lewes, Sussex.

6 *The Political Songs of England*, Volume 6, edited and translated by Thomas Wright and printed for the Camden Society, 1839.

7 *Song of Lewes*, translated and edited by C. L. Kingsford. Clarendon Press, 1890.

8 *Robert of Gloucester*. Rolls Series.

CHAPTER VII

1 *The Carousel*, from *The Battaile of Lewes*, by Arthur Lee. Baxter, Lewes, 1847.

2 *Chronicle of William Rishanger*, translated by Margaret A. Hennings, *England Under Henry III.* Longmans, Green and Company, 1924.

3 *Chronicle of John de Oxenede.*

4 *Warton's Historical Poetry*, poem of Sir Degore.

5 Chronicle of Melrose.

6 *The Political Songs of England*, Volume 6, edited and translated by Thomas Wright and printed for the Camden Society, 1839.

7 Chronicle of Walter Hemingford.

8 Lee's Lewes, 1795.

9 *Chronicle of Raphael Holinshed.*

10 *Robert of Gloucester*, Rolls Series.

11 *Sussex Notes and Queries*, XIV, May 1956.

12 T. W. Horsfield, *The History and Antiquities of Lewes and its Vicinity*. Baxter, Lewes, 1824.

CHAPTER IX

1 *Chronicle of English History*, by Peter Langtoft, translated by

Robert de Brune. *The Political Songs of England*, Volume 6, edited and translated by Thomas Wright and printed for the Camden Society, 1839.

2 *Collected Papers on Mediaeval Subjects*, by N. Denholm-Young. Blackwell, 1946.

3 *Chronicle of William Rishanger*, translated by Margaret A. Hennings, *England Under Henry III.* Longmans, Green and Company, 1924.

4 Stubbs, *Select Charters.*

5 Rymer's *Foedera*, translation from W. H. Blaauw's *The Barons' War*. The original is in Latin.

6 Robert of Gloucester.

CHAPTER X

1 Stubbs, *Select Charters.*

2 *Liber de Antiquis Legibus*, translated by Margaret A. Hennings, *England Under Henry III.* Longmans, Green and Company, 1924.

3 Chronicle of William Rishanger.

4 Rymer's *Foedera.*

5 *Robert of Gloucester*. Rolls Series.

6 *Chronicle of Melrose*, translated by Margaret A. Hennings, *England Under Henry III.*

7 G. W. Prothero, *The Life of Simon de Montfort Earl of Leicester*. Longmans, 1877.

8 Published with the *Chronicle of William de Rishanger* by the Camden Society, 1840.

9 *Chronicle of Melrose.*

10 This translation from the *Evesham Chronicle* is taken from "Simon de Montfort and his Cause, 1261–1266", edited by Rev. W. H. Hutton, 1888.

"Simon of the mountain strong,
Flower of knightly chivalry,
Thou who death and deadly wrong
Barest, making England free:

Not the holy ones of yore,
They on earth who travailed sore,
   Came to such despite and scorn;

Feet and hands dissevered,
Pierced corse and wounded head,
   Flesh and harness stript and torn.

So with God our champion be
As our whole defence in thee
   Dying, leaves the world forlorn."

Pray for us, blessed Simon, that we may be made worthy of the promises of Christ.

CHAPTER XI

1 *A History of the English-Speaking Peoples*, Volume I, by Winston S. Churchill. Cassell and Company Ltd., 1956.
2 *Robert of Gloucester.*
3 This and subsequent passages are from Stubbs' *Select Charters.*
4 G. W. Prothero, *The Life of Simon de Montfort Earl of Leicester*. Longmans, 1877.
5 John R. Green, *A Short History of the English People*. Macmillan and Company, 1874.
6 *The Evolution of Parliament*, by A. F. Pollard. Longmans, Green and Company, 1920.
7 *The Age of Chivalry*, by Arthur Bryant. Collins, 1963.
8 From a speech by Lord Chatham, 9 January 1770.
9 *The Song of Lewes*, translated by G. W. Prothero in *The Life of Simon de Montfort Earl of Leicester.*
10 *Ecclesiastical Polity*, by Richard Hooker (died 1600).
11 *Makers of the Realm*, by Arthur Bryant. Collins, 1953.
12 *Daniel's Collection of the Historie of England*, 1617.

APPENDIX

Petition of the Barons at the Parliament of Oxford, 1258

(The following is an abridged version of the twenty-nine Articles. The full text appears in the Burton Annals, Rolls Series.)

1 If the firstborn son or daughter is of age, claims his inheritance and is prepared to do homage etc., his chief lord should give seisin of his inheritance; if there are no children of the deceased, the succession shall pass in the order brother, sister, brother's children and sister's children. Reasonable relief shall be paid and homage done to the chief lord, and if the intermediate lord lays the inheritance waste, he should be fined and make reparation. If relief is due to the king, queen's gold is payable.

(Relief: a sum payable to the lord by the heir of a knight's fee for entry into his inheritance, which varied with the size of the inheritance. Queen's gold: a proportion of all feudal fines and judicial amercements, payable to the queen consort.)

2 Complaint that although the king may hold a part of the land of divers lords by virtue of his wardship of a minor who holds certain lands of him, yet the king demands full military service from each lord without allowance.

3 That barons should have custody of the lands etc. of minors, and the king should have the right of marrying the heir and custody of his person.

4 That royal castles should be kept by loyal Englishmen, not foreigners.

5 That royal castles on the coast should similarly be entrusted to Englishmen.

6 That the king should not disparage those whose marriage is at his disposal by marrying them to foreigners.

7 That land declared to be outside the forest shall not be reafforested.

(Forest: wood or moor land enclosed within bounds and subject to special laws aimed at preservation of game.)

8 That cultivated land within the forest should be liable only to wardship of the heirs and not to the full range of services.

9 That grants of free warren should not be made in land deforested.

(Free warren: the right to take certain animals, such as rabbits and hares, without incurring penalties under the forest law.)

10 That the lord of the fee should be asked for his permission before land is granted in mortmain, for thereby he loses in perpetuity services due to him.

(Mortmain: land granted to a self-perpetuating body like a religious house was not liable to the customary rights of relief etc. and was said to have fallen into the dead hand, *mort main*, of the Church.)

11 Complaint that the king claims the custody of the temporalities of vacant religious houses founded on the fees of earls, barons etc. and that new abbots etc. should only be elected by royal licence.

12 That the king should guarantee in the courts grants of escheats made by him.

(Escheat: land of a deceased falling into the king's or the lord's hands on the tenant's death.)

13 Complaint that when judicial eyres open on the same day in several counties in which earls and barons have lands, they are amerced for failure to appear personally at each unless they have the king's acquittance from attendance.

(Eyre: Latin *iter*, a journey, similar to the modern judicial circuit. Amerced: the offender had fallen into the king's mercy, and had to pay a financial penalty.)

14 Complaint that heavy beaupleader fines and fines for other crown pleas have been imposed, and that men of townships adjacent to the scene of a murder have been heavily amerced for not appearing before the royal justices.

(Beaupleader fines: penalties for failure to plead strictly according to the rigorous rules of pleading. Crown pleas: cases, particularly concerning criminal offences, reserved to the king's court.)

15 That no castle on the coast or an island should be granted at farm without the agreement of the council of the whole realm.

16 That exorbitant farms should not be demanded from sheriffs and other officers, and that men should not be amerced beyond their ability to pay.

(Farms: payments of a fixed sum, as opposed to variable but actual receipts.)

17 Complaint that sheriffs, alleging that they are justices for the time being, insist that earls and barons appear at the twice yearly tourn, and amerce them for failure to appear.

(Tourn: a court of record held (usually) twice yearly by the sheriff in each hundred.)

18 Complaint that a tenant of two acres, more or less, but without an adjacent house, is amerced for failure to appear at the tourn.

19 Complaint that the sheriffs require the attendance of all knights and freemen when an assize of *novel disseisin* or *mort d'ancestor* is to be taken, and amerce them for failure to appear.

(Assize: a quick judicial procedure introduced by Henry II, whereby a case was decided by a jury of knights. Twelve knights only were required for the jury.)

20 Complaint that if an evil doer is caught within a private jurisdiction, the sheriff will not take charge of him without payment.

21 Complaint that even if a stranger dies of hunger, Englishry not being proved, the murder fine is imposed on the men of the area.

(Murder fine: introduced after the Norman Conquest to punish the residents of a locality where a Norman had been murdered and the murderer not found; it could be avoided by proving that the deceased was English.)

22 Complaint that royal officers demand two or three times the customary prises, retaining the surplus for their own use.

(Prise: the king's right to buy at his valuation a proportion of certain goods, e.g. wine, brought into the country or offered for sale.)

23 Complaint that, as prises are scarcely ever waived, English merchants are impoverished and foreigners do not come to trade.

24 Complaint that various new suits of court, of county, hundred or private courts, are imposed.

(Suit of court: the obligation to attend and form part of the ancient communal courts of county, hundred, etc.)

25 Complaint that Jews grant debts owed and lands mortgaged to them to magnates, and lesser men thereby lose their lands; moreover, although the debtors are prepared to repay loans with interest, the magnates so postpone repayment that the debtor may die and his heirs be disinherited.

(Jews: since usury was forbidden to Christians, the Jews, before their expulsion from the country, were the chief source of early medieval credit.)

26 Complaint against Christian moneylenders resident in London, e.g. those from Cahors, for Christians are forbidden to be moneylenders; the moneylenders, moreover, by their usury and their trading, impoverish the Londoners and do not pay royal tallages when they are demanded.

27 That remedy be provided against the alienation of marriage portions. Land granted with a woman in marriage should revert to the grantor if the marriage is without heirs, but widows sell their marriage portions and there is no remedy at law.

28 Complaint that the legal system is impeded because the king acquits so many knights from sitting on juries etc.

29 Complaint that, although the writ of right lays down that if the chief lord of the fee refuses to do what is right, the suit should then go to the county court, yet successive superiors of the chief lord claim jurisdiction and unjustly delay the case.

The Provisions of Oxford, June 1258
Burton Annals, Rolls Series

It is laid down that from each county four prudent and lawful knights shall be elected, and that they, on each day that the county court is sitting, shall meet to hear all complaints of any offences or injuries inflicted on any persons by sheriffs, bailiffs or any others, and to make attachments according to the complaints made, to be kept until the first occasion on which the chief justiciar shall come into the area. That they shall also take from the plaintiff adequate pledges for his prosecution of the case, and from the defendant to ensure that he shall come and shall stand trial before the said justiciar at the first opportunity. That the said four knights shall have all the aforementioned complaints enrolled, together with their attachments, in proper order and sequence, that is to say, for each hundred, and in its own right, so that the said justiciar can, the next time he comes, hear and settle the said complaints singly and from each hundred.

And they shall inform the sheriff that they will summon all his hundredmen and bailiffs before the said justiciar the next time he comes, for a day and place of which he is to inform them. That every hundredman shall ensure that all plaintiffs and defendants from his bailiwick will come, successively, according to what the aforementioned justiciar shall bring to trial from the said hundred; also as many and such men, both knights and other free and lawful men, as can best prove the truth of the matter. They should not be troubled all at the same time; only so many should come as can help in the conduct and settlement of one day's cases.

It is likewise provided that no knight from the said counties shall, by virtue of an assurance that he is not to be placed on juries or assizes, be excused by a charter from the lord king, or be exempt from this provision, which is made for the common good of the whole kingdom.

Elected on the part of the king
The lord bishop of London, the lord bishop elect of Winchester, lord Henry, son of the king of Almaine, John the earl of Warenne, lord Guy de Lusignan, lord W. de Valence, John earl of Warwick, sir John Mansel, brother John Darlington, the abbat of Westminster, sir H. de Hengham, (the twelfth, whose name is omitted, was probably Boniface archibishop of Canterbury).

The lord bishop of Winchester, Simon earl of Leicester, Richard earl of Gloucester, Humfrey earl of Hereford, Roger Marshal, Roger de Mortimer, John Fitz-Geoffrey, Richard de Gray, William Bardulf, Peter de Montfort, Hugh le Despenser.

And if it happen that any of them of necessity cannot be present, the rest shall choose whom they will, that is, another, in the place of him who is absent, for the performance of the business.

This the commonalty of England swore at Oxford

We, so and so, make known to all men that we have sworn upon the holy Gospels, and are held together by such oath, and promise in good faith that each one of us and we all together will mutually aid each other, both ourselves and those belonging to us, against all people, doing right and undertaking nothing that we cannot, without doing mischief, saving faith to the king and the crown. And we promise under the same oath that we will not henceforth take from each other land or moveables by which this oath can be distributed or in anyways impaired. And if anyone acts against this, we will hold him as a mortal enemy.

This is the oath of the twenty-four

Each swore on the holy Gospels that he, to the honour of God, and to his faith to the king, and to the profit of the realm, will ordain and treat with the aforesaid sworn persons upon the reformation and amendment of the state of the realm. And that he will not fail for gift, nor for promise, for love, nor for hate, nor for fear of any one, nor for gain, nor for loss, loyally to do according to the tenour of the letter which the king and his son have together given for this.

This the chief justice of England swore

He swears that he will well and loyally, according to his power, do that which belongs to the justiciar of right to hold, to all persons, to the profit of the king and kingdom, according to the provision made and to be made by the twenty-four, and by the counsel of the king and the great men of the land who will swear in these things to aid and support him.

This the chancellor of England swore
That he will seal no writ, excepting writs of course, without the commandment of the king and of his council who shall be present. Nor shall he seal a gift of a great wardship, or of a great [A blank space in the MS.], nor of escheats, without the assent of the great council or of the major part. And that he will take no fee otherwise than what is given to the others. And he shall be given a companion in the form which the council shall provide.

This is the oath which the guardians of the king's castles made
That they will keep the castles of the king loyally and in good faith for the use of the king and of his heirs; and that they will give them up to the king or to his heirs, and to none other, and by his counsel and in no other manner, to wit, by honest men of the land elected as his council, or by the major part. And this form by writ lasts for twelve years. And from that time forward, by this settlement and this oath, they shall not be hindered so that they cannot freely give them up to the king and his heirs.

These are those who are sworn of the king's council
The archbishop of Canterbury, the bishop of Worcester, the earl of Leicester, the earl of Gloucester, the earl Marshal, Peter of Savoy, the count of Aumâle, the earl of Warwick, the earl of Hereford, John Mansel, John Fitz-Geoffrey, Peter de Montfort, Richard de Gray, Roger de Mortimer, James of Aldithley.

The twelve on the king's side have elected out of the twelve on that of the commonalty the earl Roger the Marshal and Hugh Bigot.

And the party of commonalty have elected of the twelve who are the king's side the earl of Warwick and John Mansel.

And these four have power to elect the council of the king, and when they have elected them they shall present them to the twenty-four; and there, where the greater part of these agree, it shall be held.

These are the twelve who are elected by the barons to treat at the three parliaments by year with the king's council for all the commonalty of the land of the common need
The Bishop of London, the earl of Winton, the earl of Hereford, Philip Basset, John de Balliol, John de Verdun, John de Gray, Roger de Sumery, Roger de Montalt, Hugh le Despenser, Thomas de Gresley, Giles d'Argentein.

These are the twenty-four who are appointed by the commonalty to treat of aid to the king
The bishop of Worcester, the bishop of London, the bishop of Sarum, the earl of Gloucester, the earl of Leicester, the earl Marshal, Peter of Savoy, the earl of Hereford, the count of Aumâle, the earl of Winton, the earl of Oxford, John Fitz-Geoffrey, John de Gray, John de Balliol, Roger de Mortimer, Roger de Montalt, Roger de Sumery, Peter de Montfort, Thomas de Gresley, Fulco de Kerdiston, Giles d'Argentine, John Kyriel, Philip Basset, Giles de Lidinton.

And if any one of these cannot or will not serve, those who shall be there have power to elect another in his place.

Of the state of Holy Church
Be it remembered that the state of the Holy Church be amended by the twenty-four elected to reform the state of the realm of England, when they shall see place and time, according to the power which they have respecting it by the letter of the king of England.

Of the chief justice
Moreover that a justice be appointed, one or two, and what power he shall have, and that he be only for a year. So that at the end of the year he answer concerning his time before the king and his council, and before him who shall follow him.

Of the treasurer and of the exchequer

The like of the treasurer. That he too give account at the end of the year.

And other good persons are to be placed at the exchequer according to the direction of the aforesaid twenty-four. And there let all the issues of the land come, and in no part elsewhere. And let that which shall seem to require amendment, be amended.

Of the chancellor

The like of the chancellor. That he at the end of the year answer concerning his time, and that he seal nothing out of course by the sole will of the king. But that he do it by the council which shall be around the king.

Of the power of the justice and bailiffs

The chief justice has power to amend the wrongs done by all other justices and bailiffs, and earls, and barons, and all other people, according to the law and justice of the land. And let the writs be pleaded according to the law of the land, and in fit places. And that the justice take nothing unless it be presents of bread and wine, and such things, to wit, meat and drink, as have been used to be brought to the tables of the chief men for the day. And let this same thing be understood of all the king's councillors and all his bailiffs. And that no bailiff by occasion of plea or of his office, take any fee in his own hand, or through the agency of another in any manner. And if he is convicted, that he be punished, and he who gives likewise. And if it be fitting, that the king gives to his justiciar and his people who serve him, so that they have no occasion to take anything elsewhere.

Of the Sheriffs

Let there be provided as sheriffs, loyal people, and substantial men and land tenants; so that in each county there be a vavasour of the same county as sheriff, to treat the people of the county well, loyally and rightfully. And that he take no fee, and that he be sheriff only for a year together; and that in the year he give up his accounts at the exchequer, and answer for his time. And that the king grant unto him out of his own, according to his contribution, so that he can guard the country rightfully.

And that he take no fee, neither he nor his bailiffs. And if they be convicted, let them be punished.

Be it remembered that such amendment is to be applied to the jewry and to the wardens of the jewry, that the oath as to the same may be kept.

Of the escheators

Let good escheators be appointed; and that they take nothing of the effects of the dead, of such lands as ought to be in the king's hand. Also that the escheators have free administration of the goods until they shall have done the king's will, if they owe him debts. And that, according to the form of the charter of liberty.

And that inquiry be made into the wrongs done, which the escheators have done there aforetime, and amendment be made of such and such. Nor let tallage on anything else be taken, excepting such as ought to be according to the charter of liberty. Let the charter of liberty be kept firmly.

Of the exchange of London

Be it remembered to amend the exchange of London, and the city of London, and all the other cities of the king which have gone to shame and destruction by the tallages and other oppressions.

Of the place of reception of the king and queen.

Be it remembered to amend the hostelry of the king and queen.

Of the parliaments, how many shall be held by year, and in what manner.

It is to be remembered that the twenty-four have ordained that there be three parliaments a year. The first at the octave of S. Michael. The second the morrow of Candlemas. The third the first day of June, to wit, three weeks before S. John. To these three parliaments the elected councillors of the king shall come, provided they are not sent for, to see the state of the realm, and to treat the common wants of the kingdom, and of the king in like manner. And other times in like manner when occasion shall be, by the king's command.

So it is to be remembered that the commonalty elect twelve honest men, who shall come at the parliaments and other times when occasion shall be, when the king or his council shall send for them, to treat of the wants of the king and of the kingdom. And that the commonalty shall hold as established that which these twelve shall do. And that shall be done to spare the cost of the commonalty.

There shall be fifteen named by these four, to wit, by the earl Marshal, the earl of Warwick, Hugh Bigod, and John Mansel, who are elected by the twenty-four to name the aforesaid twenty-four, or by the major part of them. And they shall have power to counsel the king in good faith concerning the government of the realm, and all things which appertain to the king or kingdom; and to amend and redress all things which they shall see require to be redressed and amended. And over the chief justice and over all other people. And if they cannot all be present, that which the majority shall do shall be firm and established.

These are the names of the principal castles of the king, and of those who have them in keeping.

Robert de Neville, Bamburg, Newcastle-upon-Tyne.
Gilbert de Gant, Scarborough.
William Bardulf, Nottingham.
Ralph Basset de Sapercot, Northampton.
Hugh Bigot, Tower of London.
Richard de Gray, Dover.
Nicholas de Moules, Rochester and Canterbury.
Winchester.
Roger de Samford, Porchester.
Stephen Longsword, Corfe.
Matthew de Besill, Gloucester.
Henry de Tracy, Exeter.
Richard de Rochele, Haldesham.

John de Gray, Hereford.
Robert Walrant, Sarum.
Hugh Dispencer, Horsham.
Peter de Montfort, Bridgewater.
Earl of Warwick, Devizes.
John Fitz-Bernard, Oxford.

BIBLIOGRAPHY

BÉMONT, Charles
Simon de Montfort, Earl of Leicester. Translated by E. F. Jacob. Clarendon Press, 1930.

BLAAUW, W. H.
The Barons' War including the Battles of Lewes and Evesham. Second edition, 1871. Bell and Daldy of London, and Baxter and Son of Lewes.

BLAIR, Claude
European Armour. Batsford, 1958.

BRYANT, Arthur
The Story of England: Makers of the Realm. Collins 1953.
The Age of Chivalry. Collins 1963.

BURNE, Lieutenant-Colonel Alfred H.
More Battlefields of England. Methuen and Company.

CHURCHILL, Winston S.
A History of the English-Speaking Peoples, Volume I, The Birth of Britain. Cassell and Company, 1956.

COULTON, G. G.
Medieval Panorama. Volume I, Foreground: Society and Institutions. Cambridge University Press, 1938.
Social Life in Britain from the Conquest to the Reformation. Cambridge University Press, reprinted 1956.

DAVEY, L. S.
The Street Names of Lewes, published by the Friends of Lewes Society, 1961.

DAVIS, H. W. C.
England under the Normans and Angevins. A History of England edited by Sir Charles Oman, Volume II. Methuen and Company, first published 1905.

DENHOLM-YOUNG, N.
Collected Papers on Mediaeval Subjects. Blackwell, 1946.

DUNVAN, Paul. (See LEE, William)

ELMAN, P.
The Economic Causes of the Expulsion of the Jews in 1290. The Economic History Review, Vol. VII, No. 2.
GREEN, John R.
History of the English People, Vol. I. Macmillan, 1885.
A short History of the English People. Revised Edition, Macmillan, 1921.
GILBEY, Sir Walter, Bart.
The Great Horse. Vinton and Company, 1899.
HASSALL, W. O.
How They Lived 55 B.C.–1485. Basil Blackwell, Oxford, 1962.
HENNINGS, Margaret A.
England under Henry III. Longmans, 1924.
The HIGH SHERIFF
Published by *The Times*, 1961, with a foreword by Gavin Astor.
HORSFIELD, Rev. T. W.
The History and Antiquities of Lewes and its Vicinity. Sussex Press: Printed and Published by J. Baxter, High Street, Lewes, 1824.
HUTTON, Rev. W. H.
The Misrule of Henry III, 1236–1251. Nutt, 1887.
Simon de Montfort and his Cause, 1251–1266. Nutt, 1888.
KINGSFORD, C. L.
Song of Lewes, translated and edited with introduction and notes. Clarendon Press, 1890.
LABARGE, Margaret Wade
Simon de Montfort. Eyre and Spottiswoode, 1962.
LEE, Arthur.
The Bataille of Lewes and other Legends of St. Pancras' Priory, Lewes. Printed and published by Baxter, Lewes, 1847.
LEE, William
Ancient and Modern History of Lewes and Brighthelmstone, 1795. Printed for W. Lee, the editor and proprietor, by W. Lee, Printer, Lewes. This book, usually known as 'Lee's Lewes', was in fact written by Paul Dunvan, who wished to remain obscure. It was dedicated to the Prince Regent. "I blush not to avow my honest Ambition of being known to

Posterity as the FIRST PROMOTER of a RESPECTABLE HISTORY of my NATIVE TOWN, patronized, at my humble solicitation, by the most AMIABLE AND ACCOMPLISHED PRINCE in EUROPE . . ."

The LEGACY OF THE MIDDLE AGES
Edited by C. G. Crump and E. F. Jacob. Clarendon Press, 1926.

LETHABY, W. R.
Westminster Abbey and the King's Craftsmen. Duckworth, 1906.

The JOURNAL OF GIDEON MANTELL
Edited by E. Cecil Curwen, Oxford University Press, 1940.

MARGARY, I. D.
Roman Ways in the Weald—Phoenix House Limited, 1948.

MEDIEVAL ENGLAND
Edited by Austin Lane Poole, two volumes, Clarendon Press, 1958.

MILLER, Edward
The Origins of Parliament, published for the Historical Association by Routledge and Kegan Paul.

OMAN, C. W. C.
The Art of War in the Middle Ages. Cornwell University Press, 1953.

The POLITICAL SONGS OF ENGLAND, Volume 6.
Edited and translated by Thomas Wright and printed for the Camden Society, 1839.

POLLARD, A. F.
The Evolution of Parliament. Longmans, Green and Co., 1920.

POWER, Eileen
Medieval People. Methuen, 1924.

POWICKE, Sir F. Maurice
King Henry III and the Lord Edward: the Community of the Realm in the Thirteenth Century. Oxford University Press, Volume II, 1947.
The Thirteenth Century, 1212–1307.
The Oxford History of England, Oxford University Press. Second Edition, 1962.

PROTHERO, George Walter
The Life of Simon de Montfort, Earl of Leicester, with special reference to the Parliamentary History of his time. Longmans, 1877.
RAMSAY, Sir James H., Bart.
The Dawn of the Constitution. Swan Sonnenschein and Co., 1908.
RUSSEL, Josiah Cox.
British Medieval Population. University of New Mexico Press, 1948.
SABINE, George H
A History of Political Theory. Harrap, 1937.
SAYLES, G. O.
The Medieval Foundations of England. Methuen, 1948.
A SHORT HISTORY OF FRANCE TO THE PRESENT DAY
Edited by J. Hampden Jackson, Cambridge University Press, 1959.
THE SHORTER CAMBRIDGE MEDIEVAL HISTORY
By C. W. Previte-Orton, Cambridge University Press. 1960.
SOURCES OF ENGLISH CONSTITUTIONAL HISTORY
Edited and translated by Carl Stephenson and Frederick George Marcham. Harper and Sons, 1937.
STENTON, Doris Mary
English Society in the Early Middle Ages. The Pelican History of England. Penguin Books, reprinted 1959.
STENTON, F. M.
The Road System of Medieval England. From the Economic History Review, Volume VII, No. 1.
STUBBS, William
Constitutional History of England in its Origin and Development. Volume II, third edition. Clarendon Press, 1887.
Select Charters and other illustrations of English Constitutional History to Edward I. Edited by W. Stubbs. Ninth Edition, 1913, revised by H. W. C. Davis. Clarendon Press.
SUSSEX ARCHAEOLOGICAL COLLECTIONS
Published by the Sussex Archaeological Society. Volume II, 1849. Papers by W. H. Blaauw.

Volume XV, 1863. The Rivers of Sussex by Mark Antony Lowe.

Sussex Notes and Queries

Volume XIV, 1956. The Crossing of the Ouse after the Battle of Lewes, by G. D. Johnston.

Tanner, Lawrence E.

Some Representations of St. Edward the Confessor in Westminster Abbey and Elsewhere. Reprinted from the Journal of the British Archaeological Association, Third Series, Volume XV, 1952.

Taswell-Langmead's English constitutional history from the Teutonic conquest to the present time. Eleventh Edition, by T. F. T. Plucknett. Sweet and Maxwell, 1960.

Treharne, R. F.

The Baronial Plan of Reform, 1258–63. University of Manchester, 1932.

The Personal Role of Simon de Montfort in the Period of Baronial Reform and Rebellion, 1258–65. The Raleigh Lecture on History: British Academy, 1954.

The Battle of Lewes, 1264 [with Professor Sir Maurice Powicke and Lt.-Col. Charles H. Lemmon]. Published by the Friends of Lewes Society, 1964.

Trevelyan, George Macaulay

History of England. Longmans, Green and Company, 1926.

The Victoria History of the Counties of England

Sussex: Volume I, 1905. Political history by L. F. Salzmann. Volume VII. The Rape of Lewes.

Walker, Ernest

History of Music in England, Oxford University Press, 1907.

Walne, Peter

Notes and Documents: The Barons' Argument at Amiens. English Historical Review, July 1958.

Williams, Gwyn A.

Medieval London from Commune to Capital. University of London Historical Studies, 1963.

CHRONICLES

The Burton Annals

These annals from the abbey of Burton-on-Trent, which ended in 1263, are invaluable for the period of the Barons' War because they include the constitutional enactments of the period as well as letters and other documents which throw light on the political history of the time. Edited by H. R. Luard for the Record Commission, Annales Monastici i. 181–510. London, 1864.

The Annals of Dunstable

The annals of the Augustinian Priory at Dunstable, where the first miracle play on record was performed in 1110. According to Luard "It is probably the most accurate record extant of the ordinary secular proceedings of a monastery in the thirteenth century". Edited by H. R. Luard, Annales Monastici, iii, 1–420.

Robert of Gloucester

A metrical chronicle of English history probably written by a monk of Gloucester in about 1300. He borrowed his history from other writers but he wrote in a simple and vigorous style especially about events during his own lifetime. Edited by W. A. Wright, Rolls Series, 2 volumes, London, 1887.

Chronicle of Walter Hemingburgh, *or* Hemingford

Hemingburgh was a monk of Gisburn in Yorkshire, and is sometimes called Walter of Guisborough. He died there in 1347. Much of the earlier part is drawn from other chronicles but he gives a valuable account of the reign of Edward I. Edited by H. C. Hamilton for the English Historical Society. Two volumes, London, 1848–9.

Raphael Holinshed

Holinshed was born in Cheshire and came to London early in Elizabeth's reign. His Chronicle was the work of several hands and was one of the main sources for Shakespeare's historical and legendary plots. It was published in two volumes in London in 1577; by John Hooker in 1587; and by Henry Ellis in six volumes, London, 1807–8.

Household Expenses

The Roll of the Countess of Leicester's Expenses in 1265 is in the British Museum, Add. MSS. 8877. It was privately printed for the Roxburghe Club by Beriah Botfield in 1841.

Lanercost Chronicle

A chronicle covering the period 1181–1346 written at Lanercost Abbey in Cumberland. Edited by Joseph Stevenson for the Bannatyne Club, Edinburgh, 1839.

Peter Langtoft

A chronicle of English history written in French verse and translated by Robert Mannyng, also known as Robert of Brunne in about 1300. Langtoft was a canon of the priory of Bridlington in Yorkshire. Rolls Series. Two volumes, London, 1866–8.

Liber de Antiguis Legibus

A chronicle of the City of London probably written in 1274 by Arnold Fitz-Thedmar, an alderman of the city. Translated by H. T. Riley: Chronicles of the mayors and sheriffs of London. London, 1863.

Chronicle of Mailros *or* Melrose

This chronicle gives the fullest account of Simon de Montfort but by a distinctly partisan writer. Much of the information after the middle of the 12th century is contemporary. Melrose Abbey, in Roxburgh near the River Tweed, was founded in 1136. Edited by Joseph Stevenson for the Bannatyne Club, Edinburgh 1835.

Monumenta Franciscana

Adam Marsh, whose letters are collected under this heading, was well known at court as well as among the scholars of his time. His plain speaking sometimes offended the King. As his letters show, he was an intimate friend of Simon de Montfort and wrote to him in blunt terms as well as to his wife and to the Queen. He died in 1257. Monumenta Franciscana also contains an account of the early Franciscans in England, the rule of Saint Francis, the Statutes of Franciscans, the Chronicle of the grey friars, London, 1189–1556, and other works. Edited by J. S. Brewer, Rolls Series, two volumes, London, 1858–82.

William de Nangis

An anonymous Latin chronicle, mainly the work of Jean de Venette, prior of the Carmelite convent in Paris, who died about 1370.

A chronicle by a monk of Saint Denis in Paris, continued by Jean de Venette until 1368. Nangis was especially hostile to the English armies in France. *Société de l'Histoire de France*. Paris, 1843.

John de Oxenedes

A chronicle covering 449–1293 by a monk of Saint Benet at Holme in Norfolk. Most of the material is derived from other chronicles but it is enlivened by colourful illustrations. Edited by Henry Ellis. Rolls Series, London, 1859.

Matthew Paris, *or* Pariensis

The greatest of them all. This Benedictine monk was either a native of Paris or studied there (hence his name) and was born about 1195. In 1217 he entered the Monastery of Saint Albans and in 1236 replaced Roger of Wendover as the chronicler. He travelled widely and had an international reputation as well as being intimate with such men as Richard of Cornwall and well known to the King. Part of his great *Chronica Majora* was transcribed from earlier chronicles, but from 1235 until his death in 1259 it was his own work, and his outspoken comment and humorous observation together with a large fund of information and good sense set him apart as one of the great historians. His chronicles are enriched by lively illustrations. Edited by H. R. Luard, Rolls Series, seven volumes. London, 1872–83.

POLITICAL SONGS

The evils of Henry III's reign gave rise to an outburst of political satire. Thomas Wright published a collection of these in 1839, written in Provençal, French, Latin, or a mixture of languages. Most of them were probably written by the Grey Friars of Oxford, the Franciscans who took such an active part in the political upheavals of the time. Others were probably the songs by which wandering minstrels spread gossip, like the lampoon about Richard of Almaine and his windmill after the Battle of Lewes. The most important of them all is the Song of Lewes.

WILLIAM OF RISHANGER

Little is known about this monk of Saint Albans who was born nine years before Matthew Paris died and who has sometimes been known as the "Historiographer Royal". His was probably one of several hands that continued the monastery annals, but he undoubtedly wrote the Chronicle of the battles of Lewes and Evesham which gives a valuable account of this period. Edited by J. O. Halliwell and published with The Miracles of Simon de Montfort by the Camden Society, London, 1840.

ROYAL LETTERS

Royal and other historical letters of the reign of Henry III, edited by W. W. Shirley. Rolls Series, two volumes, London, 1862–6.

RYMER'S FOEDERA

Thomas Rymer (1641–1713) was appointed Historiographer Royal in 1692, and published many historical and critical works. Pope called him "one of the best critics we ever had", and Macaulay "the worst critic that ever lived". His *Foedera* was a collection of historical material from the eleventh century to his own times. His work was carried out at public expense and published in various editions. Syllabus of documents in Rymer's Foedera by T. D. Hardy. Rolls Series, three volumes, London, 1869–85.

William de Shepisheved

This brief chronicle comes from the abbey of Crokesden and gives an interesting account of Simon's death at Evesham. MSS. Cotton Faust B.VI.

Roger of Wendover

This predecessor of Matthew Paris died in 1236 at Saint Albans. His *Flores Historiarum* begins with the story of the Creation but it gives a first hand account of the years from 1202 until his death. Edited by H. O. Coxe. English Historical Society, four volumes, London, 1841–4.

Thomas Wyke

This canon of the Augustinian Priory of Osney was strongly royalist. He wrote in a pungent style and never failed to flay the barons, believing that de Montfort wooed the lower orders in order to gain allies in his ambitious struggle against the nobility. He left an authoritative history up to 1290. Edited by H. R. Luard, Annales Monastici, iv, 6–319. Rolls Series, London, 1869.

INDEX

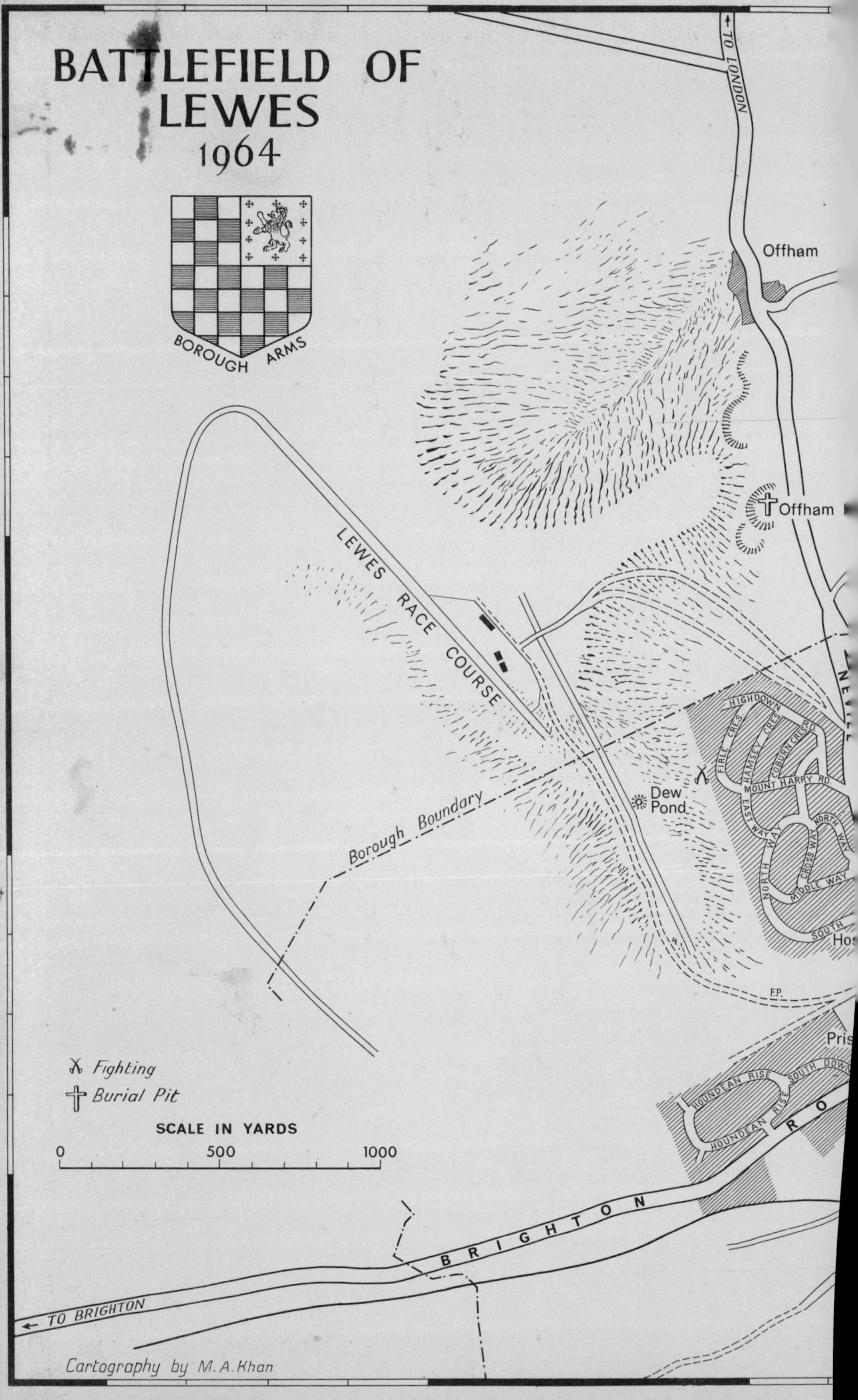

BATTLEFIELD OF LEWES
1964
BOROUGH ARMS
TO LONDON
Offham
Offham
LEWES RACE COURSE
Borough Boundary
Dew Pond
HIGHDOWN
FIRLE CRES
HAMSEY CRES
COBURN CRES
MOUNT HARRY RD.
EAST WAY
NORTH WAY
CROSS WAY
MIDDLE WAY
SOUTH
F.P.
HOUNDEAN RISE
HOUNDEAN RISE
HOUNDEAN RISE
BRIGHTON
TO BRIGHTON
Fighting
Burial Pit
SCALE IN YARDS
0
500
1000
Cartography by M.A.Khan